THE BOOK OF
WEAPONS

THE BOOK OF
WEAPONS

TOOLS OF WAR
THROUGH THE AGES

DWIGHT JON ZIMMERMAN

Tess
Press

To Mikey Fratangelo, George Burke, and Jamie Lawson, with gratitude
— D. J. Z.

The Book of Weapons was created by Black Dog and Leventhal in conjunction with Endeavor London Limited.

PHOTO CREDITS

Art Resource: 51, 57. AP: 307, 327, 371, 399, 420, 422, 439, 439 476; Corbis: 237, Department of Defense: 121, 163, 169, 177, 195, 216, 223, 258, 260, 277, 283, 288, 290, 297, 301, 304, 305, 309, 422, 306, 315, 319, 320, 321, 323, 324, 325, 326, 331, 333, 337, 338, 341, 342, 344, 345, 347, 349, 352, 355, 360, 356, 357, 361, 363, 365, 367, 369, 370, 373, 375, 379, 381, 383, 385, 387, 389, 391, 393, 395, 397, 401, 403, 404, 405, 407, 408, 409, 411, 413, 414, 415, 417, 418, 419, 420, 424, 427, 428, 429, 430, 433, 435, 436, 437, 440, 441, 447, 449, 451, 452, 453, 455, 465, 467, 468, 469, 471, 479, 481, 485, 487, 491, 493, 495, 497, 501; Gresham, John D.: 445; Library of Congress: 96, 103, 107, 115, 117, 119, 122, 135, 140, 141; National Archives: 161, 175, 191, 209 243, 247, 249. NMUSA: 306. Polmar, Norman: 211; USAF: 151, 153, 181, 182, 215, 227, 229, 231, 234, 257, 258, 273, 313, 317, 328, 498, 499; Wells, Mary: 81; WWI Signal Corps Collection: 165, 328.

All other images courtesy of Getty Images including the following which have further attributions:

Agence France Presse: 159, 459, 473, 475, 477, 483, 489; Bridgeman Art Library: front jacket (2R), title page (1R),19, 59, 99/Louvre, Paris; 21/Musee Marmottan, Paris; 27/Royal Geographical Society, London; 29/Private Collection, Rafael Valls Gallery, London; 30/Archaeological Museum of Heraklion, Crete; 5 (2L), 33, 105/British Museum, London; 35/Service Historique de la Marine, Vincennes, France; 5 (3L), 41/Palazzo Ducale, Venice; 45, 49/Pushkin Museum, Moscow; 5(2R), 57/Germanisches Nationalmuseum, Nuremberg, Germany; 63/National Gallery, London; 67/Bibliotheque Municipale de Lyon, France; back cover (1L), 69/Private Collection, Stapleton Collection, London; 71/ Courtesy of the Warden & Scholars of New College, Oxford; 73/Castello della Manta, Saluzzo, Italy; 77/Collection of the Earl of Leicester, Holkham Hall, Norfolk, UK; 95/Hermitage, St Petersburg; 147/Private Collection, Archives Charmet; Christian Science Monitor: 463; Dorling Kindersley: 25, 37; Epsilon: 299; National Geographic: back jacket (middle), 5(R), 23; Popperfoto: jacket flap, 6(R),127, 133, 145, 171, 187, 225, 239, 243, 255, 267, 271; Roger Viollet: 219, 233; Time & Life Pictures: 8(2R), 43, 55, 123, 125, 131, 139, 167, 201, 213, 261, 263, 269, 281, 293, 329, 335

This edition published by Tess Press, an imprint of
Black Dog & Leventhal Publishers, Inc.
151 West 19th Street
New York, NY 10011

Manufactured in China

HC ISBN-13: 978-1-60376-117-8
Paperback ISBN: 978-1-60376-164-2

CONTENTS

Prehistoric Weapons 14

Knife 16

Spear 18

Sling 20

Blowgun 22

Atlatl 24

Boomerang 26

Ancient Armor 28

Ax 30

Bow 32

Incendiaries 34

Trireme 36

Camel 38

Crossbow 40

Ballista 42

Elephants 44

Pigs 46

Archimedes 48

Hot Oil, Sand, and Water 50

Greek Fire 52

Faith 54

Sword 56

1,000,000 B.C.

Prehistoric
Weapons

2200 B.C.

Bow

500 B.C.

Crossbow

1079

Sword

40,000 B.C.
Blowgun

Mace	58	Congreve Rocket	96
Flail	60	Propaganda	98
Medieval Armor in Europe	62	Ship-of-the-line	100
Gunpowder	64	Dahlgren Gun	102
Medieval Siege Engines	66	Horse	104
Samurai Armor	68	Colt Percussion Revolver	106
Morning Star	70	Samuel Colt	108
Halberd	72	Sharps Rifle	110
Early Biological Warfare	74	Gatling Gun	112
Pot de Fer	76	Richard Jordan Gatling	114
Arquebus	78	USS *Monitor*	116
Beretta	80	Sea Mine	118
Bo	82	Torpedo	120
Bayonet	84	Dynamite	122
Mortar	86	Alfred Nobel	124
Brown Bess Musket	88	Mauser	126
Eli Whitney	90	Maxim Machine Gun	128
Air Rifle	92	Merchant of Death	130
Leadership	94	Lewis Gun	132

1872
Mauser

1503
Arquebus

1692
Mortar

1850
Dahlgren Gun

1911
Lewis Gun

Colt Model 1911 Pistol	134	Adnan Khashoggi	172
Big Bertha	136	M1 Garand	174
Krupp	138	Radar	176
Zeppelin	140	JU-87 Stuka	178
Fokker Eindecker	142	T-6 Texan	180
Asdic/Sonar	144	Messerschmitt Bf-109	182
Sex	146	Wilhelm "Willy" Messerschmitt	184
Albatross D. III	148	Hawker Hurricane	186
Sopwith Camel	150	Sir Sydney Camm	188
SPAD S.XIII	152	B-17 Flying Fortress	190
Fokker Dr. I Dreidecker	154	Vickers Wellington	192
Anthony Fokker	156	P-40 Warhawk	194
Birds	158	Katyusha Rocket Launcher	196
Thompson Submachine Gun	160	Combat Knife	198
M2 .50-Caliber Browning Machine Gun	162	Yak-I	200
John Moses Browning	164	Spitfire	202
Samuel Cummings	166	Reginald Joseph Mitchell	204
Bofors 40-mm Anti-Aircraft Gun	168	F4F Wildcat	206
Fairey Swordfish	170	SBD Dauntless	208

1917
Sopwith Camel

1921
Thompson Submachine Gun

1938
B17 Flying Fortress

1940
Spitfire

1917
Anthony Fokker

Edward Heinemann	210
Mitsubishi Zero	212
Jiro Horikoshi	214
Aichi D3A "Val" Dive Bomber	216
88-mm Cannon	218
T-34	220
Hawker Typhoon	222
De Havilland Mosquito	224
Consolidated B-24 Liberator	226
B-25 Mitchell Medium Bomber	228
Martin B-26 Marauder	230
Focke-Wulf Fw 190	232
Lockheed P-38 Lightning	234
Ilyushin Il-2 Shturmovik	236
Mitsubishi G4M Betty	238
Churchill Tank	240
Amphibious Landing Craft	242
V-1 Flying Bomb	244
M4 Sherman Tank	246
Flame Thrower	248
Grenade	250
Tiger	252
Avro Lancaster	254
Republic P-47 Thunderbolt	256
North American P-51 Mustang	258
Chance Vought F4U Corsair	260
Submarine (Conventional Power)	262
Panzerfaust	264
Grumman F6F Hellcat	266
Panther Tank	268
Northrop P-61 Black Widow	270
Messerschmitt Me-262	272
V-2	274
Wernher von Braun	276
Boeing B-29 Superfortress	278
Conventional Bomb	280
Battleship	282
Cruiser	284

1941
Hawker Typhoon

1941

Lockheed P-38
Lightning

1942

Sherman Tank

1942

Chance Vought F4U
Corsair

1944

Battleship

Destroyer	286	Intercontinental Ballistic Missile	324
Aircraft Carrier	288	Bell UH-IH Huey	326
Atomic Bomb	290	Reconaissance Satellites	328
Julius Robert Oppenheimer	292	Mcdonnel-Douglas F-4 Phantom	330
Centurion Tank	294	P-I5 Termit/SS-N-2 Styx	332
AK-47 Assault Rifle	296	Herbicides	334
Mikhail Kalashnikov	298	9KII Malutka/AT-3 Sagger	336
MiG-I5	300	RPG-7	338
A-I Skyraider	302	North American T-28 Trojan	340
F-86 Sabre	304	Booby Traps	342
Napalm	306	Lockheed SR-71 Blackbird	344
AIM-9 Sidewinder Missile	308	ZSU-23-4 Shilka	346
Submarine (Nuclear Power)	310	M-I6	348
B-52 Stratofortress	312	Combat Shotgun	350
Lockheed U-2	314	Leopard	352
Skunk Works	316	BMP Armored Personnel Carrier (APC)	354
Tactical Nuclear Weapons	318	Mk I9 Grenade Machine Gun	356
Tupolev Tu-95 Bear	320	LTV A-7 Corsair II	358
MiG-2I Fishbed	322	SA-6 Gainful	360

1944
Aircraft Carrier

1945
Atomic Bomb

1959
ICBM

1964
Lockheed SR-71 Blackbird

1956
Tactical Nuclear Weapons

SA-7 Grail	362
Harrier	364
Aegis Combat Weapons System	366
AS-6 Kingfish	368
MiG-23 Flogger	370
MiG-25 Foxbat	372
Saab 37 Viggen	374
Bell AH-I Cobra and Super Cobra	376
Mil Mi-24 Hind	378
Tu-22 Backfire	380
T-72 Main Battle Tank	382
Aerospatiale SA 34I Gazelle	384
FN Minimi	386
Israel Aircraft Industries Kfir	388
MD/Boeing F-15 Eagle/ Strike Eagle	390
AGM-84 Harpoon	392
Fairchild-Republic A-10 Thunderbolt II	394

E-3 Sentry (AWACS)	396
F-I6 Fighting Falcon	398
Dassault-Breuguet Super Étendard	400
Panavia Tornado	402
UH-60 Black Hawk	404
Exocet	406
General Dynamics	408
Shenyang J-8 Finback	410
Abrams Main Battle Tank	412
Lockheed Martin MC-I30 Combat Talon	414
M2 Bradley Armored Personnel Carrier	416
FIM-92A Stinger	418
MIM-I04 Patriot	420
Ohio Class SSBN	422
MiG-3I Foxhound	424
AGM-II4 Hellfire	426
FV4030/4 Challenger I	428

1973
T-72 Main Battle Tank

1972

MiL MI-24 Hind

1976

MD/Boeing F-15 Eagle

1980

Abrams Main Battle Tank

1981

M2 Bradley Armored Personnel Carrier

Mcdonnell Douglas-Boeing F/A-18 Hornet — 430

Lockheed F-117A Nighthawk — 432

MiG-29 Fulcrum — 434

Global Positioning System (GPS) — 436

AH-64 Apache — 438

Dassault-Breguet Mirage 2000 — 440

End User Certificate — 442

Ground Mobility Vehicle — 444

Chemical Weapons — 446

Biological Weapons — 448

Amphibious Assault Ship — 450

Military Robots — 452

Precision Guided Munitions — 454

Communication Devices — 456

Public Opinion — 458

Predator — 460

Non-lethal Bullets — 462

Javelin — 464

B-2 Spirit — 466

Modern Armor — 468

Night Vision Device — 470

BAE Systems — 472

Dassault Rafale — 474

Suicide Bomber — 476

Sniper Rifle — 478

Dolphins and Sea Lions — 480

Eurofighter Typhoon — 482

High Speed Vessel (HSV) — 484

Amphibious Assault Vehicle — 486

Non-lethal Weapon Systems — 488

F-22 Raptor — 490

M777 Howitzer — 492

M982 Excalibur — 494

Dogs — 496

F-35 Lightning II — 498

Expeditionary Fighting Vehicle — 500

1983

Lockheed F-117A Nighthawk

1996

Javelin

1999

Night Vision Device

2003

High Speed Vessel

2003

Amphibious Assault

INTRODUCTION

If the history of mankind is the history of war, then it follows that the history of war is in large part written by the weapons that made battle possible. *The Book of Weapons* is a survey of significant arms and armor from ancient to present day—and a little bit more.

The Book of Weapons takes a comprehensive approach, providing not only key data details but also important background and anecdotes, resulting in brief, yet rounded accounts of each entry. The chapters are arranged in chronological order according to criteria that includes archeological data, significant battlefield contribution, peak popularity, dates of birth of individuals, and, beginning in the nineteenth century when accurate record keeping became prevalent, dates of acceptance by the military.

Significantly, *The Book of Weapons* expands on the traditional approach to the subject. It takes the all-too-rare additional step of including some of the men and companies who designed, built and sold (or re-sold) weapons. To otherwise focus only on the weapons themselves is the equivalent to seeing only the final act of a play—witnessing a dramatic climax while remaining ignorant of the often-torturous journey to that point. To take just one example, it is no small thing to say that the history of post-colonial Africa would have had a different ending had it not been for Samuel Cummings and the aftermarket arms sales shadow world in which he traveled.

The Book of Weapons also includes chapters on the psychological weapons employed by rulers that harness and give purpose and direction to a people's will to use the physical weapon thrust into their hands.

The past two decades have witnessed a revolution in arms design and development and *The Book of War* presents some of the more significant systems that recently became operational or are being tested.

Yet it's worth noting that no matter how efficient, deadly, or technologically advanced, all the weapons throughout history share one immutable limitation. As World War II General George S. Patton, Jr., said, "We fight wars with machinery, but we win wars with people."

Prehistoric Weapons

Though his name is long since lost to antiquity, credit must be given to the prehistoric merchant of death who one day decided that a stone, in all its simplicity, was far more effective than his hands and teeth in felling prey or an enemy. Though it will never be proved whether the first stone weapon was thrown or tightly gripped while delivering the deadly blow, the effort produced the desired result. And it is entirely within the realm of possibility that, upon hearing of this man's success, the rest of the hunters/warriors in the tribe began outfitting themselves as rapidly as possible with these death-dealing stones, literally initiating the first arms race.

The earliest known tools and weapons (they were often interchangeable) were made of stone or bone. Flint was the preferred stone as it was plentiful, easily shaped, and held a good cutting edge. Another stone highly prized for its cutting ability was the volcanic glass obsidian. In fact, obsidian blades are still in use today as delicate surgical instruments; their cutting edges are sharper than the highest quality steel scalpel.

Prehistoric stone knives started out as hand-held blades and came in all sorts of sizes and shapes. They were generally triangular, with the wide base serving as a handle, or long and narrow. The knife was single- or double-bladed, depending on its purpose. Sometimes the blades were serrated. The first technological upgrade was the binding of the stone blade to a short bone or wooden shaft or pole, creating a knife with a handle. This extended the fighter's reach and allowed him to use the full force of his arm in a thrust.

The addition of the handle soon led to the development of adzes, axes, and clubs. Even longer poles led to the development of the spear, and, upon the creation of the bow, to arrows. The arrival of the Bronze Age (ca. 3300 B.C.) in Mesopotamia saw the replacement of these materials by tools and weapons made of forged metal. Even so, stone, bone, and wood tools and weapons were used by people well into the nineteenth century and are still in use by tribes in the remote regions of the world.

Cave art in Libya showing prehistoric hunters attacking game with spears

KNIFE

Knives are one of the most ancient and widespread of weapons. Their archeological evidence is found throughout history and around the world. The wide range of designs and styles is truly breathtaking. They run the gamut from prehistoric sharpened stones, sticks, and bones to elaborate and complex Damascus steel blades to crudely constructed shivs wrought by convicts. Their use has been equally broad—weapons, tools, and utensils; sacred objects in religion; and symbols of power, authority, masculinity, and treachery. Even when limiting the discussion to weapon knives, the design and variety are no less astonishing, ranging from single-edged bayonets, double-edged daggers, curved Japanese tanto, to the undulating "flame-bladed" kris of Indonesia.

One knife that combines religious symbolism and military utility is the kirpan—a knife with a curved blade. The kirpan has great significance in the Sikh religion. Sikh men are required to wear the kirpan at all times as a symbol both of their baptism and of their willingness to defend the helpless and fight injustice. On October 31, 2002, the Indian Ministry of Civil Aviation, which is responsible for airline security, issued a circular allowing Sikhs to carry a kirpan on all domestic airline flights, so long as the blade was no more than six inches long and that the overall length of the kirpan did not exceed nine inches.

Another knife with great social significance is the Yemeni jambiya, which is both a status symbol and a symbol of masculinity. The most important part of the jambiya is its hilt. The most famous and expensive hilt—and thus the one signifying the high status of its owner—is the saifani, made of rhinoceros horn. International treaties protecting the rhinoceros significantly cut down on the use of rhino horn, and so now the intricacy of the jambiya's design indicates the owner's status.

But of all the types of knives and no matter their rich heritage or humble history, by far the most dangerous one of all is a knife whose blade is dull.

A Javan man with knives in his belt

SPEAR

At some point, the knife-creator must have confronted a limitation of his simple but effective hand-held engine of destruction—he could only kill his prey or enemy if it were within reach. Archeological evidence of spears goes back only 400,000 years, but experts speculate that spears were created millions of years earlier. Regardless, at some point someone got the bright idea to strap a knife blade to a long pole, such as a walking stick, and while out hunting threw the thing at a fleeing animal. Of course, it can never be known whether that first attempt worked. But at some point our hunter did hit and kill his prey, and the spear entered the inventory of arms.

Spears became practical weapons of war during the Bronze Age. Spears generally fall into two categories: the thrusting spear (or pike) and the throwing spear (or javelin). One of the most famous of the ancient thrusting spears was the Greek doru. Ranging in length from six to nine feet, it was used with great effectiveness by the tightly packed Greek phalanxes. Alexander the Great used a longer pike, called a sarissa, whose length ranged from 13 to 21 feet.

The Romans perfected deadly spear designs. The inventory included the hasta, a six-and-a-half-foot-long heavy thrusting spear, a three-and-a-half-foot-long javelin called the verutum, a six-foot-long javelin called the lancea, the seven-foot-long pilum, and, in the late Roman period, a six-foot javelin called a spiculum.

In Japan, spears were objects of veneration and legend. Most notable were what came to be known as the Three Great Spears of Japan. They were the Otegine, the Nihongo, and the Tonbogiri (Dragonfly Cutter) created by the famed swordsmith Masozane and wielded by the brilliant general and hero Honda Tadakatsu. According to legend, the Tonbogiri got its name because its blade was so sharp that when a dragonfly landed on it, it was cut in two.

400,000

B.C.

Interior of an ancient Greek cup showing hunters with spears stalking the Boar of Calydon

SLING

If artillery is defined as a weapon that launches a projectile at a target, then the sling is the first artillery weapon. And because of its 100 percent biodegradable construction, it could also be considered the first green weapon!

The sling is nothing more than a pouch attached to the middle of two lengths of cord. The projectiles, called sling-stones or sling-bullets, can be as simple as round or oval stones picked up from a riverbed or lumps of baked clay or cast in lead. Though their organized military use ended during the Middle Ages, groups who have no access to firearms have continued to use slings in conflicts to the present day.

Because slings were fashioned out of leather or woven plant fibers, few ancient slings have survived. Instead, evidence of them is found in art and literature, and in archeological excavations. The earliest depictions appear in Assyrian and Egyptian bas-reliefs and walls. The oldest written mention (about 1000 B.C.) is in the Bible's Book of Judges, recounting the Battle of Gibeah that occurred several centuries earlier. Interestingly (or perhaps "sinisterly"), the Bible notes not only the number of sling throwers (700) and their skill ("every one could sling stones at a hair breadth, and not miss") but also the fact that they were left-handed. Ancient Greek writers, including the poet Homer and the Greek general and historian Xenophon, mention slings. The oldest known sling was found in Tutankhamen's tomb and is dated about 1325 B.C.

The sling's low cost, ease of construction and operation, and effectiveness (accurate to 2,000 feet, compared to contemporary arrow accuracy of about 300 feet) made it ubiquitous worldwide. Herders needing to protect their flocks used slings against predators. Ancient generals, including Alexander and Julius Caesar, included units of sling-throwers in their armies. Some cultures and societies regarded the sling as a low-class weapon. The most famous sling-thrower was the young Israelite, David, who killed the Philistine Goliath with one of five stones pulled out of a brook. David would go on to become king of Israel, a remarkable achievement for a humble wielder of the world's most proletarian weapon.

50,000 B.C.

A Renaissance illustration showing David about to use his sling against Goliath

Blowgun

Thanks to Hollywood, a popular impression of blowguns and their use is that of Amazonian warriors waiting to ambush unsuspecting European or American explorers. Their first warning of danger is a blowgun dart coated with curare poison in the neck. While there is a core of truth, Hollywood's efforts distort and diminish the story of the blowgun, one of the most ubiquitous weapons in history.

The origin of the blowgun is lost in prehistory. The earliest known blowguns, found in Asia and Africa, date back about 40,000 years and were made of bamboo, reeds, and hollowed wood. The first written record of blowguns appears in *Poliorcetus*, a work on siegecraft written by the Roman architect, Appollodorus of Damascus, in which he describes blowguns used to hunt birds. Illustrations of individuals using blowguns in Peru date back to the sixth century. Some French and Flemish illustrated manuscripts from the fourteenth and fifteenth century show boys and men using blowguns for hunting. Though lacking in power and range of other weapons such as the bow and arrow, the blowgun did have some advantages. It was extremely accurate and it was quiet. This made it an ideal weapon for hunting, ambush, and assassination.

Blowguns were used in China, India, Africa, and throughout Europe. Egyptian Mamelukes called the blowgun "zabatana," in Italy it was the "cerbottana," and in Germany it was known as the "blasrohr." They were used even as far north as Scandinavia. In North America, the Choctaw bound four or five together to create multi-barreled blowguns. In Japan, blowguns were a favored weapon of the ninja assassins.

Today, blowguns are used for sport and some hunting. Unlike so many other weapons that have survived through the ages, the blowgun has remained essentially unchanged. A bamboo blowgun made and used today, but for age, would be indistinguishable from one made hundreds or thousands of years ago.

40,000 B.C.

A native Piaroa hunter from Venezuela stands with a blowgun and poison darts

Atlatl

The atlatl, used to give extra velocity and distance for a spear throw, is a wooden shaft about two feet long, cut into a trough-like shape and cupped at one end. The spear is placed in the trough and the butt of the spear is notched in the cup. The thrower balances the spear with one hand, and with the other gripping the open end of the atlatl, launches the spear with a swing of his arm. Though the atlatl is primarily known as a device to help in spear throwing, originally it was used to hurl darts.

Experts believe the dart-throwing atlatl came into use during the Upper Paleolithic period, about 30,000 B.C.; the earliest known atlatl, found in France and made from a reindeer antler, dates back about 27,000 years. Use of the atlatl began to diminish shortly after the arrival of the bow and arrow, which proved more efficient in hunting and fighting.

The last employment of the atlatl in combat occurred millennia after it had become little more than a device used in spearing fish. During the 1500s, shortly after the arrival of the Spanish Conquistadors, the Aztecs reinvented it for use in war and, though spears hurled by the atlatl did not have the power to penetrate armor, the Conquistadors learned to fear it above all other weapons used by the Aztecs.

The atlatl is still used in some parts of the world. In Australia, the aborigines use a version called the woomera as a spear-throwing aid in hunting. And the Inuit of northern Canada use a version called the nuqaq for seal hunting. The atlatl has gained a following among some hunters and an association was formed that sponsors events and competitions worldwide. Efforts to form an atlatl-hunting season of large game, such as deer, have had some success in the United States and elsewhere.

30,000 B.C.

An Aztec apprentice warrior in armed regalia that includes in his right hand an atlatl

Boomerang

The original boomerang didn't return after it was thrown. In fact, the Australian aborigines, the most famous users of the boomerang, originally didn't even throw it—they used it as a club. The earliest known archeological evidence of a boomerang was a 30,000-year-old mammoth tusk shaped like a boomerang found in the Carpathian Mountains of Poland. And both hunting (non-returning and identified by their straight shape) and curved sport (returning) boomerangs were among the many artifacts discovered in Tutankhamen's tomb in Egypt.

Modern boomerangs come in several distinctive shapes. The basic returning boomerang looks like a flat, angled wing usually made of wood, though other materials can be used. The thrower must have a sophisticated knowledge of the technique, and of the wind speed and direction, to get the boomerang to return.

Boomerangs saw little use in combat, and were more practical as hunting weapons. Today, they are used almost exclusively in sport, with boomerang clubs and competitions organized and held throughout the world. The boomerang's popularity supports regular bi-annual international world cup competitions.

100,000 B.C.

An Australian aborigine father and son with their boomerangs

Ancient Armor

While the first weapons were dual purpose, serving as equipment for hunting and fighting, it could be argued that armor is the first equipment designed for war. The purpose of armor is to protect its wearer from injury during battle. At the same time, it has to be light enough to allow freedom of movement. Body armor was used by all the ancient civilizations. Infantries, whose close-quarter fighting required maximum protection, wore the heaviest armor. Cavalry armor during this period was either light or nonexistent, because speed and maneuverability were used defensively more than actual physical shielding. That changed during the Middle Ages.

The first armor was probably made of animal hides. In ancient Egypt, crocodile armor was favored for its toughness. Also, warriors believed it would give them the strength and ferocity of a crocodile. Its use endured well after the discovery of metallurgy enabled the creation of superior armor of bronze, brass, and iron. After Rome's conquest of Egypt, legionnaires garrisoned there took to wearing crocodile armor.

The most famous examples of armor in the ancient world are those worn by the Greek hoplites and the Roman legionnaires. The hoplites, whose ranks were formed from the upper classes in Greek society, were heavily armed and armored shock troops. The body armor of a hoplite was usually cast bronze and consisted of a helmet, a two-piece cuirass covering the chest and back, and greaves that protected the knees and shins. They also had large, circular shields.

By the time of the Roman Empire, armor development had become quite sophisticated. The *lorica segmentata* was a combination cuirass and shoulder armor composed of overlapping strips of metal that provided a lot of flexibility and protection for the legionnaire. The collapse of the Western Roman Empire in 476 A.D. saw the dramatic decline of the use of armor in Western Europe. The next great chapter in armor design and use had to wait about three hundred years with the reign of Charlemagne and the Holy Roman Empire.

Armored Roman generals in conference

Ax

With its sharp, heavy blade and sturdy haft, the ax was one of the most—if not the most—versatile implements in the prehistoric world. Its importance is reflected by the discovery of Neolithic Age "ax factories" dating as far back as 4000 B.C. found in a wide variety of places, including Ireland and Poland. They were used from cradle to grave—as religious symbols in ceremonies celebrating birth and planting, as tools in forestry and agriculture, as weapons of war, and as instruments of justice in the hands of hooded executioners.

One of the most notable axes of the ancient world was the labrys, a double-bladed ax usually associated with the Minoan civilization of Crete and principally used by priestesses in religious services. The holiest of religious symbols, the labrys was made in many sizes and metals, including gold. It was a symbol of matriarchal power and was never held or used by men.

As their name indicates, battle axes were specifically designed for combat and were single-bladed or double-bladed. Because they were cheaper and easier to manufacture than swords, they were among the most common weapons, particularly during the early Middle Ages. Hatchets are smaller, lighter axes, and the most famous weapon of this design is the tomahawk used by the Native Americans of North America.

Ax and tomahawk use began to decline after the advent of firearms. Their use as a weapon essentially ended by the conclusion of the nineteenth century. The tomahawk saw a resurgence in the U.S. military during the Vietnam War with a design that later came to be known as the Vietnam Tactical Tomahawk. This design is now classified as a "Class 9 rescue kit" and has been used by units deployed in Afghanistan as an all-purpose breaching tool.

4000 B.C.

A collection of gold miniature double axes, c. 1500 B.C., found in the Minoan sacred cave Arkalochori

Bow

The bow is another weapon whose use in war spanned millennia before finally being retired in the late nineteenth century. And—like its contemporaries the knife, spear, and sword—it has been used by civilizations throughout the world and constructed in an astonishing variety of shapes. Historians and archeologists credit the Assyrians as being the first civilization to employ a standing army. Bas-reliefs show that they employed both foot and chariot-driven archers; the latter made their first appearance about 1600 B.C.

Archers were organized into units that fought on foot or from chariots, and later, horses. Foot archers used bows that were heavier, longer, and more powerful than those used by mounted archers. The longest was the English longbow, which was more than six feet tall and had a 200-pound pull. These bows were usually made of a single piece of strong and flexible wood, preferably yew. Expert foot archers were capable of rapid fire (from ten to twenty arrows per minute) at enemies up to distances of two hundred yards or more. The longbow was so strong that it could penetrate all but the toughest steel plate armor, even at two hundred yards.

As horses became larger and stronger, archers transferred from the chariot to horseback. Assyrian bas-reliefs show horses carrying two riders, one to direct the horse and the other to fire the arrows. Eventually this was reduced to one. The most accomplished practitioners of the art of horse archery were the peoples who lived in the steppes and prairies. The short list amounts to a who's who of some of the most feared warrior tribes in history: In Asia and Europe, it was the Scythians, Parthians, Huns, Magyars, Mongols, and Turks. After the Spanish Conquistadors arrived in North America, the nomadic warrior group came to include the Sioux, Comanche, and other Plains Indian tribes.

Today the bow is used in sport and hunting. The most popular design is the compound bow, a complex arrangement of composite carbon fibers and high-tech metal, levers, pulleys, counterweights, stabilizers, dampers, and mechanical releases. It requires less strength but is just as accurate as the traditional bow of history.

An Assyrian bas-relief depicting King Ashurbanipal on a chariot and firing his bow

INCENDIARIES

A weapon of mass destruction is one that wreaks a broad swath of uncontrollable devastation. As such, it could be argued that fire, when used as part of a "scorched earth strategy" that destroyed entire towns and large tracts of cultivated land and forest, was the first weapon of mass destruction.

Even today, fire is a cost-effective weapon. All it takes is a well-placed torch or other starter and sufficiently dry conditions to create an inferno. But because fire remains vulnerable to the whims of a shifting wind, it is just as fickle a weapon as it was back when Alexander the Great and other generals of the ancient world tried to harness its destructive power for their own purposes.

Incendiaries came into their own in sieges and naval battles, where the danger of fire could be best put to use. Flaming projectiles launched by archers or catapults were made of pitch, oil, resin, animal fats, or burning sulfur or other materials. Defenders had in their thermal arsenal hot oil, hot sand, and boiling water that they poured from the parapets onto attacking troops. The most effective countermeasures in the ancient world were water, vinegar, and urine. Defenders soaked animal hides and draped some over vulnerable wooden structures. Liquids were also stored in towers, barrels, and cisterns placed in key locations.

Wooden walls and buildings were obviously vulnerable, but even stone walls and buildings were susceptible to thermal destruction. Intense heat applied along the base of a wall could crack and shatter stones, causing the wall to collapse.

One of the earliest records of the use of incendiaries was the well-documented siege of the Judean walled city of Lachish by an Assyrian army led by King Sennacherib in 701 B.C. The epic of the city's downfall and the departure of its population into captivity are recorded in the Bible, Assyrian documents, and visually in a series of bas-reliefs on the walls of Sennacherib's palace at Ninevah. The Assyrians used archers shooting flaming arrows to burn buildings, with great effect. Lachish fell when the Assyrians built a ramp that reached the top of the walls.

A 16th century engraving showing natives attacking a walled village with flaming arrows

TRIREME

The trireme—so named for the three banks of oars on each side of the vessel—was the dominant warship of the ancient Mediterranean world for four centuries (700 to 400 B.C.). The trireme's sail served only as an alternate source of power; rowers provided the main power, particularly during battle. The trireme's design and tactics reflect the experience and philosophies of generals who, when confronted with the situation where they had to fight on the water, became admirals. They were not so much warships as they were mobile platforms designed to facilitate a land battle fought on water.

Tactics centered on ramming and boarding. The bow of the trireme was fitted with one or more stout wooden rams tipped with metal. The rowers, all freemen and skilled professionals, accelerated to at least 10 knots to successfully breach the enemy's hull. In another ramming method, the attacking trireme sideswiped the other ship. At the last second, rowers in the attacking ship pulled in their oars. The attacking trireme would then shatter the exposed oars of its opponent as their hulls moved past each other, rendering the attacked trireme helpless. Triremes also carried a contingent of marines for boarding. Ship captains tried to avoid boarding attacks because the boarding trireme could just as easily find itself boarded by its enemy once the grappling hooks were in place.

Triremes participated in one of the greatest battles in naval history, the Battle of Salamis, where the Greek fleet led by Athens defeated a Persian invasion fleet about twice its size led by Xerxes I. With only forty ships lost, the Greeks destroyed about 200 Persian vessels and ended Xerxes' planned conquest of Greece.

As the Roman Empire grew in power and influence, the trireme was superseded by the larger (four-row) quadriremes and (five-row) quinquiremes. These monstrous vessels lacked stability and were difficult to maneuver. Because they were more used for boarding than ramming, the quadriremes and quinquiremes took the concept of a land battle platform operating on water to its extreme and, mercifully, its end.

An ancient Greek trireme

CAMEL

When one thinks of cavalry, the most common images that come to mind are those of soldiers mounted on horseback, or riding in armored vehicles such as tanks. But other animals have served in cavalry corps, and one of them was—and still is—the camel. Camel cavalry—or camelry—were once common units in the armies of the desert world.

The first known engagement involving camels occurred in 547 B.C. in the Battle of Thymbra. Cyrus the Great, leading a Persian army of conquest estimated to be from 30,000 to 50,000 troops, had set his sights on adding the Lydian Empire, in what is now central and western Turkey, to his own empire. Opposing Cyrus was the Lydian king Croesus—from whom we got the expression "rich as Croesus"—and an army historians estimate at about 100,000 troops.

In Cyrus's army were about 300 camels, used as pack animals. Contrary to popular opinion, camels don't spit when agitated. Instead, they projectile vomit. They also have a distinctive smell. It's this latter trait that proved decisive. As Cyrus was preparing for battle, one of his generals informed him that in an earlier battle with the Lydians, when Lydian horses picked up the unfamiliar scent of camels, they got spooked and shied away from the beasts. Cyrus promptly organized his camels and their handlers into a cavalry corps with instructions to charge the Lydian cavalry upon his command.

Shortly after the battle was joined, Cyrus gave the signal. The camel units, stationed on both flanks, charged the Lydian cavalry. When they caught the smell of the camels, the Lydian horses panicked. The ensuing chaos in the Lydian ranks helped turn the tide in favor of the Persians. The battle ended in a decisive victory for the Persians, and the Lydian empire was soon incorporated into the Persian.

Though camels continued to be used as cavalry, and are being employed in small units in Iraq and Afghanistan by United States and United Nations troops today, the cavalry branch came to be dominated by horses. In the 1850s, Jefferson Davis, then a U.S. senator from Mississippi and chairman of the Senate Committee on Military Affairs, sponsored the formation of a camel cavalry corps for use in the desert military posts in the West. The effort ultimately failed, primarily because of the outbreak of the Civil War.

An engraving showing a train of camels from the short-lived U.S. Camel Corps of the 1850s

CROSSBOW

Simply stated, the crossbow is a ballista writ small. Instead of muscle power, the launching force of the crossbow is mechanical. The drawstring, or cord, is pulled back by a winch and released by a trigger. Such is the power of the crossbow that its small, cheaply made bolts could penetrate the best armor. In addition to having greater power, the crossbow could be fired from a variety of positions. Its only real disadvantage was that it was much slower than the regular hand-drawn bow.

The earliest known crossbows are believed to have originated as much as three thousand years ago in China. They came to play a major role in battles in the Middle East and Europe for centuries until the development of practical firearms in the seventeenth century.

The crossbow has the distinction of being among the first weapons to be banned. Because little skill was needed to shoot a crossbow with deadly efficiency, a lowly commoner could easily kill an armored knight. This murderous affront to nobility was a factor in leading to a series of bans forbidding its use, beginning with Pope Urban II in 1097. This was followed by a modified ban promulgated in the Second Latean Council of 1139 in which Pope Innocent II forbade its usage against Christians (the Kingdom of Jerusalem was being seriously threatened, and the Second Crusade would be launched within eight years). The ban was expanded to include archers in general and sling throwers, but that never gained much traction.

Conrad II, the disputed Holy Roman Emperor (he was involved in a civil war), banned the crossbow before he took off on the Second Crusade. Needless to say, the bans proved ineffective. Richard the Lionhearted was killed by a gangrene infection as the result of a crossbow wound suffered in battle in 1199.

Today crossbows are primarily used in sport and hunting. A few countries around the world—including China, Turkey, Greece, and Serbia—are reported to have units trained in their use, but they are the exception.

The Capture of Constantinople

Ballista

The ballista (plural, ballistae) and the catapult are the two great mechanical artillery pieces of the ancient world. The ballista looks like a gigantic crossbow whose drawstring, a thick tightly woven cord, is stretched by a large windlass that cocks, or prepares, the ballista for firing. When triggered, the cord propelled the ballista's projectile with great force. The projectile was usually a large spear, though blunter objects were sometimes used. Modern recreations of the ballista have demonstrated that the fieldpiece's effective range extended to about five hundred yards.

Though war engines had existed for several centuries, their use was limited to static sieges because their large size and heavy weight made them difficult to move. This changed shortly after Philip of Macedon came to the throne in 359 B.C. Philip, the father of Alexander the Great, ingeniously saw a way for the ballista to "live off the land" during a campaign. He disassembled a ballista and determined that the essential parts could all be loaded on a single pack animal. Everything else, in other words the heavy and bulky items, could all be cut and shaped from trees from local forests. Alexander used his father's tactical innovation with such great success that other armies soon began copying the Macedonian's method.

The ballista reached its height during the Roman Empire. One popular variation was a "repeating" ballista known as the polybolos; it was capable of firing as many as eleven bolts a minute. Another popular model was the small "scorpion" which could be operated by just two men. Though use of the ballista continued into the Middle Ages, it entered a stage of gradual decline after Rome fell in the mid-sixth century.

Though archeologists have been able to recreate modern, functioning versions of the ballista, they have been unable to recapture the ancient secret of preserving the cords' elasticity.

ELEPHANTS

Hannibal's crossing of the Alps with his army in 218 B.C. during the Second Punic War made military history. What made it legendary were the war elephants accompanying him. It is one of the most famous images in the history of warfare. War elephants were the ultimate shock cavalry of the ancient world. Their use extended beyond the battlefield. For centuries elephants served as trucks, tractors, bulldozers, forklifts, and cranes. Even after their use was rendered obsolete by the advent of firearms, elephants continued to perform valuable military service in construction and supply. During World War II, for example, elephants were used to help build the Ledo Road, a supply route that connected India with China. Their status in the military continues to this day. The Green Berets classify elephants as pack animals in their field manual.

It's not known for certain when elephants were first used in war. The earliest records reveal that war elephants were used in India as early as 1100 B.C. and that their use spread west into the Persian Empire. One of the first Western encounters with war elephants occurred during the battle of Gaugamela in 331 B.C., where Alexander the Great defeated the Persian army led by Darius III. Though Darius fielded only fifteen elephants in that battle, their presence and use made a huge impression on Alexander. His horse cavalry was rendered almost useless because the horses panicked over the unfamiliar smell and size of the animals. Once he had conquered the Persian empire, he incorporated war elephant units into his army.

War elephants were integral parts of several armies in Southeast Asia. War elephants were used extensively in a war between Burma and Siam, present day Myanmar and Thailand, in the early 1590s. The war ended in a Siamese victory after the conclusion of a personal combat fought on elephants when Siamese King Naresuan killed Burmese crown prince Minchit Sra. The day of that duel, January 18, 1593, is observed as Armed Forces Day in Thailand.

A sixteenth century painting of the Battle of Zama (202 B.C.) showing Carthaginians using war elephants against Roman legionaires

PIGS

Of all the animals used in war, it's hard to find one more abused than the pig. A weapon in the arsenal of the armies of the ancient world, they served only one purpose in battle: a countermeasure to war elephants. But it was how they were deployed against the pachyderms that was, well, beastly.

Elephants are scared of the noise pigs make. In his famous book, *Natural History*, Roman author and naturalist Pliny the Elder wrote that elephants were terrified of even the smallest grunts and squeals of hogs. One of the earliest accounts of pigs versus elephants occurred during the siege of Megara in the Wars of the Diadochi (322–301 B.C.), when civil war broke out between Alexander the Great's generals (collectively known as the Diadochi) in their division of his empire. The Macedonian general Antipater had war elephants in his army. The Megarans lifted the siege when, during one assault, they poured oil over the backs of a bunch of pigs, ignited the oil, and chased the flaming, squealing, pigs straight at the elephants. The elephants bolted in terror, wreaking havoc among the ranks of the Macedonian army.

The Romans also used flaming pigs, most notably against the war elephants in the army of the Greek general Pyrrhus of Epirus, from whom we get the term "pyrrhic victory" describing a battlefield success achieved after excessive cost.

Tar, pitch, and olive oil were the most common flammable materials used to set the pigs on fire. It almost goes without saying that fire pigs were not reliable. They could just as easily run into the ranks of those who set them afire, and no doubt some did, though history is sadly silent on that subject.

The only other recorded case of similar battlefield abuse of animals happened in World War II on the Eastern Front when Soviet troops strapped anti-tank mines to dogs trained to attack tanks. As it turned out, the dogs did not distinguish friend from foe, and enough of them disabled and destroyed Soviet tanks that the program was quickly ended.

ARCHIMEDES

(287–212 B.C.)

Archimedes of Syracuse was a mathematician, physicist, engineer, inventor, astronomer, and the greatest weapons-maker of the ancient world. He was single-handedly credited with preventing the Roman capture of Syracuse for two years.

Archimedes was already famous and well into his seventies when the city's rulers sided with Carthage against Rome in the Second Punic War. In 214 B.C., General Marcus Claudius Marcellus arrived with a large Roman army and navy to capture the walled city, and the stage was set for the greatest siege since the Trojan War.

Marcellus tried a series of sea and land assaults. Archimedes' defensive efforts ranged from the simple to the complex. Roman ships that sailed close to shore were driven away by bowmen firing through holes pierced in the harbor's walls under Archimedes' orders. Rapid-fire catapults that hurled heavy stones huge distances repulsed Marcellus' attacks by land or sea.

Archimedes also designed large cranes to defend the harbor. Some were capable of dropping heavy loads of stone onto approaching ships. The most amazing crane was called "Archimedes' Claw." It had a gigantic hook attached to a long, heavy rope. It could grab a vessel, lift it into the air and swing it against the rocky shore or plunge it back into the sea. Another invention was his "burning mirrors"—curved plates of polished metal. The mirrors were arranged so that they reflected and concentrated sunbeams onto ships to ignite them.

Archimedes so traumatized the Romans that at one point well into the siege he successfully routed an attack through sheer bluff. As the legions approached Syracuse's walls, the citizens threw some ropes over the parapets. Thinking that another Archimedes invention was about to rain death and destruction on them, the troops retreated in panic.

Marcellus surrounded the city to starve it into submission. After eight months, Syracuse surrendered. Marcellus gave orders that Archimedes was not to be killed. The most common account of what happened next is that a legionnaire found Archimedes in his home working on a mathematics problem and killed him when he refused to leave his work. He was buried in a tomb engraved with a sphere within a cylinder, a representation of his favorite mathematical proof.

Hot Oil, Sand, and Water

What the peoples of the ancient world may have lacked regarding technological innovation in weaponry, they more than made up for it with imaginative destructive uses of what they had at hand. Hot oil, hot sand, and hot water have all been used in battle. Oil was the most expensive and sand was, at the risk of making a bad pun, dirt cheap. An advantage all had was their ability to not just penetrate armor, but by heat transference, turn the soldier's armor into a burning weapon. It's impossible to say when any of them were first used in battle, but military history is filled with accounts of their use.

One effective example of the use of hot oil occurred during the Siege of Jotapata (67 A.D.) in the First Jewish-Roman War. Jews led by Josephus had taken refuge in the citadel of Jotapa, which was surrounded by steep cliffs and could be approached from only one direction. Vespatian, leading three legions, surrounded the place and, after some fruitless attacks, breached a section of the north wall, the only place that could be easily attacked. The Romans were moments away from invading Jotapa. In his book, *Last Days of Jerusalem*, historian Alfred J. Church wrote, "Then Josephus, being in a great strait (when men are wont to be best at devising that which is needful), commanded that they should pour hot oil on the shields of the Romans. Of this the Jews had a plentiful store, and when they poured it down upon the Romans, these cried aloud for the pain of the burning, and brake their order, and fell back from the wall, for the oil crept under the armour from their heads even unto their feet, and consumed them even like fire; and the nature of oil is that it is easily kindled but hardly quench." Church went on to recount how the Jewish defenders followed this by then pouring hot water laced with herbs onto the wooden planks, making them so slick that the Romans couldn't keep their footing, and many fell to their death. The victory proved short-lived, for the city fell through treachery after holding out 47 days.

A fifteenth century illustration showing castle defenders pouring hot oil onto attacking ships

Greek Fire

The chemical compound originally known as Byzantine fire and Roman fire eventually came to be called Greek fire and is one of the legendary weapons of the ancient world. A hellish liquid concoction that was fueled by water (causing it to also be known as "sea fire" and "liquid fire"), Greek fire was the ultimate weapon of its time. So great was the fear its use inspired that armies were known to retreat from battle when the nozzles of Greek fire siphons were pointed in their direction.

Greek fire was invented in about 706 A.D. by the architect Callinicus at the behest of the Byzantine emperor Constantine IV who sought weapons to defend Constantinople from invaders, particularly the resurgent Saracens. The weapon's great test occurred in 673 when a combined Saracen land and water expedition was launched against the city. The armada managed to force passage into the Dardanelles Straits. With the great city in sight and with only the thin shield of a small Byzantine fleet barring its advance, it seemed that the fall of Constantinople was just hours away. But moments before the Saracen warships smashed into the Byzantine galleys, strange bronze tubes stationed on the Byzantine prows emitted jets of liquid fire that splashed onto the wooden decks and water around the ships. Immolated Arab marines rolled around in agony as their ships were engulfed in flames fed by the water of the straits. The Saracens retreated and attempted a four-year siege that ended in a costly failure. Among the peace terms the Saracens agreed to was the restoration of all their recent conquests to Byzantium and the payment of an annual tribute of 3,000 pounds of gold for thirty years.

The Byzantines valued Greek fire so highly that its formula became a state secret ultimately lost to history. Based on eyewitness descriptions, speculation of Greek fire's composition included a mixture of petroleum, niter, and sulfur; naptha, quicklime, and sulfur; or phosphorous and saltpeter. While similar types of flaming liquids predated the invention of Greek fire, none proved as effective. Historians generally agree that had it not been for Greek fire, the Byzantine empire would not have survived as long as it did.

A twelfth century illustration of a Byzantine ship shooting Greek fire at an enemy vessel

σκλᾶσϊϋπρωολόωϊπυρί ·

τωνἱηαηπφλον ·

FAITH

The adage "faith has the power to move mountains" is somewhat misleading. Faith has the power to move the foot that steps on the shovel that moves the mountain. Rulers, religious leaders, generals, and frontline soldiers and sailors from time immemorial have called upon divine assistance in wars and battles. Muhammad's triumph over the Meccans at Badr (624) and Joan of Arc leading the French to victory over the British at Orléans (1428) are just two of the most spectacular (and, in their case, history-changing) examples of the power of faith in battle.

In the aftermath of success the victors often offered worshipful sacrifices. Frequently the vanquished were offered the choice of life, provided they agreed to worship the victor's gods, or death. This binding of spiritual authority to temporal power went on for millennia. It was a practice that promoted unity and stability in the conquered lands through integration, though some empires chose another route. For instance, the Roman Empire tolerated local religions and customs so long as they did not conflict with Roman authority and rule, and dealt harshly with those that did.

Wars of religion elevated the spiritual commitment (or lowered it, depending on the point of view) by making faith a *casus belli*. The Crusades to "free and preserve" the Holy Land from Muslim rule are the most famous of these. The Protestant Reformation begun in 1571 unleashed about two hundred years of religious wars in Europe between Roman Catholics and Protestants.

Muhammad's death in 632 inspired a century of Arab expansion in a jihad (struggle) that spread the Muslim faith. This reached its zenith with the Umayyad Caliphate, whose empire stretched as far east as Pakistan and, by 718, as far west as Spain.

Jihads continue to be invoked to this day. The most notorious was the jihad called by the terrorist Osama bin Laden against the United States that resulted in the terrorist attacks on September 11, 2001.

Joan of Arc

SWORD

When it comes to elegant simplicity in a weapon, nothing beats the sword. Stripped to its essentials, the sword is nothing more than a single piece of shaped metal consisting of a long blade and hilt (handle), and sometimes a quillon (crossguard)—essentially, a very long knife (it was developed from the dagger). Of the group of classic ancient weapons that included the club, knife, ax, bow and arrow, and spear, the sword was the last, appearing only after smelting and metal-working skills had sufficiently developed to make long-bladed weapons possible. Over the millennia, swords have been fashioned in widely varying designs according to military necessity and cultural tastes. Blades have been single- and double-edged, curved and straight, flat and tapered, and single-handed and double-handed. Though other weapons have matched the sword for longevity on the battlefield, none—not even today's weapons—come close to equaling its prestige.

It is no expression of hyperbole to state that swords of legend and fact glitter throughout the chapters of history. Among the many legendary swords there are the Sword of Damocles, Roland's Durandal, Charlemagne's Joyeuse, and King Arthur's Excalibur in the West. Zulfiqar (Spinecleaver) was a gift from the prophet Muhammad to Ali. In Hindu mythology, the god Shiva presented the sword Chandrahas (Moon-blade) to the ten-headed king of Sri Lanka, Ravana. One historical sword that has been elevated to mythic status is Japan's Kusanagi-no-Tsurugi, one of the Three Sacred Treasures of Japan that make up the Imperial Regalia. Reportedly kept in the Atsuta shrine, it is never displayed in public and is only used in the imperial enthronement ceremony.

Another sword that achieved legendary status is Tizona, the sword of Rodrigo Díaz de Vivar, the eleventh-century national hero of Spain who is better known as El Cid (The Lord). Tizona's blade contains Damascus steel (itself a legendary metal because of its high quality) and was used in many battles against the Moors, including the Battle of Cabra (1079). Tizona survived its master and is presently on display in the Museum of Burgos in Spain.

An Albrecht Durer portrait of Holy Roman Emperor Charlemagne holding his sword *Joyeuse*

karoliis impaint magniis Annis .142

Mace

The mace is a club-like staff weapon. It is believed to be the first weapon specifically designed for killing humans. The mace head's shape makes it possible to deliver a stunning or lethal blow from any side. Maces were used by infantry and cavalry and had a variety of heads. Though the mace remained in the military inventory well into the seventeenth century in the Indian subcontinent, gunpowder had rendered it obsolete in Europe. Its decline as a weapon was followed by its elevation for ceremonial uses. Today ornate maces, often of gold or silver and encrusted with gems, are used to signal the opening and closing of legislative sessions or university convocations, and as symbols of ecclesiastical or academic authority and jurisdiction. Military use of maces has evolved into that of a parade instrument. A drum major, standing at the front of the band, uses it like a baton to signal orders.

The earliest known maces date back to about 12,000 B.C. These were for the most part made of stones strapped to the end of a stick. The development of metallurgy in the Bronze Age, beginning in 3300 B.C., significantly advanced the utility and reliability of maces. Before that, mace heads often came loose, and occasionally the stone head shattered upon impact.

Once they were cast in metal, mace shapes, styles, and shaft length increased. Mace head designs included simple and ornate metal balls, balls studded with round bumps or spikes, and a variety of flanges. The flanged mace became popular in Europe beginning in the 1100s because of its ability to dent or penetrate even the thickest armor.

Mace handles for infantry were generally short, about two feet long. Cavalry mace handles were longer and either designed for single-hand or double-hand use, with the double-handed maces being the longest.

Even children had maces. One example from the eighteenth century was found in India. It's a flanged, metal mace with bird's-head details, thirteen inches long and just a half-pound. Speculation is that it may have been used for early military training.

The painting *Two Knights Fighting in a Landscape* by Eugene Delacroix , the foremost French Romantic painter, shows the knight on the right wielding a mace

Flail

The flail is an example of what happens when a perfectly useful and otherwise harmless farm implement falls into the hands of an inventor with a fiendish outlook on dealing death. Originally the flail was nothing more than a hand-held threshing tool. Then, in the 1200s, someone got the bright idea to take the tool concept a step further, finding that something wonderfully capable of beating the husks out of grain could, with a little bit of tinkering, do a similarly efficient job separating a foe's brain from his skull. It may even be that a modified farm tool itself went into battle. Levies of farmers and peasants were often impressed to aid a feudal lord and, as they were generally too poor to own a sword or other weapon, they took with them what they had. In the case of a flail, they simply added some stones or pieces of metal to make them more effective brain bashers.

The standard European military flail is a stick that has a spiked metal ball and short chain attached to one end. Flails started out as an infantry weapon. It was particularly useful against someone with a shield, as the business end of the flail could arc over or around the edge of the shield and still wound or kill. Flails were soon added to the arsenal of the cavalry because the chain does not transfer impact force and vibration back to its wielder, reducing the risk of being unhorsed. A disadvantage was that troops using flails had to spread out to avoid injuring each other.

The nunchaku is a Japanese variation of the flail. Japanese warriors also had a three-section staff version called a sansetsukon. An Indian version, the cumberjung, was used in the Maratha Empire. This was a flail that had chained quoits or balls attached to both ends of the stick. The quoits had a sharp, circular edge that entirely encircled the ball. The wielder spun it to gain momentum before flinging it at an enemy. Extremely dangerous, it required a considerable amount of skill in order to be used effectively.

A late nineteenth century engraving showing a farm laborer using a flail to thresh grain

MEDIEVAL ARMOR IN EUROPE

Medieval armor falls into two categories: mail and plate. Mail armor appeared first, with the earliest examples dating from the fifth century. Plate armor made its appearance in the fourteenth century and by the late fifteenth century had largely replaced mail armor. Armor use swiftly declined when it proved incapable of protecting against bullets shot from firearms. The Spanish Conquistadors of the sixteenth century were among the last soldiers to use plate body armor.

Mail armor was commonly composed of alternating rows of welded and riveted rings of iron or mild steel connected together in a four-to-one system, where each ring is linked to four others, forming a mesh. A complete mail shirt extending from shoulder to knees contained as many as 30,000 links. A complete suit of mail consisting of a coif (head) and hauberk (knee-length shirt) could weigh as much as thirty pounds.

Mail armor was used by cavalry and infantry on both sides in the Battle of Bovine (1214). This climactic battle was part of a dynastic struggle between the English army and its allies led by King John and the French army led by Philip II. The French victory reasserted France's sovereignty over the Normandy and Brittany and led discontented barons who had lost their possessions in Normandy forcing King John to sign the Magna Carta.

Plate armor, after having fallen into disuse after the collapse of the Roman Empire, began reappearing in the thirteenth century. Because it was expensive and difficult to make, only the nobility and royalty were able to afford and maintain complete sets.

The idea that a knight's armor was so heavy that he would be unable to pick himself up after he had fallen is false. Mark Twain's vivid description in *A Connecticut Yankee in King Arthur's Court* of an armored knight having to be mounted on his horse with the help of pulleys did much to perpetuate this fallacy. In fact, a complete suit of plate armor could weigh as little as 45 pounds. In comparison, paratroopers in World War II went into action carrying combat gear weighing more than one hundred pounds. Even today it is not unusual for some soldiers to carry body armor and gear weighing ninety pounds or more.

A detail from the fifteenth century triptych *The Battle of San Romano* showing mounted armored knights fighting

GUNPOWDER

The original gunpowder mills of El-du Pont de Nemours & Co, where the first powder to be manufactured in the U.S. was made in 1802

A simple mixture of sulfur, charcoal, and potassium nitrate (saltpeter) revolutionized weaponry. Though the first firearms were crude, heavy, inaccurate, low-powered, and as dangerous to their users as they were to their intended targets, they thunderously ushered in a new chapter in humanity's quest for greater destruction.

Like a number of important inventions, gunpowder was discovered by accident. Alchemists in ninth century China, searching for an elixir of immortality, instead found one that accelerated mortality. The first weapons using gunpowder appeared in the tenth century. By the thirteenth century, gunpowder use had spread throughout Asia and into Europe.

The first mention of gunpowder in Europe appeared in documents written in 1267 by the Franciscan friar Roger Bacon. He wrote, in part, about a firecracker, "a child's toy of sound and fire made in various parts of the world with powder of saltpeter, sulphur and charcoal of hazelwood." He speculated that "if an instrument of large size were used, no one could stand the terror of the noise and flash. If the instrument were made of solid material, the violence of the explosion would be greater."

Europe had to wait just eight decades to see the fulfillment of that prophecy. Primitive cannons used by English King Edward III, though few in number, proved decisive in his victory over the French in the Battle of Crécy (1346). Within four years, gunpowder artillery units were integral in armies throughout Europe.

An important technological breakthrough was achieved in the 1880s with the formulation of smokeless gunpowder. Until then, discharged gunpowder created thick clouds of smoke. Successive firings of cannon and shoulder arms invariably obscured a battlefield with foul-smelling smoke, making it difficult or impossible for generals to direct the flow of battle.

Gunpowder played an important role in the dawn of a new age of explosives. On July 16, 1945, the *Albuquerque Tribune* reported, "An ammunition magazine, containing high explosives and pyrotechnics, exploded early today in a remote area of the Alamogordo air base reservation, producing a brilliant flash and blast." But the flash was not caused by gunpowder. It was the first successful detonation of the atomic bomb.

A fourteenth century engraving showing an early cannon used at the Battle of Crecy in France during the Hundred Years War

Medieval Siege Engines

As the Western Roman Empire declined, siege engines fell into greater disuse. With Rome's collapse in 476, most of the specialized technology needed to make siege engines was lost. The subsequent five hundred years that constituted the early Middle Ages saw a fits-and-starts revival of the classic siege engines of antiquity including the ram, bore, catapult, and ballista. But it was not until the twelfth century, the beginning of the Late Middle Ages, that Europeans developed a new siege weapon, the trebuchet.

Like the ballista and catapult, the trebuchet uses mechanical energy to propel its missile. But unlike the other two, it operates on the principle of counterpoise instead of torsion. The trebuchet consists of a horizontal beam that pivots on two great uprights. One end of the beam is fitted with a sling or spoon-shaped cavity that contains the missile. At the other end of the beam hang weights of iron or stone that supply the power of propulsion when the beam is triggered. The missile, usually a large stone, describes a parabolic arc in flight. A winch is used to pull the sling back to the ground for reloading.

Trebuchets were capable of flinging a missile of great weight. Though the average weight of a trebuchet missile was two hundred pounds, some were designed to hurl stones as heavy as three thousand pounds. Trebuchets were the most efficient siege engine during the Middle Ages. Richard the Lionheart used trebuchets in the Siege of Acre (1191) and christened two of them "God's Own Catapult" and "Bad Neighbor."

The development of cannon artillery using gunpowder caused the trebuchet to fall into gradual decline. The last known use of the trebuchet occurred in the New World in 1521 when Hernán Cortés put the Aztec capital of Tenochtitlán to siege. Because of a shortage of gunpowder, he decided to soften up the city using a trebuchet. But by then the skills of using a trebuchet were gone. The first shot was a misfire that landed back on the trebuchet, destroying it.

Siege of Antioch by William of Tyre

Samurai Armor

Inevitably, after a weapon or type of armor established its usefulness, "dressed up" models would appear. Sometimes the reasons were practical, such as establishing unit identity or intimidating a foe. Other times it was a statement of status, elaborate arms and armor being more expensive than plain ones. Museums around the world have in their collections spectacular examples of the art of war. In many cases, these elaborate etchings and precious inlays came at such a cost to battlefield utility that the weapons and armor could only be used in ceremony. But there were exceptions. The *ne plus ultra* of flashy form and practical function might very well be the *ô-yoroi* (great armor) of the Japanese samurai.

For about a thousand years, from the seventh century until their abolishment in 1876 during the Meiji Restoration, the samurai were the warrior elite of Japan who fought in service of the emperor or nobles (the exception was the *ronin*, a masterless samurai). Because samurai were originally archers, their first armor was a simple cuirass chest piece and helmet. By the thirteenth century, when samurai added swords to their arsenal (the *katana* and shorter *tachi*, and a dagger, the *wakazashi*), samurai armor had extended to cover the entire body and was incredibly elaborate. One significant feature of the *ô-yoroi* is that in cross-section viewed from above, the armor forms the letter "C" because it is completely open on the right side. A persistent rumor is that samurai armor contained wood and bamboo, but that is incorrect. Some very early Japanese armor, not attributable to samurai, was composed of assembled turtle shells. But samurai armor, regardless of style, was composed of leather and metal.

The square, box-like *ô-yoroi* was heavy and very expensive. As such only the most elite warriors could afford to wear them. Lighter models, *dô maru* and *haramaki*, which were more form-fitting and had more skirt plates, were developed for lesser warriors and other retainers.

In contrast to European helmets, which tended to make the wearer anonymous, the helmets of elite samurai warriors were distinctively elaborate and exotic. This became such a part of samurai mystique and Japanese history that, reportedly, all a Japanese historical film has to do is show a helmet, and the audience will immediately identify the warrior.

Samurai with raised sword, c. 1860

MORNING STAR

The morning star, also known as the "holy water sprinkler" because of its resemblance to the aspergillum used in the Catholic mass, was another of the simple but deadly weapons to come out of the Middle Ages. The morning star resembled the mace, except the club end is tipped with spikes. The most distinctive of these is a long one that protrudes directly out of the top.

Morning stars came into use during the fourteenth century and were primarily an infantry weapon. As it was inexpensive and easy to make and use, many thought it to be a peasant's weapon, but professional soldiers of the period possessed well-crafted morning stars in their arsenal.

One of the most famous groups to use the morning star was the guildsmen of Flanders. In the Battle of Courtrai (1302), the Flemish guildsmen used the morning star to such great effect against the French cavalry and infantry that some accounts claim that more than ten thousand Frenchmen were killed and wounded, at nominal cost to the guildsmen. So many French knights fell in the battle that it also came to be known as the Battle of the Golden Spurs, for the more than a thousand spurs taken from the feet of dead knights. These spurs were hung on display in the Church of Our Lady in the Flemish town of Kortrijk for eighty years, until the French were able to retrieve them following the Battle of Westrozebeke.

The morning star began falling out of favor in the fifteenth century. By the sixteenth century it no longer appeared in any arsenal.

1302

A detail of the Courtrai Chest depicting two scenes from the Battle of the Golden Spurs fought in Courtrai in 1302 (wood) (detail)

HALBERD

The halberd was one of many two-handed staff weapons used by the infantry that was developed during the Middle Ages. Its name is taken from the German words "halm" (staff) and "barte" (ax). The halberd is three weapons in one. Ranging in length from three to eight feet, its hardwood shaft was tipped with a heavy steel head that had the blade of an ax, the point of a spear, and a hook for pulling a rider out of the saddle. Strips of metal called langets extended down from the weapon-head and were added to provide protection and strength for the staff. In the hands of a brawny halberdier, it was a murderous tool of war that could cleave the best plate armor.

The Swiss are credited with inventing the halberd in the thirteenth century. It was well suited for mountain dwellers whose foes at the time were encroaching horsemen. The Swiss victory over Austrian cavalry in the Battle of Morgarten (1315) proved the value of the halberd against armored horse cavalry and its widespread use by the Swiss eventually made it that country's national weapon. Other notable groups to use the halberd were the Spanish Tercios of the Renaissance, who played a key role in the Spanish victory over the French in the Battle of Pavia (1525). Another group was the German mercenaries known as Landsknechts who fought in so many battles during the fifteenth and sixteenth centuries that they came to be known as the universal mercenary of the Renaissance.

The halberd remained in use only about three hundred years. Its decline in the battlefield coincided with its rise as a ceremonial weapon. Today, the Swiss Guards of the Vatican include the halberd in their arsenal of ceremonial weapons.

A detail of a fifteenth century fresco showing Crusader, and later King of Jerusalem, Godfrey de Bouillon holding a halberd

EARLY BIOLOGICAL WARFARE

The use of biological weapons is almost as old as the history of warfare itself. Its use was recorded in both history and literature. Though they could be extraordinarily effective, it was a rash general indeed who did not take extra care in their use. Today, moral outrage and international law has proscribed (but not eliminated) its use. Before the twentieth century, uncontrollable nature could cause it to just as easily fell friend as it did foe.

The Hittite Empire is credited with being the first in history to use biological weapons. Hittite texts dating between 1500 B.C. and 1200 B.C. record accounts of Hittite armies driving plague victims and diseased animals into enemy lands. Roman legions between 300 and 100 B.C. were recorded as having catapulted hives of bees and hornets at enemy troop formations. And the great Carthaginian general Hannibal achieved his victory in the Battle of Eurymedon (190 B.C.) with the help of pottery jars filled with poisoned snakes that were catapulted onto the decks of his opponent's ships.

Sometimes just knowing the lay of the land was sufficient. Syracuse was one of the most fought-over cities in the ancient world. In 415 B.C. an Athenian siege of the city was lifted because the Syracusian generals succeeded in forcing the Athenian army to encamp near marshes full of malaria-carrying mosquitoes. The Athenian army, decimated by disease, eventually had to lift the siege.

The most devastating consequence of biological warfare occurred in 1344 in Genovese-ruled city of Kaffa in the Crimea. The city had been under siege for three years by the Mongol army under Jannibeg Khan. Jannibeg had decided to lift the siege and move on when merchants arriving from China infected his army with bubonic plague. In one of his last acts before lifting the siege, Jannibeg ordered that plague infested corpses of his troops be catapulted into the city. The citizens dumped the bodies into the sea, but the damage had been done and soon the people of Kaffa began dying as well. Four Genoese ships thought to be untainted by plague departed for Europe. The ships anchored at Messina, Venice, Genoa, and Marseille. By 1348 the Black Death was sweeping through Europe and would eventually claim the lives of a third of the population.

An ancient Greek vase showing men being stung by bees

Pot de Fer

The bottle-shaped gunpowder firing oddity that appeared on the battlefield in the early fourteenth century was just under three feet long, a little more than one foot at its widest point, and weighed about 900 pounds. It fired a four-and-a-half-foot arrow 600 feet, about the same distance as an arrow shot by an archer using the English longbow (who could also fire more of them in the span of a minute). But though the tiny pot de fer ("iron pot" in French) was heavy, had a slow rate of fire, and short range, this first cannon laid the foundation for the military branch that would become the king of the battlefield—artillery.

Pots de fer were some of the first pieces of gunpowder-firing artillery in the Middle Ages. The list came to include the larger bombards, mortars, and the culverin. All were cast in metal, with bronze and iron being the most common. Artillery gunners considered themselves members of a guild or craft rather than an arm of the military service. A spirit of freemasonry prevailed among these specialists who passed on their knowledge to apprentices under oaths of secrecy. Part of this had to do with gunpowder itself, which was associated with alchemists. Gunpowder formulas were a master gunner's most jealously guarded secret, and master gunners were able to demand and receive high pay and servants for their services.

The earliest mention of the pot de fer appears in the 1327 illuminated manuscript by Walter de Milamete. The first important battle that featured the pot de fer occurred during the Hundred Years War in 1346 at the Battle of Crécy. According to accounts, the English King Edward III possessed just six pots de fer, but they were enough. When the French cavalry under Philip IV charged, Edward gave the signal to fire. According to one chronicler, the pots de fer "made a sound like thunder." Another chronicler recorded that the English "struck terror into the French Army with five or six pieces of cannon, it being the first time they had seen such thundering machines." The sound, fire, and acrid smoke from the pots de fer probably did more to panic the knights and horses than the actual impact by the fired shots. The battle ended in an English victory when Edward finished off the French with his longbowmen and other troops.

A fifteenth century illustration of the Battle of Auray (1364) showing troops using gunpowder artillery in the lower middle foreground.

ARQUEBUS

The arquebus was a low-velocity heavy firearm that was widely used from the fifteenth to the seventeenth centuries. The arquebus was a muzzle loader—it was loaded through the front of the firearm. The muzzle was flared, making it easier for the arquebusier to add gunpowder and a bullet, which were then tamped down with a ramrod. The arquebus had two firing mechanisms. The first was the matchlock, where a slow-burning match-cord held in a clamp was triggered to touch a flash pan near the base of the barrel that was filled with priming powder. The primer would ignite "in a flash" and travel trough a small touch hole drilled in the barrel to the main charge of gunpowder inside the barrel, discharging the weapon. The second firing mechanism was the wheelock which used a rotating steel wheel to ignite the powder. The principle is similar to that used in cigarette lighters.

Despite its disadvantages of being heavy, clumsy, and having a slow rate of fire, arquebuses were used by armies throughout Europe and Asia. Aquebusiers were a formidable force when properly supported by infantry carrying the pike or halberd in what came to be called a "pike and shot" formation.

One of the first examples of this new tactic in warfare was demonstrated in the Battle of Cerignola (1503) during the Second Italian war, a dynastic struggle between France and Spain, each who sought hegemony in the peninsula. A Spanish army of eight thousand, including about a thousand arquebusiers and 20 cannons, had taken up defensive positions in the high ground near Cerignola off the Adriatic coast in southern Italy. Attacking the Spaniards was a French army of thirty-two thousand, mostly heavy cavalry and mercenary Swiss pikemen and supported by about 40 cannons. The Spanish general, Gonzalo Fernández de Córdoba, arranged his arquebusiers and pikemen into mixed units called "Coronelías" to protect his flanks. This pike and shot formation proved murderously effective. Attacks on the flanks by first the French cavalry and later by the Swiss mercenaries were repeatedly repulsed with heavy losses. The French retired in defeat, having suffered more than four thousand dead and an unknown wounded. The Spanish suffered only about a hundred casualties. Historians regard the Battle of Cerignola as being the first engagement won by firearms.

BERETTA

Though much is known about the weapons of the ancient and medieval world and how they were made, comparatively little is known about the business side—the companies that build weapons in quantity. The equipping for war was for many years, with obvious exceptions as Roman legions, left primarily to the individual. That started to change during the Renaissance, beginning in the fourteenth century. It is notable that one of the oldest corporations in the world is also one of the first firearms manufacturing companies—Fabbricia D'Armi Pietro Beretta S.p.A., better known as Beretta.

During the medieval and Renaissance ages, guilds dominated weapons manufacturing, as they did other trades. Bartolomeo Beretta, the company's founder, was himself a master gunsmith from a family of gunsmiths. He lived in Gardone, a village in the Val Trompia of Lombardy in northern Italy. Iron mines in the region had supplied ore dating back to Roman times, and the area was the location for guilds specializing in weapons manufacture. The company was founded on October 3, 1526, when Beretta signed a contract with the ruling Doges of Venice to supply 185 arquebus barrels for its arsenal. Within two hundred years, Beretta was the area's second-largest barrel producer with an output of 2,883 barrels a year.

Napoleon's conquest of the region in 1797 led to the abolishment of the guild system. This resulted in a dramatic expansion of the company, and within a few years, it was producing about 40,000 guns a year. Over time, Beretta expanded into the sporting arms field and today it is more known for its sport firearms than its military weapons.

In 1985, Beretta once again became a major manufacturer of military arms when the U.S. Department of Defense, in a cost-saving move, replaced the Colt .45 with the Beretta Model 92 9mm as the military's standard sidearm.

The Beretta symbol, three arrows and circles trademarked in the 1950s, was originally the personal trademark of the Italian poet, novelist, and war hero Gabriele d'Annunzio. Even after five hundred years, Beretta has the distinction of still being a private, family-controlled company.

Bo

Stick weapons were among the earliest weapons in history. The first stick weapons were most likely saplings trimmed of their leaves and branches. Stick weapons and stick fighting were known and practiced throughout Europe and Asia. In England, the stick weapon was known as the quarterstaff; in Ireland it was the shillelagh; in Japan it was called the bo.

Like most long stick weapons, the bo was a shaft about six feet long, tapered at both ends, and made of hardwood such as red or white oak. The martial art of stick fighting with a bo is called bojutsu and is associated with Okinawan kobudo or Japanese Koryu budo systems. The bo is believed to have developed from the farm implement known as a tenbin. Baskets were suspended from each end, and the carrier would place himself in the middle, with the bo resting on his shoulders. The bo is the earliest known weapon indigenous to Okinawa and it is regarded as the king of Okinawa weapons.

The martial arts style of fighting using the bo originated in Okinawa in the early seventeenth century. When Okinawa was conquered by Japanese samurai of the Satsuma Clan in 1609, a weapons ban was instituted, making it a crime for Okinawans to carry or own metal weapons such as swords and spears. In their search for a way to defend themselves against samurai aggression, the Okinawans took to developing fighting techniques using farm implements such as the bo, which the samurai could not confiscate. Out of this came bojutsu.

The bo was most often used by monks and commoners and in their skilled hands they were the equal of any samurai with a katana.

A Japanese pilgrim holding a wooden staff on his way to Mount Fujiyama, 1880

BAYONET

The development of shoulder firearms initiated the decline of the arsenal of pole weapons that had come to include pikes, halberds, axes, poleaxes, bardiches, war hammers, and maces. But because the early firearms had slow fire rates, their users were vulnerable to attacks at close quarters. In the late sixteenth century or early seventeenth century, someone hit upon the idea of combining the two, creating the bayonet.

The bayonet (originally spelled "bayonette") developed from the dagger. There are several versions of its origin, with some ascribing it to the French city of Bayonne, near the Pyrennes Mountains. According to one, the citizens, having run out of gunpowder, rammed the hilts of their long hunting knives into the muzzles of their muskets.

The first bayonets were plug types, with bases that fit inside the muzzle. Plug bayonets made their first appearance in 1671 when they were issued to French regiments. The disadvantages of plug bayonets soon became apparent: They prevent the gun from firing. Within twenty years, the bayonets of a socket design, in which the base of the bayonet was secured around and not in the muzzle, began to appear, creating a true dual-purpose weapon. By 1703 the design had been sufficiently perfected for bayonets to become general-issue weapons.

Early bayonets were much longer than ones that saw use in World War II. In the nineteenth centuries, bayonet sizes ranged from 25 to 45 inches, with the longer ones being known as "sword bayonets." The most famous of the modern bayonets is the MI Bayonet used by the American military forces in World War II (1939–1945) and the Korean War (1950–1953). It entered production in 1942, had a ten-inch blade, and was fitted over the MI Garand rifle.

A turning point in the Union victory in the Battle of Gettysburg (1863) came as the result of a bayonet charge. Outnumbered, low on ammunition, and about to be overrun, Union colonel Joshua Lawrence Chamberlain ordered the surviving members of his 20th Maine Regiment on Little Round Top to fix bayonets and charge. The desperate counterattack forced the Confederates to retreat and the vulnerable Union army flank was saved.

A line of soldiers, bayonets fixed on their rifles, during the Spanish American War, c. 1899

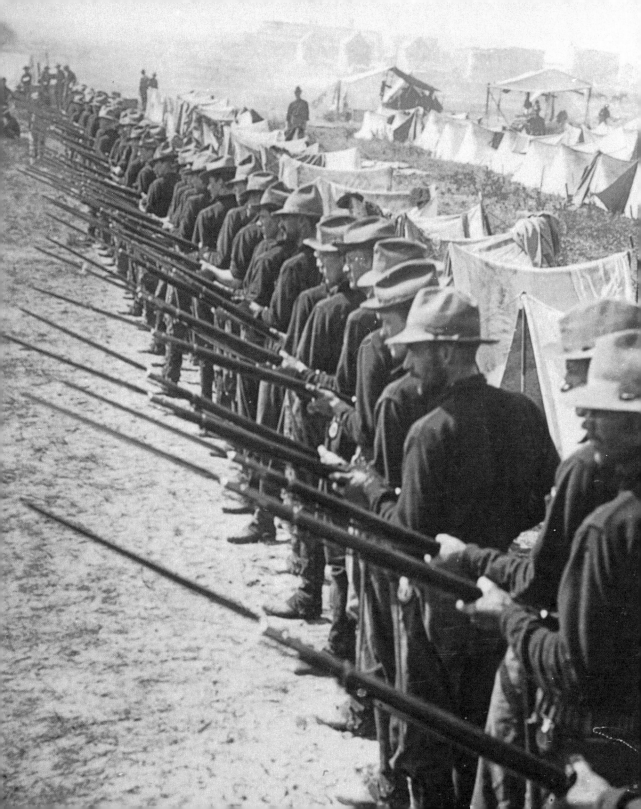

Mortar

The mortar is one of the simplest of the gunpowder weapons. It's basically just an angled tube that fires a muzzle-loaded projectile in a high ballistic arc at a target, a method known as indirect fire—direct fire being the method where a weapon is aimed directly at the target. For many centuries mortars were primarily siege weapons, with the largest weighing thousands of pounds. During World War I (1914–1918), smaller portable mortars were developed in quantity for close support in localized infantry operations, a role they continue to hold to this day.

Siege warfare reached a high point in the seventeenth century. The greatest practitioner of siege warfare both in defense and attack was the French engineering genius Sébastien le Prestre de Vauban. His only worthy rival, nicknamed "Hollandish Vauban," was the Dutch soldier and engineer Menno van Coehoorn. The two squared off in 1692 during the siege of Namur, where van Coehoorn built a fortress and then defended it against Vauban. Vauban captured the fortress after a 36-day siege at a cost of 2,600 killed and wounded. Van Coehoorn's garrison suffered about 5,200 casualties. Three years later, the roles were reversed. Though Vauban was not present for this siege, he had spent the three years redesigning the fortress. Van Coehoorn invested Namur after a 60-day siege, suffering 18,000 casualties. The French lost 8,000 men.

Vauban's siege of Namur in 1692 is important because he was the first to use ricochet fire. Before this, attacks focused on straightforward breaching of fortress walls. Cannon shots were directed at a particular spot, eventually punching a hole in it. Vauban's new tactic consisted of mortar fire using smaller charges of gunpowder to propel the ammunition. This caused the ball to drop just over the lip of the parapet and bounce along the level space, or terreplein, where the gun batteries were mounted. The effect was similar to a bouncing bowling ball knocking over pins, though more deadly. When accurately aimed, it caused enormous destruction and it was many years before effective defenses against it were developed.

An early siege mortar, c. 1500

Brown Bess Musket

The British Land Pattern Musket, better known by its nickname "Brown Bess," was the primary long, or shoulder, arm used by British troops in the eighteenth and nineteenth centuries. During a time when firearms were custom made and individually purchased and supplied, it was among the first to be built to a standard design. Because it was used by British troops throughout the world, it became a symbol of the expanding British Empire.

At least seven different models of the Brown Bess were manufactured during its long life; all fired a .75-caliber bullet and could be fitted with a 17-inch bayonet. Production began in 1722 with the Long Land Pattern, a long-barreled (46-inch) musket that was 62.5 inches long and weighed 10.5 pounds. This model was gradually phased out by shorter variants including a 39-inch barrel for regular infantry and a carbine model for cavalry units that had a 26-inch barrel. Because it was a smoothbore and had no rear gun sights, accuracy dropped off dramatically after fifty yards. Maximum range was a hundred yards, but hitting a target at that distance was more a circumstance of luck than a good shot.

The origins of the nickname "Brown Bess" are unknown. The word *brown* is thought to refer to the color of the musket's stock or to the rust-colored barrel, the result of a preservative process called "browning." The origins of *Bess* range from a reference to Queen Elizabeth I ("Good Queen Bess") to a derivative from firearms predecessors arquebus or blunderbuss. The generally accepted origin is that it's the Anglicized version of the German *brawn buss* ("strong gun") or *braun buss* ("brown gun") because King George I, who commissioned the Brown Bess, was from Germany.

No one knows for certain how many Brown Bess muskets were made over the course of its production run, which ended in the 1860s. The English Army began phasing out the Brown Bess following the end of the Crimean War (1853 to 1856). It continued to be use by a number of armies before finally retired in the 1880s.

A detail of the painting *Defeating Braddock* by Edwin Willard Deming showing Native American warriors using muskets in ambush British troops during the French and Indian War

ELI WHITNEY

(1765–1825)

American inventor Eli Whitney is most famous for creating the cotton gin, a device that efficiently separated seeds from cotton bolls. He also made an important contribution to arms manufacturing with what came to be called the "American System," a process that paved the way for mass production.

It was ironic that his entry into the arms industry was forced upon him by the invention that made him famous. In the late 1790s, Whitney was on the verge of bankruptcy as the result of patent rights litigation over the cotton gin. When the War Department issued contracts to supply the army with muskets, Whitney secured a contract in 1798 for the delivery of as many as fifteen thousand muskets in two years.

Though he had never before manufactured firearms, Whitney built a new manufacturing plant near New Haven, Connecticut, and devised a system of interchangeable parts created through the use of power machinery and specialized division of labor. Though it took him until 1809 to deliver all the muskets, he was so successful in promoting his American System that it was copied by other industries. Soon other firearms manufacturers established businesses in the state. By the 1850s, Connecticut had a thriving firearms industry that included such famous American brands as Colt, Winchester, Spencer, and Sharps, among others.

AIR RIFLE

Though gunpowder became the dominant propellant force for weapons, another propellant also proved useful on the battlefield: compressed air. Though more complex, expensive and delicate than firearms, air rifles of the period had a number of advantages over contemporary flintlocks. They could be fired in wet weather, they were quieter, had no muzzle flash, were smokeless, and had a higher rate of fire. Though pneumatic technology was known as early as the fifteenth century, it was not until 1779 that an air rifle suitable for military use appeared: the Girandoni air rifle.

Designed by Bartholomäus Girandoni, a watchmaker, mechanic, and gunsmith from the Tyrol region in what is now Austria, his air rifle was about the same size and weight as a musket (four feet and ten pounds). It had a gravity-fed magazine capable of holding twenty .51-caliber balls. A hollow butt contained the compressed air reservoir and was good for thirty shots before having to be recharged with a hand pump. Maximum range was about 150 yards, decreasing as the compressed air was released. An experienced air rifleman could fire as many as 22 shots per minute, about five times the rate of fire from a muzzle-loading musket.

Called the "Windbüchse" (wind rifle), it was used by the Austrian army from 1780 to 1815. Because it did not give away the shooter the way firearms did with their loud report and gout of fire and smoke, it became the favored weapon of snipers.

The Girandoni air rifle, capable of sustaining air pressure of 800 psi (pounds per square inch), was one of the weapons in the Lewis and Clark Expedition (1803–1806). It was used both for hunting and in demonstrations for the tribes they met. Captain Meriwether Lewis made one such demonstration for the warlike Yankton Sioux on August 30, 1804. Expedition member Private Joseph Whitehouse recorded in his journal that Lewis fired several times at a tree, with the balls deeply penetrating the trunk. Whitehouse wrote "the sight and the execution" of firing without having to reload and the power of the bullets' impacts "surprised them exceedingly."

An early nineteenth century illustration depicting members of the Lewis and Clark expedition meeting some Chinook Indians

LEADERSHIP

In a letter to his son then attending West Point, General George S. Patton, Jr. wrote, "I have it—but I'll be damned if I can define it." The "it" was leadership. Stripped to its basics, leadership is the ability of one individual to inspire the concerted action of others to achieve a defined goal.

The consequences of military leadership failures are often catastrophically spectacular. A few notable examples are the defeats of Emperor Darius at Gaugamela, Major General Ambrose Burnside at Fredericksburg, General Robert Nivelle's disastrous World War I offensive bearing his name that resulted in a mutiny of the French army, and the collapse of the entire French military high command in 1940 that led to France's surrender to Nazi Germany.

But when leadership succeeds, the results can be equally spectacular. One of the greatest examples of leadership occurred on March 27, 1796, between 27-year-old General Napoleon Bonaparte and his republican French army. The bankrupt revolutionary government had been unable to pay or supply his men for weeks. His planned invasion of Italy was about to fail before it could begin. Hungry and clothed in rags, his troops were on the verge of mutiny when he issued the following proclamation, "Soldiers, you are naked, ill fed! The Government owes you much; it can give you nothing. Your patience, the courage you display in the midst of these rocks, are admirable; but they procure you no glory, no fame is reflected upon you. I seek to lead you into the most fertile plains in the world. Rich provinces, great cities will be in your power. There you will find honor, glory, and riches. Soldiers . . . would you be lacking in courage or constancy?" As former Army Chief of Staff General Maxwell D. Taylor wrote, Napoleon's proclamation "gave the French soldiers an élan which carried them to six victories in a fortnight and launched their commander on his career of conquest."

Baron Antoine Jean Gros' painting *General Bonaparte on the Bridge* of Arcole depicting a dramatic moment during the general's Italian campaign of 1796

CONGREVE ROCKET

The Congreve rocket, designed in 1804, was the most famous invention designed by prolific inventor Sir William Congreve, a future member of Parliament and a baronet. It was inspired by British army experiences in India against rocket-firing Indian troops during the Anglo-Mysore Wars of the late eighteenth century. The Congreve rocket was used in campaigns against Napoleon and in the War of 1812 (1812–1814), before being retired.

The rocket consisted of an iron case divided into two parts (warhead and propellant) attached to a wooden guide pole. It was launched in pairs off half troughs mounted on A-frames. Ten different sizes were built, ranging from three to 300 pounds. Parliament authorized Congreve to form two rocket companies, and they saw service throughout the Napoleonic War. A Congreve rocket company participated in the Battle of Leipzig (1807), the only British unit to participate in that battle.

Though it made a spectacularly dramatic statement in flight, especially at night, it was neither very powerful nor very accurate—after witnessing a demonstration, the Duke of Wellington was unimpressed. When it was used in battle, it was done more to boost morale of troops than in the hope of actually hitting and damaging something.

Both traits of the Congreve rocket came dramatically together in an unexpected way when a British fleet staged a bombardment of Baltimore harbor's Fort McHenry in 1814. The combined cannon and Congreve rocket bombardment lasted through the night and was witnessed by Francis Scott Key, an American hostage aboard one of the British ships. When dawn broke the next day, the fort still stood, having suffered slight damage. Once again the Congreve rocket had been ineffective as a weapon, and a terrific morale booster, though not in a way the British expected. Key was so inspired by what he had seen that he wrote a poem about his experience. Set to the tune of a popular British drinking song, "The Star Spangled Banner" immortalized the Congreve rocket and its "red glare."

A print showing Francis Scott Key standing on the top of a stepladder, watching the siege of Fort McHenry

PROPAGANDA

Propaganda is a deliberate attempt to persuade people to think and behave in a manner desired by the source (usually a government). Propagandists seek to accomplish this by exploiting two primal emotions, hope and hatred, separately or together. At all times, the core message must be simple and direct so that even the most uneducated can understand it.

The word "propaganda" comes from *Congregatio de Propaganda Fide* (congregation for the propagation of the faith), the papal office established in the seventeenth century and charged with overseeing the religious reconquest of Europe as part of the Counter-Reformation and to also spread the Roman Catholic faith in newly discovered lands. To be effective, propaganda has to reach a large amount of people relatively quickly. Two technological revolutions made that possible. The first occurred in the fifteenth century with the invention of the movable-type printing press. The second appeared in the twentieth century with the inventions of radio, film, and television.

Though the bias inherent in propaganda always made it a suspect source of information, propaganda did not become demonized until the twentieth century through the policies of Nazi Germany.

One of the great masters of propaganda was Emperor Napoleon I of France. His primary vehicle was the official newspaper *Moniteur Universe!*—usually referred to as *Moniteur*—which published his bulletins. During his reign, *Moniteur* published 183 bulletins, among other messages. Most bulletins reported news about himself, his armies, and its operations. Information in them was so controlled and slanted that the reports inspired the phrase "to lie like a bulletin."

An excerpt from his Sixty-third Bulletin of the 1807 Campaign is instructive. "Captain Auzouy . . . mortally wounded in the battle of Eylau, was lying on the battlefield. His comrades came to take him up and carry him to the hospital. He recovered his senses only to say to them, 'Let me alone, my friends; I die contented, since we have victory and that I can die upon the field of honor, surrounded by the cannons taken from the enemy, and the wrecks of its defeat. Tell the Emperor that I have but one regret, which is that in a few moments I shall be no longer able to do anything for his service, and the glory of fine France . . . to her my last breath.'"

An example of art as propaganda, a detail of the painting "Napoleon on the field of Eylau" by Baron Antoine Jean Gros. Note that even a wounded soldier on the ground in the lower right is reaching out to the Emperor.

Ship-of-the-line

When the Age of Sail began in about 1500, the major nations of Europe found themselves facing maritime challenges of enormous complexity. New trade routes circled the globe. New colonies were scattered throughout the world and from pole to pole. To defend their vast, far-flung interests, these rival nations embarked on a massive warship-building program. Soon brigs, sloops, frigates, galleons, and other warships were sailing out of shipyards and into harm's way. The largest and most powerful of all these warships was the ship-of-the-line.

Ships-of-the-line were the battleships of their day and ruled the seas until the end of the Age of Sail, about 1850. They derived their name from the naval tactic of the day that called for a fleet to secure advantage over its opponent by forming a line, called a line of battle, so that the ships could fire at the enemy the maximum amount of cannons, a "broadside." Ships-of-the-line came in various sizes and were categorized by the amount of cannons, or guns, they carried. The smallest was the two-decker (two decks of cannons firing through side ports on both sides of the hull) which carried anywhere from 50 to 90 guns. The ships also came in three- and four-decker sizes with 98 to 140 cannons. The most common ship-of-the-line size was the "74," carrying 74 cannons.

Ships-of-the-line fought in some of the greatest battles in naval history. Of these, none was more important than the Battle of Trafalgar (1805) during the Napoleonic War between the British and the French. British Admiral Horatio Nelson led 27 ships-of-the-line against a combined French and Spanish fleet containing a total of 33 ships-of-the-line (18 French). Excluding frigates and other vessels, this meant the British had 2,132 cannons and the French-Spanish fleet had 2,484 cannons.

When the smoke cleared, the British had faced its most serious challenge in the war and won. Nelson died in the battle, living just long enough to learn of his victory, one that made him Britain's greatest naval hero.

A detail of a nineteenth century print showing British ships-of-the-line in the Battle of Trafalgar (1805)

Dahlgren Gun

The Dahlgren gun was named after its inventor Rear Admiral John Adolph Bernard Dahlgren, the "father of American naval ordnance." Entering production in 1850, it was the primary deck cannon of the U.S. Navy during the Civil War (1861–1865). It was also one of the most unusually shaped cannons ever produced. Because its fat breech and tapered gun tube gave it the appearance of a bottle lying on its side, it was nicknamed the "soda bottle gun." Eleven models were manufactured, with the largest one weighing fifty tons and capable of firing a hundred-pound shell.

Dahlgren entered the navy in 1826. Ironically for a naval officer, he suffered throughout his life from seasickness, sometimes terribly. In 1847 then-Lieutenant Dahlgren was assigned to ordnance duty at the Washington Navy Yard. It was there that he rose in rank and responsibility, becoming commandant of the navy yard in 1861 and chief of the Bureau of Ordnance in 1862.

A brilliant inventor and engineer, Dahlgren was a stickler for quality control. He created the first sustained weapons research and development program and organization in U.S. naval history. Dahlgren's heavy muzzle-loading smoothbores were derived from scientific research in ballistics and metallurgy, and they were manufactured and tested under the most comprehensive program of quality control in the navy to that time. In an age when cannon misfires were not unusual, Dahlgren guns were extraordinarily reliable. Captain James Alden, whose stellar naval career included a circumnavigation of the globe and service in the Mexican War (1846–1848) and the Civil War before his retirement in 1873 with the rank of rear admiral, said that the 9-inch Dahlgren gun (referring to the diameter of the round it fired) was "the best . . . ever made."

Shortly after receiving his promotion to rear admiral in 1863, Dahlgren took command of the South Atlantic Blockading Squadron. For the next two years he led naval forces besieging Charleston, South Carolina. During this period, he had the unpleasant experience of being shot at by his own invention, for a number of fieldpieces in the Confederate arsenal were captured Dahlgren guns.

Rear Admiral John Dahlgren standing before one of the cannon he designed

Horse

Of all the animals put to use in war, the horse has been the most important. It has been used for every purpose from carrying and pulling supplies and weapons, to carrying armed troops into battle, and at times, for food.

The impact and influence of the horse on battles, campaigns, even peoples, is impossible to gauge. Without the horse, the Mongols and the Huns would have been far less fearsome and dangerous. The introduction of the horse to the New World by the Spanish Conquistadors in the early 1500s transformed Native American society within a hundred years and provided one of the iconic images of the West, the Plains Indian warrior on horseback. Though the horse was obsolete for battlefield use by Word War I (1914–1918), horse cavalry units existed on the active duty rolls of the armies of the major combatants when World War II broke out in 1939. In fact, during World War II, Germany used almost three million horses for supply and transport, more than it had in World War I.

Some warhorses achieved fame in their own right. The list includes Bucephalus, ridden by Alexander the Great; Traveler, an American Saddlebred that was General Robert E. Lee's favorite horse; Little Sorrel, a Morgan ridden by Lieutenant General Stonewall Jackson; and Cincinnati, a thoroughbred ridden by General Ulysses S. Grant. Comanche, a mixed mustang/Morgan gelding, became famous for being the only survivor of Lieutenant Colonel George Custer's command in the Battle of the Little Big Horn (1876).

A combination of incompetence, miscommunication, and outright hostility between top commanders conspired to create one of the great—though tragic—cavalry charges in history: the Charge of the Light Brigade during the Battle of Balaclava on October 25, 1854, in the Crimean War. Immortalized by British poet laureate Alfred, Lord Tennyson, almost seven hundred British cavalry riders attacked the heart of Russian defensive positions in what was called "The Valley of Death." The slaughter, in which almost half the horses were killed and about a third of the troops fell, caused observer French field marshal Pierre Bosquet to make his famous comment, "It is magnificent, but it is not war."

A detail from *The Cavalry Charge at Balaclava*

COLT PERCUSSION REVOLVER

One of the great sidearms of the Civil War was the percussion cap revolver produced by the Colt's Patent Firearms Manufacturing Company (now Colt's Manufacturing Company). Colt manufactured two models during the war, the Army Model 1860, a .44-caliber six-shooter of which more than 200,000 were made, and the Model 1861 Navy, a .36-caliber six-shooter of which almost 39,000 were produced. These succeeded earlier Dragoon and Navy models that also saw wide use in the war. If the production runs of those earlier models are included in the total, though its unlikely that as many as 500,000 Colt pistols were used in the conflict, what is true is that they so outnumbered all other revolvers that the name "Colt" became synonymous with the word "revolver."

These early model Colts were muzzle loaders. The "cartridge" was composed of three parts: a bullet, a measured amount of black powder, and a small copper percussion cap containing fulminate of mercury. The percussion cap was placed on a hollow nipple located at the base of the chamber. Firing occurred when the hammer struck the percussion cap. This in turn ignited the gunpowder charge in the chamber. Pulling back the hammer rotated the cylinder for the next shot.

Though all services and branches were issued pistols, because it was the favored weapon of the cavalry, the story of the revolver's use in the Civil War is primarily a cavalry story. Both sides used them, with the Confederates eagerly confiscating Colt revolvers from captured Union prisoners or arsenals.

Confederate partisan leader Colonel John Singleton Moseby thought they were indispensable. His Rangers favored the Army Colt and carried at least two (it was not unusual to see men with as many as six). Moseby and his Rangers became the terror of Union troops who had to fight them in Loudoun County, Virginia. In fact, the exploits of Moseby's men were so successful that Union general Ulysses S. Grant was driven to issue the order that "where any of Moseby's men are caught, hang them without trial." After the war, Moseby boasted, "I think we did more than any other body of men to give the Colt pistol its great reputation."

Three Union soldiers carrying Colt revolvers

SAMUEL COLT

(1814–1862)

The flamboyant Samuel Colt was one of the greatest firearms inventors of the nineteenth century. So popular were his revolvers, including the Colt Single Action Army "Peacemaker" produced after his death, that they became iconographic symbols of the United States in the second half of the nineteenth century. Among the many who owned a Colt pistol was General George S. Patton, Jr., who carried—and used in battle—a customized ivory-handled Peacemaker all his life. During the Mexican Punitive Expedition (1916), he got into a gunfight and used it to kill two followers of bandit Pancho Villa.

Sam Colt conceived of the idea for his revolver while an apprenticed sailor. During a voyage from India, he whiled away his time carving a wooden model that would become the basis for his famous design. The first Colt revolvers were produced in 1835, but the company failed due to lack of business. Colt's fortunes revived with the outbreak of the Mexican War (1846–1848). The combination of Army contracts and an expanding market in the American West and Europe led to such a surge in business that in 1845 he began a large armory and factory in his hometown of Hartford, Connecticut. "Coltsville," as it came to be known, was a state-of-the-art facility that became a showplace of American industry and the training ground of inventor-entrepreneurs. At the outbreak of the Civil War, Colt's company was the second-largest arms manufacturer in the country, exceeded only by the Federal government's own Springfield Armory.

Colt's inventive genius and keen sense of showmanship made him one of the most famous industrialists of the time. The workaholic Colt kept up such a grueling schedule that by the time of the outbreak of the Civil War, his health began to fail. He died of rheumatic fever in 1862 at the age of forty-seven, leaving behind an estate that in today's dollars had an estimated value of almost four billion dollars.

Sam Colt

SHARPS RIFLE

Even though only about 100,000 Sharps rifles and shorter-barreled carbines were used in the Civil War, they are the most famous long arms of that conflict. The reason for their notoriety lies in their firing system. Patented by inventor Christian Sharps in 1848, they incorporated the first successful breech-loading system in which the cartridge was chambered into the barrel from its base. Before this, all firearms were muzzle-loaders, with the ammunition inserted through the front, or muzzle, of the barrel.

One reason so few Sharps shoulder arms were manufactured is because the breech-loaders had to overcome bitter opposition. Traditionalists favored muzzle-loaders and were preferential to a repeating rifle manufactured by Colt that was inferior in design.

In the Union army, the Sharps rifle was used by two special regiments, the 1st and 2nd Sharpshooters, commanded by Colonels Hiram Berdan and Henry A. Post, respectively. This has led to much confusion because the name "Sharpshooter" did not come from the weapon. Instead, it came from the fact that their ranks were composed of outstanding marksmen who received training and participated in missions similar to today's Special Forces. At first, the units were issued Springfield muzzle-loading rifles. It took the personal intervention of President Abraham Lincoln, after a spectacular demonstration of the superiority of the Sharps rifle by Colonel Berdan, for them to be issued the Sharps rifle.

The Sharps carbine was issued to the cavalry, where its short barrel and high rate of fire (up to ten rounds a minute) made it an ideal weapon.

Following the end of the war, increased competition and some bad business decisions caused a precipitous decline in Sharps business. In 1881 the company shut its doors.

American Civil War Weapons; from top to bottom; a Confederate 58 caliber musket, a Sharps 52 caliber carbine single-shot equipped with target sights, a Joslyn 52 caliber carbine, a Burnside 52 caliber carbine and a Sharps and Hankins 52 caliber carbine

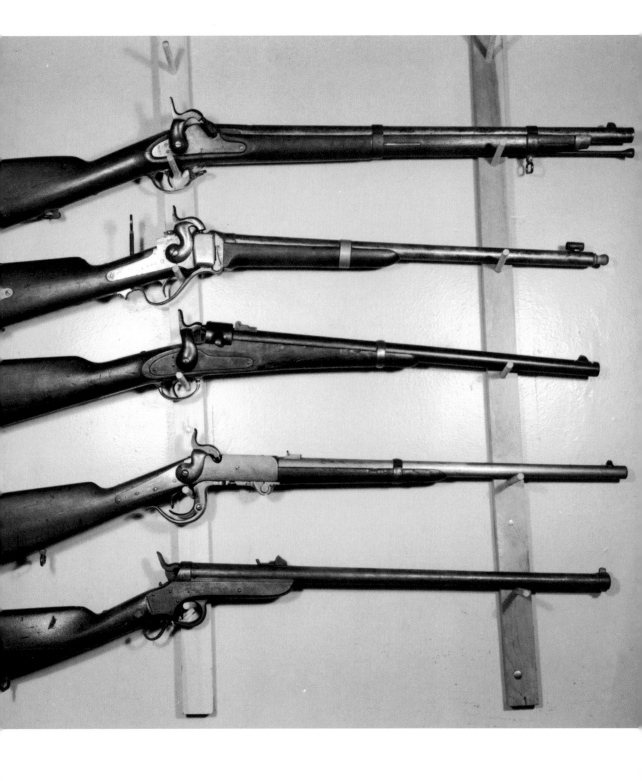

GATLING GUN

The Gatling gun is one of the most recognizable pieces of weaponry produced in the United States. Invented in 1862 and adopted by the Army in 1866, it saw service in campaigns throughout the world. Declared obsolete in 1911, designs based on Gatling's multiple rotating barrel were developed in the 1940s using electric motors instead of a hand crank to rotate the barrel. Today, almost 150 years after its debut, modern versions of the Gatling gun are capable of rates of fire beyond anything that its inventor could have imagined.

The Gatling gun's design was both simple and revolutionary. The original 1862 model consisted of six rifled barrels revolving around a central axis, turned by a hand crank. This assembly was mounted on a modified artillery-type carriage. The advent of all-metal cartridges solved a number of design problems, but the Army Ordnance department was not impressed by trial tests conducted during the war. Though officially turned down by the army, Major General Benjamin Butler was sufficiently impressed to order twelve weapons. Admiral David Dixon Porter also purchased one. But it was not until after the war was over that the Gatling gun would see service.

Machine gun development using blowback designs began making their appearance in the late nineteenth century and had been perfected sufficiently to cause the Army to declare the Gatling gun obsolete shortly before the outbreak of World War I (1914–1918).

Interest returned to the multi-barrel concept thirty years later when designers sought to build a weapon capable of sustaining high rates of fire for long periods of time. If existing machine guns were fired too long (more than 500 rounds at a time), the barrel overheated and warped. In contrast, the M61 Vulcan, a 20-mm six-barreled rotary cannon, is capable of firing 6,000 rounds per minute.

A nineteenth century hand-cranked Gatling gun

Richard Jordan Gatling

(1818–1903)

When the Civil War started, Richard Gatling was already a well-established inventor, whose list included patents for a crop planter, a steam plow, and five farm-related inventions. His most famous invention, the multi-barreled machine gun that bears his name, was invented in 1862 and accepted by the army in 1866. Today, almost 150 years later, highly sophisticated variants are produced with rates of fire thousands of times higher than the original.

Born and raised in North Carolina, Gatling and his family were living in Indiana at the outbreak of the Civil War. Probably because he had married a Northerner, Gatling chose to remain in the North, instead of returning to his native state. After the declaration of war, he focused his attention on creating a weapon of increased firepower. It is speculated that his idea arose out of a discussion he had on the subject with his friend, the future president Benjamin Harrison, then the commander of a regiment of Indiana volunteers. He also believed his invention would help reduce war fatalities because he saw that more soldiers were dying from disease than gunshot wounds. In 1877, he wrote, "It occurred to me that if I could invent a machine—a gun—which could by its rapidity of fire, enable one man to do as much battle duty as a hundred, that it would, to a large extent supersede the necessity of large armies, and consequently, exposure to battle and disease would be greatly diminished." Gatling was not the first inventor, nor would he be the last, to have his invention increase instead of decrease the cost of war.

Gatling continued to invent and his forty-eight patents include toilets and tractors. He was the first president of the American Association of Inventors and Manufacturers. He died in New York City in 1903, a wealthy and world-famous man.

USS MONITOR

The beginning of the end of the Age of Sail occurred when "Fulton's Folly"—Robert Fulton's steamship *Clermont*—sailed up New York's Hudson River in 1807. By the time the Civil War began, wooden-hulled, sidewheel steamships, possessing both sails and steam power, were traveling and guarding the sea lanes. Then came the fateful day of March 9, 1862, when the ironclad warship CSS *Virginia* was confronted in the waters of Hampton Roads off the coast of Virginia by the latest addition to the Union fleet, the ironclad USS *Monitor*. The *Monitor* was the weirdest looking warship imaginable, derisively described by contemporaries as "a cheese box on a raft" and called "Ericsson's Folly" after inventor John Ericsson. The two vessels closed and, though the battle ended inconclusively four hours later, a new age of naval warfare had arrived.

Swedish-born Ericsson chose the name *Monitor* from the Latin word *monere*, meaning to warn or advise. He said this type of vessel "will admonish the leaders of the Southern Rebellion that the batteries on the banks of their rivers will no longer present barriers to the entrance of the Union forces." The *Monitor*, and the class of shallow-draft warships for which it was named, was 172 feet from bow to stern and 41 feet wide. Its flat deck was wood covered with iron plating an inch thick and rode just 18 inches above the waterline. It displaced about 1,000 tons, which meant it drew less than eleven feet of water, a draft that allowed it to operate in any major harbor. Its armament, two 11-inch Dahlgren guns, was located in the center and was protected by a 9-foot-high gun turret covered in iron plating eight inches thick.

The *Monitor*'s success changed American shipbuilding priorities. Armored warships become the focus of American ship construction for the rest of the Civil War. Ericsson designed four more classes of ironclads and all made important contributions to Union victory. In a patriotic gesture after the war, Ericsson turned over his unpatented plans to other engineers to facilitate the production of new vessels. Within a few years, ships like the *Monitor* were being construction for navies around the world, and were on active duty well into the twentieth century.

A Currier and Ives print showing the USS *Monitor* (left foreground) battling the CSS *Virginia* (center)

THE FIRST FIGHT BETWEEN IRON CLAD SHIPS OF WAR.

TERRIFIC COMBAT BETWEEN THE "MONITOR" 2 GUNS & "MERRIMAC" 10 GUNS.

IN HAMPTON ROADS, MARCH 9TH 1862.

Sea Mine

Originally called "torpedoes," mines are a passive defense system used on land and underwater. Mines, particularly land mines, are inexpensive to make. They consist of an encased explosive charge connected to a triggering device. Naval mines were invented by Robert Fulton, of steamboat fame, during the War of 1812 (1812–1814). Mines were first used in the Crimean War (1854–1856) and have been used in war ever since. Because of the poor record of belligerents in cleaning up mine fields after the cessation of hostilities, mine fields, some dating back to World War I, periodically kill or maim unsuspecting civilians who enter them. In the last decades of the twentieth century, international pressure from human rights groups has led to the cleaning of old mine fields and the decline of mine use.

Confederates used sea mines extensively during the Civil War (1861–1865) to protect the harbor entrances of their blockade-running ports. The mines weren't perfect. They could be swept away by currents, and detonators could get water-logged and fail. But they were efficient enough to inspire terror, called "mine fever," in sailors. By the end of the war, Confederate sea mines had sunk seven Union iron-clads and twenty-two wooden gunboats and damaged another fourteen warships.

Sea mines figured prominently in the Battle of Mobile Bay (1864). Union admiral David Farragut made the risky decision of running the mine field that had been laid in the mouth of Mobile Bay and was guarded by three forts. When the first ship in his formation, the USS *Tecumseh*, struck a mine, the ships behind halted in confusion, making them vulnerable to cannon fire from forts Gaines, Morgan, and Powell. With the destruction of his command imminent, Farragut, in his flag-ship the *Hartford*, regained control of his fleet with his order, "Damn the torpedoes. Full speed ahead." The ships resumed their attack and successfully crossed the mine field. Farragut would capture the forts and seal off the mouth of the bay. Though the port of Mobile was never captured during the war, Farragut's triumph ended its usefulness to the Confederacy.

Torpedo

Originally a "torpedo" was any explosive device that was stationary and could be hidden, what would now be called "mines." Giovanni Luppis, a naval officer working for the Austrian Empire, developed a prototype of the self-propelled forerunner of today's torpedo in 1864. He presented his design, which he called a *salvacoste* ("coastsaver"), to engineer Robert Whitehead, manager of the factory responsible for making naval weaponry for the Austrian government. Whitehead successfully tested the first torpedo in 1866. By 1890, torpedoes were a part of the inventory of navies throughout the world.

Torpedoes are complex weapons. They need to be watertight, have a propulsion unit complete with fuel capable of speeds in excess of the target, have sufficient buoyancy to maintain proper depth during the attack, and finally, have a warhead that will detonate on impact. When all these things work in harmony, success can be deadly.

The Germans proved how deadly with their U-boat submarine attacks using torpedoes in World War I (1914–1918) and World War II (1939–1945). German success in World War I led to the victorious Allies using the Versailles peace treaty to ban U-boat construction and possession by the German government. During World War II, the Germans' successful use of the U-boat almost forced British capitulation. And in the Pacific theater of World War II, the Japanese Long Lance torpedoes were used in the devastating attack on Pearl Harbor and helped sink the British battleship *Prince of Wales* and battlecruiser *Repulse* and American carriers *Lexington*, *Yorktown*, *Wasp*, and *Hornet*, among other ships, in the open seas.

Today torpedoes are designed to carry a variety of warheads, including nuclear warheads, and use propulsion systems that make them capable of reaching speeds of more than 200 knots.

DYNAMITE

Dynamite gun

Dynamite was the result of a search to find a way to safely handle the incredibly powerful, but dangerously unstable, explosive nitroglycerine.

Alfred Nobel, through his worldwide promotion efforts and factory building, had almost single-handedly built the international nitroglycerine industry. But his success literally threatened to blow up in his face. Though the force of the explosive, greater than the most powerful gunpowder, made it the prime choice for use in mining, excavation, and other uses requiring explosives, nitroglycerine was equally unstable. Accidental explosions had become so frequent and so destructive that France and Belgium had outlawed it. Great Britain shunned it. And the U.S. Congress was considering a law sentencing irresponsible shippers of it to death by hanging.

Suspecting that the cause behind these accidents was careless spillage, Nobel began experiments designed to prevent that. After numerous tries, he discovered the ideal absorbent, in kieselguhr—a diatomaceous earth formed from the tiny silica skeletons of algae. It absorbed three times its weight in nitroglycerine and, crucially, made the explosive safe to handle. Unlike liquid nitroglycerine, it wouldn't explode even if dropped. Initially sold as "Nobel's Blasting Powder," in a canny decision of salesmanship, he decided to name these explosive sticks "dynamite"—the Greek word for power.

Patented in 1867, his paper tubes, eight inches long and about an inch in diameter, packed with kieselguhr and nitroglycerine, were far outselling the gunpowder products of his closest rivals. Because of the nature of its explosive force, dynamite use in the military is confined to demolitions or excavation. The so-called "dynamite gun," used in the military from the 1880s to about 1904, didn't use the explosive at all. Its projectiles were launched using compressed air. These guns saw limited service during the Spanish-American War (1898). They proved to be mechanically unreliable and inaccurate and were soon phased out of use.

A miner holding seven sticks of dynamite in his left hand. In his right hand is a primer used to detonate the dynamite.

ALFRED NOBEL

(1833–1896)

The man who invented dynamite and used the fortune it created to establish in his name annual prizes in literature, science, and world peace, was the son of a Swedish entrepreneur who, invented plywood, among other things. A lifelong bachelor, he was a sickly, moody youth with a fondness for romantic poets; Shelley was a favorite. Thanks to his father, he had a first-class education in chemistry and spoke five languages. The knowledge and skills would serve him well as an adult.

Alfred Nobel focused his attention on the development of explosives after the death of his younger brother Emil in an industrial accident making nitroglycerine in 1864. His efforts bore fruit three years later when, in 1867, he filed a patent for "Nobel's Blasting Powder" which was later named "dynamite."

Dynamite's success in industry and public works and Nobel's salesmanship abilities soon made him famous, respected, and enormously wealthy. So it came as an immense shock to him when, one day in Paris, he opened a newspaper and found himself reading his obituary, headlined "The Merchant of Death is Dead." As it turned out, his brother Ludvig had recently died. But the journalist who wrote the obituary thought it was Alfred who had passed away. Calling him a "merchant of death"—the first time the term was used—for inventing dynamite, the journalist went on to accuse Nobel of hastening the destruction of mankind instead of aiding in its development.

Nobel was so shaken by the condemnation that he began to think of what he might do to reverse his legacy. On November 27, 1895, he signed a new will, establishing the Nobel Prizes, annual international awards recognizing outstanding achievements in literature, science, and world peace. Two weeks later, he was dead of a stroke. Today, as he had hoped, Alfred Nobel is more famous for his awards recognizing the advancement of mankind than he is for an explosive capable of aiding in its destruction.

Mauser

Mention "six-shot revolver" and the name Colt comes to mind. For bolt-action rifles, the name is Mauser. The first successful Mauser bolt-action rifle was designed by brothers Peter Paul (referred to as Paul) and Wilhelm Mauser in 1872 and licensed to the Imperial German government for manufacture. Two years later, the Mauser brothers formed the partnership Mauser Brothers and Company. It soon became the primary source of rifles for Germany, a position it maintained until the end of World War II, and a major supplier of rifles to nations around the world.

In the rough-and-tumble international arms race of the late nineteenth and early twentieth centuries, no opportunity was overlooked in order to clinch a deal. Mauser scored important foreign sales inroads through the clever device of naming a particular model after its principle buyer. These models, which for the most part had only minor variations compared to each other, included the 89 Belgian, the 91 Argentine, the Turkish Mauser, the Swedish Mauser, and the Spanish Mauser.

Mausers were used in almost all the major conflicts between 1872 and 1945. Spanish Mausers were the primary weapon used by Spanish troops during the Spanish-American War (1898). German and other nations' troops carried the Mauser during the rescue mission to Peking during the Boxer Rebellion (1899–1901) and Dutch Boers used South African Mausers with deadly efficiency in the Second Boer War (1899–1902).

The most successful Mauser was the Model 98, produced in 1898. Updated through the years, millions were manufactured. The Karabiner 98k was the primary rifle of the German Army in World War II.

After Germany's defeat, Mauser was forced out of the arms industry for several years. Three engineers from the company—Edmund Heckler, Theodor Koch, and Alex Seidel—left during this time and founded the arms manufacturer Heckler and Koch.

Surplus military Mausers proved easy to adapt for hunting, and soon converted Mausers entered the market. Among the more notable were the Safari rifles in Africa, Mausers rechambered from the standard 8 mm size to take larger ammunition up to .50 caliber (12.7 mm).

Three Boers with their Mausers

Maxim Machine Gun

The Maxim machine gun was the first single-barrel gun in which the functions of loading, firing and ejecting the cartridge were performed automatically by using the recoil force. It was invented by American-born and later British subject Sir Hiram Maxim, who also invented the common mousetrap and the inhaler for use by asthmatics (he suffered from bronchitis), and who has a case for claiming to be the inventor of the light bulb.

According to legend, Maxim claimed that he first thought of designing his machine gun in 1882, as the result of a conversation he had with a fellow American during an exposition both were attending. The person he was talking to said, "If you want to make a pile of money, invent something that will enable these Europeans to cut each others' throats with greater facility." The Maxim gun had a rate of fire of 600 rounds per minute, far greater than the hand-cranked Gatling gun. Its debut occurred shortly after the period of African colonization by European powers known as the Scramble for Africa (1880–1914). The Maxim gun played a key role in the continent's conquest. Debuting in battle during the First Matabele War (1893–1894) between the army of Cecil Rhodes' British South Africa Company and the Ndebele people who lived in what is now Zimbabwe, the Maxim gun's role in the war proved decisive. In one battle alone, 50 soldiers possessing four Maxim guns were able to defeat a force of five thousand warriors. After a few such battles, the mere appearance of a Maxim gun was sufficient to instill fear and obedience in native populations. The impact of the Maxim gun in stamping British control over its African colonies caused the prolific writer Hilaire Belloc to famously quip, "Whatever happens, we have got/The Maxim gun, and they have not."

The Maxim gun saw extensive service with the British army in World War I (1914–1918). Though the British Army began phasing it out following the war, it saw a brief revival with combatants in the Russian Civil War (1917–1921) and was in the arsenal of the Soviet Red Army well into the 1930s.

Hiram Maxim and his Maxim machine gun

Merchants of Death

In 1888, a French journalist wrote the line, "The merchant of death died" in an obituary that erroneously announced dynamite inventor Alfred Nobel's passing. Though the journalist's name has long-since been forgotten, the phrase he coined expanded to include the entire arms industry.

The arms industry is, in one respect, a necessary evil. If one takes the perfectly logical position that "war is bad," then anyone having anything to do with arming combatants—regardless of how justifiable or necessary that role may be—is morally compromised. Yet so long as people continue to fight, someone will be needed to supply arms to one side or the other, or, as has occasionally happened in history, simultaneously to both. The latter became an international scandal when details of the intricately interconnected world of international arms manufacture and sales came to light after World War I (1914–1918). Many details were revealed in the 1934 bestselling exposé, *Merchants of Death*, written by H. C. Engelbrecht and F. C. Hanighen.

For instance, in a series of transactions beginning in the 1870s, Remington, already a supplier to the U.S. Army, sold arms and ammunition to Cuban rebels and the Spanish army. When the United States joined the Cuban side in the Spanish-American War (1898), some Spanish troops took aim at American soldiers over the gunsights of Remington rifles. And during the naval Battle of Jutland (1916), German warships fired cannon shells made by the German steel giant Krupp at British warships protected by Krupp armor plate.

Merchants of Death revealed, "The arms merchant does not see himself as a villain, according to his lights he is simply a businessman who sells his wares under prevailing business practices. The uses to which his products are put and the results of his traffic are apparently no concern of his." After surveying the business practices of other industries during that period, the influential historian Harry Elmer Barnes, one of the founders of the field of revisionist history, noted, "The only way in which the armament makers are at all unique is that they are engaged in an industry where the death of human beings is the logical end and objective of their activity."

Samuel Cummings (right, with rifle), the largest private arms dealer of the twentieth century in his Interarmco weapons reconditioning factory

LEWIS GUN

While all other post-Gatling gun machine gun designs had the weapon mounted on either a carriage or a tripod, inventor Samuel McClean and Colonel Isaac Newton Lewis took a different route. The Lewis light machine gun that they created somewhat resembled a very large-bore shotgun mounted on a bipod. Instead of belt-fed ammunition, the Lewis gun used a drum magazine containing 47 or 97 rounds. It saw service in World War I (1914–1918) and World War II (1939–1945). Even though by then it was obsolete, it was still in use by some nations during the Korean War (1950–1953) and, amazingly, was one of the weapons used by the Communist Viet Minh in its battles against the French and later the United States in Vietnam.

One important aspect of the Lewis gun was its weight. At just 28 pounds, it was about half as heavy as other machine guns, yet had a rate of fire that was about the same (five hundred to six hundred rounds per minute). Also, one person could use it, whereas other machine guns needed a team of two or more to operate it. Its ease of handling and reliability made it a useful anti-aircraft weapon.

The gun also served as secondary armament on Allied airplanes during World War I, with the first Lewis machine gun-mounted aircraft becoming operational in the summer of 1915.

Like other inventors whose weapons were either technological innovations or otherwise departed from the norms of accepted design, the U.S. Army at first refused to purchase the Lewis gun and its inventors were forced to sell the gun under manufacturing license to other nations. Belgium was the first country to purchase Lewis guns, followed by Great Britain and France. Only after a hundred thousand had been purchased and had seen significant action in World War I did the U.S. Army place order—for a total of 3,550 guns.

Sailors manning a Lewis gun aboard a British ship

COLT MODEL 1911 PISTOL

"Necessity is the mother of invention." This variation of Plato's idiom described the American army experience in the southern Philippines after the end of the Spanish-American War (1898). Rebellious native Moro warriors, incited to a suicidal frenzy in pre-battle rituals that included drugs, often proved unstoppable even in death. Their momentum would carry them into American lines where the soldiers who has slain them were killed or maimed by the wavy-bladed kris swords and daggers. The army needed a close-quarter sidearm with stopping power.

The Army held a design competition in 1904. Six companies submitted designs. The winner was the Colt Model 1911 .45-caliber semi-automatic pistol designed by John M. Browning, fires a .45-caliber ACP (Automatic Colt Pistol) round. It is one of the most successful handguns in the history of weaponry. By the time its use was discontinued by the U.S. military in 1985, more than 2.7 million Model 1911s of various types had been manufactured. It continues to be used by law enforcement agencies and military units throughout the world, and holds an esteemed reputation with enthusiasts.

Soldiers issued the sidearm discovered that the Colt Model 1911 delivered as promised. It was rugged, reliable, and powerful. Initially it was only manufactured by Colt, but demand for the pistol became so strong that in order to keep up with orders, during World War I the company had to license manufacture of it to the government's Springfield Armory; and, during World War II, to six arms companies.

In the 1970s, political pressure from NATO allies to get the United States to conform to the 9-mm NATO-standard pistol cartridge used by other member nations forced the United States to search for a replacement for the Model 1911. After tests over several years, the Beretta 92F was chosen. But, the smaller cartridge also meant reduced stopping power. This was the primary reason that United States Special Operations Command chose to re-adopt the Model 1911 as its standard sidearm for some of its units.

BIG BERTHA

Dicke Bertha (literally, Fat Bertha) is the name the Germans gave to the 420 mm M-Gerät howitzer they used during World War I. The cannon got its name from a real-life Bertha: Bertha Krupp von Bohlen und Halbach, the heir to the Krupp steel and weapons manufacturing dynasty. The Allies translated the name into "Big Bertha" and, because of the Krupp "cannon king" reputation, came to use it as the generic term for all large-caliber German artillery, particularly the 210 mm "Paris Gun" used to shell Paris in 1918.

Fat or Big, the original Big Bertha certainly was a monster. Almost 20 feet long and weighing 43 tons, it could fire a shell weighing 1,808 pounds almost eight miles. Its success destroying the walls of Belgian and French forts at the beginning of the war sealed its reputation. The German press enthusiastically called it a *Wunderwaffe* ("miracle weapon"). Twelve were built. Two survived the war, with one of them being put on display at the United States Army Ordnance Museum in Aberdeen, Maryland.

The other Big Bertha was the *Paris-Geschütz* (Paris Gun), a cannon so big and complex only one was built. It weighed 256 tons, was about 92 feet long, and had to be transported to the front by railroad. It fired a 210-pound shell 81 miles. The shell's ballistic arc was an incredible 25 miles, which meant that it was the first man-made object to reach the stratosphere. The caliber of the cannon started at 210 mm. Wear and tear of the cannon barrel's bore after each shot was so great that each succeeding shell was larger that its predecessor. Each of the ever-larger shells was sequentially numbered to exactly fit the barrel's increasing diameter. Only 65 shells could be fired before the barrel had to be restored.

It was used for only six months in the last year of the war and caused a large amount of damage to Paris. The cannon and its construction plans were destroyed to keep them from falling into Allied hands. The Paris Gun was among the German weapons specifically banned by the Versailles peace treaty.

The Big Bertha firing on Paris, which the Germans bombarded for 20 months during 1917.

KRUPP

The Krupp family and company became famous—and infamous—as the armorers of Imperial and Nazi Germany, the Second and Third Reichs. But originally arms were a sideshow for Krupp, and an unprofitable one at that. The transformation of the family-run steel foundry whose signature product was the patented seamless railroad car wheel into that of "Cannon King" for the Kaisers, Hitler, and other nations became an extreme example of the interdependence between armorers and governments.

The Krupp responsible for the company's transformation was Alfred Krupp, the Cannon King, who at fourteen inherited a company near bankruptcy. Through obsessive hard work and some luck, he turned the company's fortunes around. At first, cannons were a small part of the company's product mix. That changed after Germany defeated France in the Franco-Prussian War (1870–1871). Krupp cannons played a key role in Germany's victory and soon industrialized nations around the world were placing large orders for high-quality Krupp cannons and other arms. When Alfred died in 1887, his company was a national institution and his descendents were treated like an industrial royal family.

Krupp had become so large and powerful, its agents acted as if they were diplomats of a sovereign nation. A representative of the World Peace Foundation bitterly observed in 1911, "King Krupp of Essen has ambassadors of his own in every great capital of the world, from Tokyo to Constantinople, and from St. Petersburg to Buenos Aires. He has even in Sofia, Bulgaria, a representative who knows more about local politics and has a larger acquaintance with politicians than all the legations put together."

Krupp's role as armors of Germany in both world wars caused its top officers to be indicted as war criminals. For Alfried Krupp, Jr. who succeeded as the head of the company in 1943, the charges included crimes against humanity. He was sentenced to twelve years in prison and had to forfeit all property. The sentence was pardoned and confiscation was rescinded in 1952 by John McCloy, the top American authority during the post-war period of Allied occupation of Germany. He pardoned a number of industrialists so they could help restore moribund German industry.

Alfried Krupp shortly after his apprehension by American troops at the end of World War II

ZEPPELIN

Count Zeppelin

For the civilian population in England, the large cigar-shaped Zeppelin slowly flying overhead was the most terrifying weapon of World War I (1914–1918). Zeppelin raids on English soil began within weeks after the war's outbreak and did little damage. But those first air raids in 1914 aroused such panic that the British government ordered the Royal Navy to attack Zeppelin bases in northern Germany as soon as possible. The result was a dramatic aircraft carrier raid (the second in history) conducted against the Zeppelin base at Cuxhaven on December 25, 1914.

"Zeppelin" is the trademark name for the rigid airship design patented in the late nineteenth century by Count Ferdinand von Zeppelin of Germany. The design became so popular and dominant in the airship industry that the term "zeppelin" came to be used to describe all rigid airships. Blimps, like the ones seen today over sports arenas, have no skeletons.

The first successful Zeppelin flight test took place in 1899 near Lake Constance in southern Germany. This was a time when man was making the first attempts to fly, and Zeppelin's airship success quickly captured the imagination. By 1909 Zeppelins were being used to transport passengers.

When World War I began, the German army and navy had fourteen Zeppelins. Though Zeppelins were mostly used in reconnaissance of Allied shipping lanes and naval activity in the North and Baltic seas, they became famous for their raids on England. A typical raid consisted often to twelve Zeppelins, with each Zeppelin capable of carrying at the most nine tons of bombs.

The golden age of the Zeppelin began in the late 1920s when Zeppelin passenger airships capable of transatlantic flight majestically soared the skies. It all came to a fiery end on May 6, 1937, at Lakehurst, New Jersey, when the *Hindenburg*, filled with hydrogen, burst in flames while attempting to land.

A Zeppelin in flight—note the two gondolas and covered walkway beneath the gas bag.

ZEPPELIN AIRSHIP JULY 4,'08 - 6.21 a.m.
ZEPPELIN AIRSHIP

462-6

Modell
Z.2.1908   4.Juli vorm. 6.21

54.

FOKKER EINDECKER

The Great War (1914–1918), as World War I was originally known, contained many firsts. One was the use of combat aircraft. The first combat airplanes were small and fragile and had little strategic impact, but they were the harbingers of the future of aerial combat. One of the most significant of these early combat aircraft was the Fokker Eindecker ("one wing"), a monoplane fighter.

At the beginning of the war, aircraft on both sides were unarmed and used only for reconnaissance. In the first aerial combats, such as they were, pilots and passengers shot at each other with handguns, rifles, or shotguns. These in turn were replaced by machine guns light enough for use in aircraft. The first machine guns were used by passengers or were forward-mounted on the top wing of biplanes so they could fire above the propeller. Some aircraft had a machine gun mounted above the engine. Because the machine gun was not synchronized with the propeller's rotation, the wooden propellers were attached with metal plates to protect them from bullet impacts—an inefficient arrangement as much a danger to the shooter as to the target.

The Eindecker, designed by Dutch aviation engineer Anthony Fokker, was the first fighter aircraft to be fitted with a synchronized gear that allowed the pilot to fire his machine gun without the bullets hitting the propeller blades. When it debuted over the skies of Western Europe in July 1915, its impact was so dramatic that the next several months, until the Allies developed similar fighters in 1916, were known as the "Fokker Scourge."

There were just five Eindeckers in the first squadron, but three of the five pilots flying them would become among the most famous German aces of the war. They included Lieutenant Kurt Wintgens, credited with being the first fighter pilot to score an aerial victory over an opponent; First Lieutenant Max Immelman, who perfected the combat maneuver that bears his name; and Captain Oswald Boelcke an outstanding tactician and leader. (The term "ace" first came into use during World War I, describing a pilot who shot down at least five enemy planes. It's established in five-plane increments, thus a "double ace" shot down ten planes, "triple ace" shot down fifteen, and so on.) All three received Imperial Germany's highest military decoration, the Pour le Mérite, the equivalent of the Medal of Honor, and all three died in combat.

A German Fokker E-III, the first warplane to be equipped with a synchronised machine-gun

ASDIC/SONAR

All too often during World War I, the first indication a ship's crew had that it was under submarine attack was seeing a torpedo wake just minutes or seconds before impact. The German U-boat's ability to hide beneath the surface of the sea made it one of the deadliest weapons of the war. As the number of merchant ships sunk by U-boats increased, the British government commissioned scientists and engineers to find a countermeasure. The efforts bore fruit in 1916 with an underwater sound detection device code-named ASDIC.

ASDIC was a forerunner of SONAR. It was developed by Canadian physicist Robert William Boyle and British physicist Dr. Albert Beaumont Wood working in the British Board of Invention and Research's Anti-Submarine Division. To maintain secrecy regarding the experiments with sound waves and the use of quartz piezoelectric crystals, the word "ASD"ic (taking the first letters of "Anti-Submarine Division") was created as a substitution for the word "supersonic," and "ASD"ivite for the quartz material. Very quickly the device came to be called simply ASDIC.

Though ASDIC-equipped ships were used by the United States and England in 1918, they arrived too late to have much of an impact against submarines. Far more effective were defensive tactics that included grouping merchant ships into convoys and providing heavy warship protection. ASDIC, and later SONAR, would become important anti-submarine weapons during World War II.

In 1939, the British Admiralty was contacted by the staff of the Oxford English Dictionary who wished to include the word "ASDIC" in their latest edition and requested the origin of the word. The Admiralty responded with a spurious tale that it was the acronym for the group that designed and built the device, the Allied Submarine Detection Investigation Committee. This misleading origin is still widely believed, though no committee with that name has ever appeared in Admiralty archives.

An operator on a Royal Naval Patrol service trawler listens on the Asdic

Sex

Any study of the weapons of warfare is incomplete without the weapon of sex. Through the simple act of "doing what comes naturally," countless women were able to influence the outcome of battles and campaigns and alter the course of history.

One of the most famous stories of sex as a weapon of statecraft occurred when Cleopatra dramatically presented herself to Julius Caesar with the flourish of emerging from an unrolled carpet. He intended to annex Egypt for Rome. Instead, Cleopatra seduced him, bore him a son, and maintained Egypt's independence throughout Caesar's lifetime.

Before the twentieth century, a woman's opportunity to exercise political power directly was limited. Had Jeanne-Antoinette Poisson, the Duchess Pompadour and mistress of French King Louis XV, been a man, she would have made a poor diplomat. As it turned out, she was a woman—and a poor diplomat. Her influence led to France's disastrous participation in the Seven Years War (1756–1763), known in North America as the French and Indian War, where France lost almost all its North American colonies.

The most famous seductive female spy appeared on the world stage during World War I (1914–1917). She was the Dutch exotic dancer Margarethe Geertruida Zelle, a double agent who worked for both Germany and France. The French discovered her duplicity and executed her in 1917. Zelle's stage name "Mata Hari" became the definition of a beautiful, seductive female spy.

During World War II (1939–1945), the pro-German, Anglophobe Countess des Portes held enormous influence over French Prime Minister Paul Reynaud and was instrumental in arranging the French government's capitulation to Germany in 1940.

One of the most mysterious female spies of World War II was an Irish woman who worked for British intelligence. She succeeded in penetrating German chancellor Adolf Hitler's personal entourage. Code-named "Mata O'Hara," she was the mistress of SS Lieutenant General Hermann Fegelein, the brother-in-law of Hitler's mistress. For years, she passed to the British sensitive information indiscreetly revealed following an afternoon or evening of indulgence.

Albatros D. III

With an elongated teardrop fuselage, a top wing whose outer edges flare out like the tips of a bird's wing, and graceful tail, the Albatros D. III is one of the most beautiful warplanes built during World War I. Unlike the blunt-nosed air-cooled warplanes produced by Fokker, SPAD, and Nieuport, the Albatros used a water-cooled engine, allowing its nose to have a more aerodynamic shape. The manufacturer Albatros-Flugzeugwerke built a total of four D. models: D. I, D. II, D. III, and D. V, with a total production of more than 4,500 fighters, making it one of the most successful lines in the war.

The Albatros D. II and D. III ruled the skies over the Western Front from September 1916 to June 1917, easily outclassing or overwhelming their Allied opponents. German air superiority reached its peak in April 1917, "Bloody April," when German squadrons shot down a total of 245 British aircraft, while German losses from all causes totaled just 66 aircraft.

Though Baron Manfred von Richthofen, Germany's greatest ace, is most famous for flying the Fokker D. I triplane, he scored 61 of his 80 aerial victories flying Albatros aircraft, with 23 of them in the D. III.

After the war, the Polish government obtained 38 Albatros D. III and used them in ground attack operations during the Polish Soviet War (1919–1920). The Polish government was so pleased with the aircraft's performance that it sent a letter of commendation to the factory.

Albatross aircraft from Baron Manfred von Richthofen's Flying Circus

SOPWITH CAMEL

Thomas Octave Murdoch Sopwith's F-1, more popularly known as the Camel, became the symbol of British military aviation in World War I. The Camel was the successor to the Sopwith Pup and the Sopwith Triplane; fighters that had become outclassed by the German Albatross and Fokker fighters appearing over the Western Front in 1916. Testing on the Camel prototype was conducted in December 1916 and the first combat squadron became operational in June 1917. Originally designed as a scout, the Camel became England's most successful fighter and was ultimately credited with shooting down more than 2,800 enemy aircraft.

The Camel was the first British warbird armed with twin Vickers machine guns firing synchronized through its propeller. A fairing enclosing the machine guns created a hump, causing the F-1 to get its more popular name. The Camel was a powerful, sturdy airplane with excellent performance and maneuverability in combat. It was also temperamental and required the constant attention of its pilot. The result was that it had a high incidence of accidents, particularly among inexperienced student pilots.

A total of 5,734 Camels were built and flew in the service of air forces from six Allied nations. Three American squadrons flew the Camel, the 17th, 41st, and 148th, with some of those pilots making ace. The F-1 was the main production model. Other variants included a naval version, a night fighter, a variant with tapered wings, and one designed for strafing trenches.

The Camel achieved aviation immortality on April 21, 1918, when the Canadian ace Captain Arthur "Roy" Brown got into a dogfight with Germany's greatest ace, Baron Manfred von Richthofen, the "Red Baron." Brown was officially credited with shooting down the Red Baron, for which he was awarded a bar to his Distinguished Service Cross. Later it was determined that von Richthofen had been killed by ground fire.

Decades later, the Camel returned to the world stage in an unexpected venue, the American syndicated comic strip *Peanuts*. The Sopwith Camel was the aircraft flown by the "World War I flying ace" known as Snoopy.

SPAD S.XIII

The SPAD S.XIII was the last in the line of successful biplane fighters designed by the French manufacturer Société Pour L'Aviation et ses Dérivés (SPAD). Almost 8,500 of the S.XIII model were built, with almost 900 going to the United States Army Air Service, making it one of the most-produced warplanes in World War I.

The SPAD S.XIII mounted two synchronized Vickers machine guns above the engine and was a powerful, rugged high-performance fighter with excellent diving characteristics. Though it rewarded a skilled pilot who knew how to fly it, novice pilots found it temperamental and difficult to control. But the S.XIII outperformed the best German aircraft and was equally a match to its British contemporary, the Sopwith Camel.

Seventeen American squadrons flew the SPAD. America's top ace in the war, Captain Eddie Rickenbacker, scored 20 of his 26 air victories in an S.XIII. Rickenbacker would receive a Medal of Honor and an extraordinary seven Distinguished Service Crosses, as well as the French Legion of Honor and Croix de Guerre, for his achievements in the skies above the Western Front.

On September 25, 1918, he was flying a voluntary, solo patrol over the city of Billy in northern France when he spotted five Fokker fighters escorting two Halberstadt photoreconnaissance planes. Despite the odds, Rickenbacker attacked, downing one fighter and one photo-recon plane, forcing the rest to return to their airfield. For his "conspicuous gallantry and intrepidity above and beyond the call of duty," then-lieutenant Rickenbacker was presented with the Medal of Honor.

Replica of Eddie Rickenbacker's SPAD

FOKKER DR. I DREIDECKER

Though it arrived late in the war (September 1917) and few were built (320), the Fokker Dr. I Dreidecker triplane is arguably the most famous German warplane of World War I for two reasons. One was that it was painted in the eye-popping colors favored by Germany's leading squadron, *Jagdgeschwader* I, nicknamed the Flying Circus, led by its greatest ace, Baron Manfred von Richthofen. And it was in a bright red Dr. I that the Red Baron, as he was known because of his 80 aerial victories, was killed.

The Dr. I was Germany's response to the high performance and highly maneuverable British Sopwith Triplane that appeared in the skies over the Western Front in early 1917. The first triplanes to see action were actually two pre-production models labeled F.I. They were delivered to Richthofen's squadron in September 1917 and within the span of two days, the Red Baron flying an F.I had shot down two enemy aircraft, his sixtieth and sixty-first victories. Richthofen had fought the Sopwith Triplane in April 1917, when he was flying the Albatros D. III. In his report after his victories in the F.I, Richthofen stated that the Fokker triplane was superior to the Sopwith and that fighter squadrons be equipped with the new Fokkers as quickly as possible. After a five-month period flying the Albatros D. V in which he only shot down two planes, in March 1918 Richthofen was in the air with the new Dr. I. He made up for lost time racking up one victory after another, reaching a confirmed victory total of 80 planes shot down by April 20.

The Dr. I was highly maneuverable and many pilots regarded it fondly. But it was an unforgiving aircraft and prone to accidents during landings. It also had serious structural problems that made it vulnerable to wing failure. This last deficiency was the major reason why only 320 were ordered.

On April 21, while flying over Australian lines along the Somme River in northern France, von Richthofen pursued and engaged in combat two Sopwith Camels. It was during this dogfight that Richthofen was fatally shot. He crash-landed behind Australian lines and his plane was soon stripped by souvenir hunters. The credit for downing the Red Baron was given to Canadian Captain Arthur "Roy" Brown, a pilot of one of the Camels. Studies made decades later determined that Richthofen was killed by ground fire.

Two re-enactors pose in front of a replica of a Fokker Dr. I

Anthony Fokker

(1890–1939)

One of the great pioneers of early aviation, nicknamed "the Flying Dutchman," was born in the Dutch East Indies (now Indonesia). His first exposure to aviation was in France in 1908 when he witnessed a flying exhibition performed by Wilbur Wright. Two years later, at age 20, he designed and built his first airplane called the Spider, which promptly crashed. In 1912, he founded the aircraft company bearing his name and began full-scale production.

With the onset of World War I, the German government nationalized his company, though he remained as a director and chief designer. His company produced more than 40 different aircraft for the German air force, including the Eindecker, a monoplane that was the first fighter capable of synchronized machine gun fire through the propeller, and the Dr. I triplane flown by Germany's greatest ace, Baron Manfred von Richthofen.

Fokker was an accomplished pilot with a strong engineering background who often test-flew prototypes. He was also an important contributor to the design and development of the synchronization gear that enabled machine guns to safely shoot bullets though a spinning propeller without hitting the blades.

After Germany's defeat, the restrictions of the Treaty of Versailles prevented Germany from building aircraft. Fokker left Germany for his native Holland where he established a new aircraft manufacturing company. Later he went to the United States, where he founded the subsidiary Atlantic Aircraft Corporation. The most famous airplane built by his new company was the Fokker Trimotor, introduced in 1925. Arctic explorer Richard E. Byrd used one when he became the first man to fly over the North Pole in 1926. Other notable achievements with the aircraft included the first solo trans-Pacific flight in 1928 and, in a pioneering effort using aerial refueling, the setting of an endurance record of 150 hours of continuous flight in 1929.

Fokker immigrated to the United States and died in 1939 at age 49 from complications following nose surgery.

Anthony Fokker in his glider at the Fokker Glider Exhibition in Germany in 1922

BIRDS

For centuries, the most reliable means of swift communication between front line units and headquarters was the carrier pigeon. The ancient Persians are credited with the first to identify the keen homing ability of the rock pigeon and domesticate the breed for messenger duty. Julius Caesar made extensive use of carrier pigeons in his conquest of Gaul. Carrier pigeons continued to be a regular part of a number of armies long after reliable electronic communications systems were developed. Carrier pigeons saw regular use as late as World War II and were officially a part of the British security service MI5 as late as 1950.

Carrier pigeons were used extensively by both sides during World War I. The most famous was Cher Ami ("Dear Friend"), a registered Black Check Cock homing pigeon donated to the U.S. Army by an English pigeon club. Cher Ami is credited with saving more than five hundred American soldiers, later named the "Lost Battalion" after it became separated during its advance in the Battle of the Argonne in October 1918. The force, led by Major Charles Whittlesey, was soon surrounded and subjected to heavy enemy fire. The Lost Battalion's situation became dire when it came under friendly fire by allied artillery, a situation now known as blue-on-blue fratricide. Two earlier attempts to use carrier pigeons had failed when the Germans shot them down. Only Cher Ami was left.

Whittlesey composed a third message, put it into Cher Ami's canister and sent him aloft. The Germans once again opened fire. Men of the Lost Battalion saw him get hit and fall to the ground. Cher Ami returned to the air and successfully reached headquarters, 25 miles away.

Cher Ami had been shot through the breast, had lost an eye and one leg, but army medics saved his life. He became a decorated hero, receiving the French Croix de Guerre with palm, and achieved widespread fame. Cher Ami died of his wounds in 1919 and was mounted and enshrined in the Smithsonian Institution. In 1931 he was inducted into the Racing Pigeon Hall of Fame.

A replica of Cher Ami. Strapped to the pigeon is a small automatic camera used to take battlefield photographs.

THOMPSON SUBMACHINE GUN

The Thompson submachine gun was one of the first, most successful, and most famous hand-held automatic weapons of the twentieth century. Initially it saw service with the United States Marines and United States Post Office guards during the 1920s. But it was organized crime and Hollywood that gave the Thompson submachine gun its popular-culture cachet.

The Thompson submachine gun was designed by John Taliaferro Thompson, a retired army brigadier general. As World War I descended into static trench warfare, Thompson began experimenting with automatic small arms designs searching for what he called a "trench broom" that would sweep enemy trenches with gunfire. The war ended before Thompson's design was perfected. Marketed in 1921 as the first "submachine gun," it was made available to the civilian market. It fired a .45 caliber ACP cartridge from a box magazine that carried up to thirty rounds or a drum magazine containing fifty or a hundred rounds. It had a high rate of fire (depending on the model, from 600 to 1,200 rounds a minute), but was inaccurate beyond fifty yards and suffered from a lack of penetrating power. The "Tommy gun," as it soon became known, was the weapon of choice of gangsters, both real and the Hollywood version, during Prohibition and the Depression. A series of federal laws were passed prohibiting civilian possession of fully-automatic submachine guns beginning with the National Firearms Act of 1934.

The Thompson submachine gun was used by the U.S. military in World War II and the Korean War, where it was most often carried by commissioned and non-commissioned officers. It was also the weapon of choice for special operations troops who needed an automatic weapon with a high rate of fire.

Thousands of Thompson submachine guns were shipped to the Nationalist Chinese forces under the Lend-Lease program during World War II for use against the Japanese army. When the Communist Chinese took over the country after the war, most of the Thompson submachine guns landed in their arsenal. During the Korean War, American troops were stunned to discover Chinese troops using those submachine guns against them. Any recaptured weapons were promptly returned to service by their "original owners."

A soldier on a battlefield in Western Europe with his Thompson submachine gun

M2 .50-Caliber
Browning Machine Gun

"Ma Deuce"—the Browning M2 .50-caliber air-cooled heavy machine gun—is perhaps the most versatile automatic weapon ever invented. Designed by John Browning, one of the greatest arms designers in the world, it entered service in the U.S. military in 1921 and remained in service, with surprisingly few modifications (specialized roles excepting), ever since. It has been used by ground troops, as well as mounted on vehicles, and in airplanes—one variant is a semi-automatic sniper rifle.

The M2 is a belt-fed machine gun capable of sustained rates of fire from 450 to 1,200 rounds per minute depending on the variant. It has a maximum range of four-and-a-half miles. Unlike some weapons, the M2 can be fed from either side, with the conversion taking less than two minutes.

One of the deadliest configurations was the Quad .50, a mounting of four M2s on an armored half-track for anti-aircraft defense. The Quad .50's role was soon expanded to include ground defense. It became the weapon of choice to neutralize suspected sniper sites in trees and against mass charges; the back–and-forth sweep of its four machine guns in heavy sustained fire all but annihilated the attacker.

The M2 was used by troops in Iraq in 2003, making it the oldest weapon in use today by the U.S. military. Efforts have been made to phase out the M2, but no subsequent heavy machine gun has proved to be more efficient or reliable.

1921

A disassembled M-2 .50 caliber machine gun ready for maintenance

John Moses Browning

(1855–1926)

The "Thomas Edison of firearms" was an inventive genius who created a record that remains unmatched, and unmatchable, in the history of firearms manufacture. He owned 128 gun patents covering eighty different firearms. He produced gun designs for firearms companies Remington, Colt, Savage, Winchester, and Fabrique Nationale de Guerre, based in Liège, Belgium. He invented the automatic pistol, rifle, and shotgun, and was a pioneer in the development of machine guns and automatic cannons.

Browning was the first to design a pistol with a recoiling slide, the Colt M1900 (designed 1897), a feature that since became standard on almost all semi-automatic handguns. His Colt-Browning M1895 (patented 1890) machine gun, nicknamed "the potato digger" because of its unusual operating mechanism, was the first successful gas-operated machine gun. Browning designed other machine guns as well, but his most successful design, with updated versions still in use today, was the Ma Deuce—the M2 .50 caliber air-cooled machine gun that went into service in 1921. It saw use on land with infantry and in armored vehicles, was installed in all American combat aircraft during World War II, in jet fighters in the Korean War, and aboard ships for anti-aircraft defense.

Browning died of a heart attack while working a new sport pistol in his Fabrique Nationale office in Liège. That design was completed and produced as the Browning Hi-Power 9 mm self-loading pistol.

Inevitably, because Browning designed so many different firearms for the military and sport use, some fell into notorious hands. Depression-era gangster Clyde Barrow (of Bonnie and Clyde fame) used for a time a BAR (Browning Automatic Rifle) light machine gun that he stole from a National Guard armory. But Browning's most infamous gun was probably the Browning FN Model 1910 semi-automatic pistol, serial number 19074. This was the pistol used by Serbian nationalist Gavrilo Princip when he assassinated the heir to the Austria-Hungary Empire, Archduke Franz Ferdinand and his wife, Sophie, on June 28, 1914, causing the outbreak of World War I. That pistol was given to Jesuit priest Father Anton Puntigam, who gave last rites to the dying archduke and his wife, and was kept in a Jesuit monastery until 2004 when it was donated to the Vienna Museum of Military History.

John Moses Browning holding a Browning Automatic Rifle (BAR), one of his many gun designs

SAMUEL CUMMINGS

(1927–1998)

In an industry obsessed with the (ever more expensive) new and improved, Samuel Cummings was a recycler. For almost fifty years, Samuel Cummings was the world's biggest private dealer in small arms. Though at just $100 million a year in sales his company Interarmco was a minnow compared to the multi-billion-dollar giants in the trade, Samuel Cummings, with an office in Alexandria, Virginia, and a warehouse in England, knew his niche and he happily filled it.

Born in Philadelphia of British parents, Cummings continually enjoyed recounting how his interest in arms began. When he was five years old, he found a rusting German World War I machine gun in the trash outside an American Legion post. When he brought it home, his indulgent parents allowed him to keep and play with it. He fought in World War II and, in 1950, was recruited into the fledgling CIA. In the four years he was officially with the agency, he was its most cunning arms dealer. Masquerading as a Hollywood producer buying guns for the movies, he snapped up $100 million worth of surplus World War II German arms in Europe and shipped them to a grateful buyer in Asia. In these and other deals, he saw that enormous profits could be made in the arms aftermarket. He left the CIA in 1953 and set up his first arms company. Suspicion remained that he never completely cut his ties with the CIA. As such a connection helped business he did nothing to discourage the speculation—going so far as to name a subsidiary Cummings Investment Associates.

The small wars around the world from the 1950s through the 1980s made Cummings rich. He was not above selling to both sides of a revolutionary struggle. He sold arms to Cuban dictator Fulgencio Batista. In 1957, when it was obvious Fidel Castro was going to seize control, Cummings delivered arms to the guerillas that were paid for by the CIA. Cummings later recalled, "Castro was handy with an Armalite."

Though his stock of weapons would occasionally dip, at some point a government would conveniently declare a stockpile surplus, and Cummings would be there, check in hand. Over the years he gained a reputation as a philosopher-king of the industry. In interviews, when asked about his career as a merchant of death, he replied, "The arms business is based on human folly." And he added, "Human folly goes up and down, but it always exists, and its depths have never been plumbed."

Bofors 40-mm Anti-Aircraft Gun

The Swedish-designed Bofors 40-mm anti-aircraft gun was the most popular medium-weight anti-aircraft gun of World War II (1939–1945). Used by both sides, it saw service on land and aboard ship in all the theaters of operation. Introduced in 1934 and upgraded periodically, it has remained in production ever since. Almost 70 countries from the United States and Great Britain to Latvia, Dubai, and Singapore, have included the Bofors gun, as it is usually called, in its military inventory of arms.

The Bofors gun was originally developed for the Swedish navy, who in 1929 made a request for a compact, medium-weight anti-aircraft cannon it could install on its ships. Designs were drawn up and prototypes tested with encouraging results. In 1935, Bofors presented a copy of its first production model, the L/60, in its company display at an arms convention in Belgium. It caused a sensation, with orders for the gun promptly coming from the Netherlands, Poland, Norway, and Finland. England obtained a license to build the Bofors gun in 1937. It became a standard anti-aircraft gun in the British army. It was considered a crucial element in British defenses during the Battle of Britain (1940). During D-Day (1944), Bofors guns were vital in the defense of the strategic Pegasus Bridge south of Sword Beach and were credited with shooting down seventeen German aircraft.

The Bofors gun was adopted by the United States military in the late 1930s and became the standard anti-aircraft gun for all ships in the U.S. Navy. There were many reasons for its popularity. It was relatively inexpensive, reliable, accurate, easy to transport and operate, and depending on the variant, could be operated by as few as two people (a loader and a gunner). It also had high rates of fire—120 rounds per minute on the L/60 and 330 rounds per minute for the L/70 (the "60" and "70" referring to barrel length in inches).

In a reversal of roles, the U.S. Air Force mounted Bofors guns in the late 1960s and early 1970s into their AC-130 gunships for use in air to ground operations. Updated with modern technology, today's models include state-of-the-art tracking and automatic firing systems.

Sailors on a patrol boat manning a Bofors anti-aircraft gun

FAIREY SWORDFISH

The Fairey Swordfish was one of the most unusual warplanes of World War II. It was designed in 1934 as a gunfire spotter, torpedo, and reconnaissance aircraft for the British Royal Navy. A biplane in an age where monoplanes had taken over the skies, the Fairey Swordfish was already obsolete when the war began in 1939. Yet, instead of being retired, the Swordfish participated in British carrier operations throughout the war, finally being retired shortly after the war's end in Europe in May 1945.

The Swordfish carried a crew of three and served as a torpedo-bomber, an anti-submarine and convoy escort, a shore-based mine layer, a rocket projectile aircraft, night-operations, and trainer. With a maximum speed of 138 miles per hour, the Swordfish was slow. But its lack of speed and sophistication proved to be a virtue—so long as it operated in areas outside the range of much faster enemy fighters. The Swordfish proved an excellent torpedo bomber, and its stall speed of under 45 miles per hour added to the safety of its landing on carrier decks during adverse weather conditions.

The Swordfish participated in naval operations along the Norwegian coast shortly after Germany invaded that country in 1940. It became famous during the Battle of Taranto on November 11, 1940. Twenty-four Swordfish launched from the HMS *Illustrious* conducted a daring nighttime attack on the Italian fleet anchored at Taranto, sinking one battleship and heavily damaging two battleships, a heavy cruiser and a destroyer. Within an hour, the power of the Italian fleet had been reduced by half. Only two aircraft were lost. The attack was closely studied by the Japanese who used it as a model for their attack on Pearl Harbor the following December.

The Swordfish's second great success also occurred early in the war. In May 1941, Swordfish flying from the HMS *Ark Royal* damaged the rudder of the German pocket battleship *Bismarck*. Unable to steer, the crippled warship was later sunk by a combination of gunfire and torpedoes.

Almost 2,400 Swordfish were built, an extraordinary number considering that production continued well into the war. It received the affectionate nickname "Stringbag" by its crews because of the cargo and equipment it was authorized to carry. Crews compared it to the then-popular housewife string shopping bag that could expand to carry goods.

A Swordfish takes off from the HMS *Courageous*

ADNAN KHASHOGGI
(1935–)

For many people, the most complicated purchase they make in their lives occurs when they buy a house. That's bubblegum in a candy store compared to the transaction of an international arms deal. There's just too much prestige, politics, and—above all—money and jobs involved. Agents, middlemen familiar with the needs and customs of both sides, are regarded as crucial. The biggest—and arguably the most notorious—arms agent of the late twentieth century was Adnan Khashoggi of Saudi Arabia.

Urbane, cultivated, genial, eloquent, and connected to the power brokers of the Arab world, Khashoggi was the son of the doctor to King ibn Saud, the founder of Saudi Arabia. The key to Khashoggi's three decades of influence in the international arms arena from the sixties to the eighties lay with his unique relationship with the ruling royal Saudi family.

Khashoggi was just twenty-six, and already an agent for British and French arms manufacturers (helicopters and tanks respectively), when in 1964 he was approached by Lockheed to be its agent to help negotiate the sale of Hercules transports to the Saudi government. In 1970, he signed an agreement to be Northrop's agent to sell Tiger fighters to the Saudis. Along the way he also became the agent for a Belgian ammunition manufacturer, among others. His success in securing deals for his clients led, in 1973, to *Business Week* publishing an article about him in which he was called "the only man in the Middle East you can trust." He also became rich—*very* rich.

He adopted a playboy lifestyle so flamboyant that popular writer Harold Robbins used him as the inspiration for the protagonist in his bestselling potboiler *The Pirate*. It later emerged that in the late 1970s he was a regular client of a high-priced call girl named Heather Mills. Mills would later marry, and divorce, singer Paul McCartney.

Khashoggi was later accused of taking excessive commissions and for bribing Middle East officials. The charges were not unfounded. As early as 1976, Khashoggi was recorded as saying, "If one offers money to a government to influence it, that is corruption. But if someone receives money for services rendered afterwards, that is a commission."

He was implicated in the Iran Contra arms scandal (1988) and the BCCI Swiss banking scandal (1988). He is essentially retired, living quietly in Monaco.

MI Garand

The eight-shot MI semiautomatic rifle was the standard small-arms rifle of the U.S. military in World War II (1939–1945) and the Korean War (1950–1953). It saw limited service in the Vietnam War (1965–1972) before being completely replaced in 1966 by the M-16 assault rifle. Created in the government's Springfield Armory by Canadian-born designer John C. Garand, the MI became one of the most famous semiautomatic rifles of the twentieth century. During its service life, more than 5.4 million rifles were built by a total of seven manufacturers (one of them, International Harvester, was a truck and farm equipment company). Today, surplus MIs are one of the most popular rifles in the civilian sports and hunting market.

Prototype models of the MI built in the early 1930s were originally designed to fire a .276-caliber cartridge. But General Douglas MacArthur, then Army chief of staff, ordered that changed so the rifle would fire the .30-06 cartridge because the army had enormous stocks of that ammunition left over from World War I. The MI was accepted as the Army's standard rifle in 1936. The Marine Corps initially resisted conversion from the bolt action Springfield 1903. It was concerned about the MIs reliability and long-range accuracy. This latter was a particular sticking point as Marine sharpshooters received extra pay they would otherwise lose. These fears were not allayed until after the United States had entered World War II.

The MI proved to be an excellent rifle throughout its service. It was the first widely available semiautomatic rifle in use by troops in World War II. In comparison, the armies of Great Britain, Germany, Italy, and Japan, bolt-action rifles were standard (French troops were supplied by American weapons and equipment). This gave American soldiers and Marines an important firepower advantage over their adversaries—particularly against Japanese banzai mass charges in World War II, and later mass charges by Communist troops in the Korean War. The MI's cartridge proved to have incredible penetrating power, and, in the close-quarter jungle fighting of the Southwest Pacific, it was not unknown for a round to penetrate as many as three Japanese soldiers.

Because John Garand was a government employee, he received no royalties off the MI. An effort was made by Congress to pay him $100,000 but failed to pass. He was, however, honored with the Medal for Meritorious Service (1941) and the Presidential Medal of Merit (1944).

Soldiers holding M1s as their landing craft crosses the Rhine River in 1945

RADAR

RADAR is the acronym for Radio Detection And Ranging. Radar uses a regulated series of high-frequency pulses of electromagnetic energy sent and received by special antennas. These pulses, when analyzed, can determine the position, motion, and identity of an object in the air. Radar was one of the most important technological innovations of World War II. Today military branches around the world use a wide variety of specialty radars on land, sea, and in the air for detection, weapons guidance, and defense.

Scientists in a number of countries were conducting experiments in radar during the 1930s. The man credited with being the inventor of radar is Sir Robert Alexander Watson-Watt, who presented the first practical designs in 1935. With memories of Zeppelin air raids during World War I still fresh, and fears of a greater air attack by a re-arming Nazi Germany as a goad, the British government made radar development a top, and top-secret, priority. It was a decision that helped save England. After Nazi Germany's conquest of France in the summer of 1940, it appeared that England's defeat was inevitable. Compared to Germany's military might, England's Royal Air Force was weak and its ill-armed army was in dreadful shape. Germany launched its air campaign in the August 1940 as a prelude for the amphibious landing.

Soon dubbed the Battle of Britain, the air campaign became one of the greatest contests in the war. Thanks to the early warning provided by radar stations located strategically throughout the country, the Royal Air Force was able to position its slender resources of fighters where and when needed most against German bomber formations. German squadrons suffered such heavy losses that by the end of September, German Chancellor Adolf Hitler ordered a suspension of operations and a change in tactics. Though the air war would continue with a series of night attacks beginning in November, Operation Sealion, the planned invasion of England, was over. England was saved.

A radar control station aboard the aircraft carrier USS *Enterprise*

JU-87 Stuka

The ultimate dive-bomber in the early years of World War II had the jawbreaker of a name, Sturzkampfflugzeug ("dive bomber"). Small wonder then that Germany's Junkers Ju-87 was more popularly known as the "Stuka." Designed in 1935, it had its baptism of fire in the lead-up to World War II, the Spanish Civil War (1936–1939). Its distinctive inverted gull wings fixed under carriage and shrieking toy whistles called *Jericho-Trompetes* ("Jericho Trumpets") made the Stuka the terror of the skies during the German blitzkrieg successes in the first two years of the war.

The Stuka played a key role in the early blitzkrieg tactics that emphasized close coordination between air, armor, and infantry units. With a range of only five hundred miles, the Stuka operated over or just behind enemy lines, dropping bombs on command and communications installations, and transportation centers with deadly efficiency, on average missing a target by no more than forty yards. A typical Stuka payload was five bombs totaling about 1,100 pounds.

The Battle of Britain (1940) revealed critical deficiencies in the Stuka. It was slow, sluggish, and insufficiently armed. Unless it had heavy fighter protection, it was sure to be shot down by modern enemy fighters. By 1943, Stukas had been reconfigured into a new role as an anti-tank weapon. Deployed on the Eastern front, the Stuka would regain a measure of superiority.

The greatest Stuka pilot was "the Eagle of the Eastern Front," Colonel Hans-Ulrich Rudel, the most decorated German soldier in the war. He was an extraordinary pilot and a man filled with incredible energy and enthusiasm. Wounded five times (once so severely that his right foot had to be amputated), shot down thirty times, he flew 2,530 sorties, more than any other pilot in *any* war. He was a real "tank buster" whose tally included the destruction of more than 519 tanks, the sinking of the Soviet battleship *Marat*, a cruiser, a destroyer, and seventy landing craft. In January 1945, he would be the only individual to receive from German Chancellor Adolf Hitler the Knight's Cross of the Iron Cross with Golden Oak Leaves with Swords and Diamonds.

After the war he moved to Argentina, where he lived for several years. He returned to West Germany in 1953 where he became a successful and controversial figure because of his long-held Nazi sympathies. He later played a key role in the design of the American A-10 Thunderbolt II ground-attack aircraft.

T-6 Texan

In the early days of flying, it was not unusual for a student pilot to learn how to fly by training in the aircraft he would use in combat. But new and more powerful aircraft designs made such a procedure not only impractical, but also dangerous. The most famous of the early trainers was North American's NA-15, renamed the T-6 Texan, chosen by the U.S. Army Air Corps in the early 1930s.

Nicknamed "the pilot maker" because so many pilots qualified for their wings in it, the Texan is a cantilever low-wing monoplane. It had a top speed of 205 miles per hour, a ceiling of 21,500 feet, and a range of 750 miles.

The Texan had landing and takeoff characteristics that made it a challenge to operate, but once in the air its stable flight characteristics made it well-suited for its purpose: training inexperienced pilots. This latter point was crucial, because in the years leading up to World War II, the Air Corps revised its flight program in order to qualify the maximum amount of pilots. In 1940, training periods were reduced to seven months and two hundred hours of flight time; of that amount, seventy-five were allotted to the Texan.

Though its primary purpose was that of a trainer, the Texan did see limited combat action. During the Korean War (1950–1953) and the Vietnam War (1965–1972), it was used as a forward air control aircraft, code-named "Mosquito."

By the time it was phased out by the U.S. Air Force in the 1960s, more than fifteen thousand Texans had been built and were on the inventories of more than fifty nations.

The Texan became a popular attraction in air shows. It also saw new life in an acting career. Very few Japanese warplanes survived the war, and those that did wound up in museums or in private collections. The Texan had a profile very similar to those of Japanese World War II warplanes. With slight modification and repainting, some have been modified to resemble the Japanese Zero fighter, Val dive bomber, and Kate torpedo bomber, amongst others. They appeared in *Tora! Tora! Tora!*, and *Midway*—in fact, any Japanese warplane appearing in any movie, unless the production company uses actual combat footage, is really a disguised Texan.

MESSERSCHMITT BF-I09

Messerschmitt

It began its existence in 1935 under a cloud of controversy and suspicion that its innovative and advanced design made it too risky to fly. But when World War II ended in 1945, the German Messerschmitt Bf-109 became the standard by which all other World War II fighters would be judged.

The Bf-109 served the Luftwaffe in almost every capacity possible for an aircraft including interceptor, fighter-bomber, night-fighter, photo-reconnaissance, escort, and ground attack. With more than thirty thousand built, more 109s were produced and in more variants than any other aircraft then and today. Featuring modular construction and a decentralized manufacturing system, the Bf-109 was designed to survive the destruction of the individual factories that built it. Light, maneuverable, with an advanced aerodynamic design, a structure able to handle high-speed stresses, the 109 achieved air superiority in the first year of World War II, and proved itself a better combat aircraft than early model British Hurricanes and Spitfires.

The Bf-109 had a maximum speed of more than 350 miles per hour, a cruising range of almost 300 miles, and a quick rate of climb of about 3,000 feet per minute. Basic armament was two 7.9-mm machine guns mounted on the nose over the engine and two 20-mm cannons, one on each wing. Later models included a 30-mm cannon that fired through the center of the propeller spinner.

The German ace of aces, with 352 confirmed aerial victories, was Major Erich Hartmann. He was known as the "Blond Knight of Germany" in his native country, and the "Black Devil of the Ukraine" by the Soviets, who placed a 10,000-ruble bounty on him. Hartmann flew with the Luftwaffe's most successful fighter wing, Jagdgeschwader 52, and earned one of Germany's highest decorations, the Knight's Cross of the Iron Cross with Oak Leaves, Swords, and Diamonds. Hartmann's squadron was known as the "Sweetheart Squadron" for the distinctive bleeding heart pierced by an arrow painted on its fuselage. Hartmann further identified his airplane with the painting of a black tulip. Soviet pilots had such respect for Hartmann's ability that, instead of trying to collect the bounty, squadrons would fly away when saw that black tulip on the fuselage. Hartmann subsequently erased the black tulip—and once again began racking up victories. Never shot down and never wounded, Hartmann survived the war and, after release from a Soviet prison camp in 1955, became a pilot in the West German air force.

A crashed Bf-109 is towed past the Houses of Parliament in London during World War II, circa 1943

Wilhelm "Willy" Messerschmitt

(1898–1978)

Messerschmitt was one of the greatest aircraft designers of the twentieth century. He is most famous as the designer of the Bf-109, one of the most outstanding fighters in the war. His company was also responsible for designing and putting into operation during World War II the world's first turbojet fighter, the Me-262. His Me-110, intended as a long-range fighter, was used by German Chancellor Adolf Hitler's deputy Rudolf Hess on his self-inspired, quixotic peace mission to Britain in May 1940.

Messerschmitt, who learned how to fly at fifteen, designed his first plane, a glider, in 1916 when he was eighteen years old. Mentored by airman Friedrich Harth, Messerschmitt became successful enough that he was able to start his own aircraft design company in the 1920s. In 1926, he produced his first all-metal plane. In 1937, he received the prestigious Lilienthal Prize for research in aviation.

One of his most famous designs was the Bf-109, an aircraft that almost didn't get made. Messerschmitt found himself caught in a political turf battle between Deputy Chancellor Rudolf Hess, a wartime pilot and Messerschmitt's friend, who promoted the Bf-109, and Luftwaffe General Erhard Milch, the head of German aircraft production, who didn't like Messerschmitt and found the Bf-109 design too radical. The design was approved in 1935 and the first production Bf-109s debuted in a ceremony over the Berlin Olympics in 1936. Later that year the Bf-109 got its chance in the Spanish Civil War (1936–1939) as part of the Condor Legion.

Messerschmitt was interned after the war and convicted by a German court in 1948 of being a Nazi "fellow traveler." With Germany forbidden agreement from building airplanes, Messerschmitt was reduced to building cabins and prefabricated houses. But cold war tensions between the United States and other Western countries and the Soviet Union caused the Western nations to lift the ban, and Messerschmitt returned to the business of aircraft design and production. A successful businessman once again, he died in a Munich hospital at the age of 80.

Hawker Hurricane

Though the Supermarine Spitfire became the most famous British fighter in the Battle of Britain, the real hero of that conflict was the Hawker Hurricane. Becoming operational in 1937, the rugged, easy-to-maintain Hurricane was the Royal Air Force's first truly modern fighter. It was the service's first monoplane fighter with an enclosed cockpit, retractable undercarriage, and eight-machine-gun armament, and it was the first capable of exceeding a speed of three hundred miles per hour (early tests clocked it capable of more than four hundred miles per hour, an astonishing speed for the time). More than 14,500 Hurricanes would be built, making it one of the most numerous planes in the war. Variants included fighter-bomber and cannon-equipped ground attack fighters. It would see service in all the theaters of the war and, like its compatriots the Spitfire and the German Bf-109, fight the war from start to finish.

The Hurricane's first important action occurred during the Battle of France in the spring of 1940. Ten squadrons were deployed to France where the outnumbered squadrons suffered heavy losses. Even so, the Hurricanes succeeded in shooting down two German aircraft for every one they lost. The surviving pilots and fighters were evacuated shortly before French capitulation in June.

The Hurricane's next big challenge occurred just two months later. When the Battle of Britain commenced, the RAF had 32 Hurricane squadrons and 19 Spitfire squadrons. The Hurricane became the workhorse in battle, for the most part attacking German bombers and dive-bombers while the Spitfire took on the escort fighters. The campaign concluded in September 1940 with the RAF having fought off the Luftwaffe and ending the threat of Operation Sealion, the German amphibious invasion of England. A tally revealed that the Hurricane had shot down more aircraft than the Spitfire, 1,593 to 1,146. In recognition of the role the pilots of the Hurricanes and Spitfires had in saving England, British Prime Minister Winston Churchill in a speech to Parliament praised them, saying, "Never was so much owed by so many to so few."

A Hawker Hurricane in flight over Bengal, April 1943

Sir Sydney Camm

(1893–1966)

Sir Sydney Camm was one of Great Britain's most distinguished aircraft designers. His most famous design was the Hawker Hurricane, a World War II fighter that was a hero in the Battle of Britain. The range of Camm's designs is impressive, going from biplanes built in the 1920s to jet aircraft in the 1950s.

Camm spent his career with the Hawker Aircraft Company, later Hawker Siddeley, which he joined in 1925 at the age of thirty-two. He was described as a brilliant man with a fiery temper and an obsessive desire to get the design right. Robert Lickley, who was a member of Camm's design staff, recalled, "Camm had a one-tracked mind—his aircraft were right, and everybody had to work on them to get them right. If they did not, then there was hell. He was a very difficult man to work for, but you could not have a better aeronautical engineer to work under."

With the Hurricane, Camm decided on a different approach to the design. In the past, designers would draw up plans for an airplane and then find an engine that would fit it. But one of the specifications for the Hurricane was to have an ability to have an operational speed as low as a hundred miles per hour and as fast as three hundred miles per hour. This ability to stop and start on a dime in a dogfight caused him to decide to obtain first an engine capable of such performance, and then build around it a suitable aircraft. The engine was the Rolls-Royce Merlin, the same engine that would help the Spitfire and later the American P-51 Mustang achieve spectacular success.

Camm's other successful World War II aircraft were the Typhoon and Tempest, whose contributions are largely unknown in the United States, having become operational after the U.S. Army Air Force had become the dominant Allied airpower.

After the war, Camm became heavily involved in the jet development. He made important contributions to the Hawker Kestrel, which was a progenitor of the vertical take-off and landing Harrier.

Knighted in 1953, Camm received awards and honors including the British Gold Medal for Aeronautics, the Gold Medal from the Royal Aeronautical Society, and a leading American aeronautical award, the Guggenheim Gold Medal. At the time of his death in 1966 at age sixty-eight, he was working on designs for a jet capable of traveling four times the speed of sound.

Factory workers assembling the wing elements of Hawker Hurricane airplanes

B-17 FLYING FORTRESS

The B-17 Flying Fortress was the most celebrated bomber ever flown by the U.S. Air Force. It got its distinctive name when a reporter for the *Seattle Times* covering the story of the prototype exclaimed that it looked like "a flying fortress." The B-17 was originally designed to help the United States defend itself from hostile threats at sea. To a limited extent it did serve that purpose against the Japanese in the Pacific theater. But it is most famous for its role in the strategic air campaign against Germany.

Designed in 1934 and made operational in 1938, it was the United States' first strategic bomber and, at the time, the country's largest warplane. It embodied the strategic bombing beliefs expressed by airpower advocate retired Brigadier General Billy Mitchell. Depending on the variant, the B-17 had a top speed of more than three hundred miles per hour, an operational ceiling of thirty-two thousand feet, an average range of two thousand miles, and it carried ten to thirteen .50-caliber machine guns for defense and a bomb load up to fifteen thousand pounds. Flying in tight formation for mutual support, its supporters believed that it would fulfill the oft-spoken dictum that "the bomber will always get through."

It proved an over-optimistic belief. Though the B-17 was able to reach targets and return, the Luftwaffe had developed tactics that savaged the bomber formations. The low point in the strategic campaign was reached during the Schweinfurt raids in August and October 1943 in which the U.S. Army Air Force lost about 25 percent of the bombers participating in the attacks, an appalling figure. Only after long-range escort fighters such as the P-51 Mustang became operational were the losses reduced.

With the heavy bombers of the Royal Air Force attacking targets at night, and the American air force bombing those targets during the day, the Allies conducted an offensive against Germany called "around-the-clock bombing." By the end of the war, this offensive had effectively destroyed most German industrial cities.

A number of famous people either trained or flew in B-17s, including actors Jimmy Stewart and Clark Gable. Stewart would later see action as a pilot of a B-24 Liberator heavy bomber. Both were decorated for bravery; German Chancellor Adolf Hitler offered a reward to anyone who shot down and captured Gable. Additional famous people who flew B-17s were television producer Norman Lear and Gene Rodenberry, the creator of *Star Trek*.

B-17 and crew post mission

VICKERS WELLINGTON

The Vickers Wellington twin-engined medium bomber carried the brunt of the Royal Air Force Bomber Command's night bombing offensive against Germany during the early years of World War II. The Wellington became operational in 1938, a year before the war began. After it was superseded by heavy bombers such as the Avro Lancaster, the Wellington continued to see service in other duties, particularly anti-submarine warfare.

Named after the hero of the Napoleonic War, the Duke of Wellington, the Wellington bomber was affectionately nicknamed "Wimpy" after the hamburger-loving J. Wellington Wimpy, a supporting character in the *Popeye* syndicated comic strip. The Wellington had a crew of six, a maximum speed of 235 miles per hour, a ceiling of eighteen thousand feet, and a range of 1,805 miles. An average bomb load was 4,500 pounds and defenses consisted of six to eight machine guns. About sixteen variants were produced and a total of 11,464 were built. The most striking feature was its geodesic framework design that gave it extraordinary structural strength and stability, yet it was extremely light. This feature enabled the Wellington to survive extraordinary battle damage.

One of the most unusual variants was the Type 418 Wellington DWI Mark I, designed for minesweeping duties. The Wellingtons were fitted with a two-ton, 48-foot diameter electromagnetic hoop mounted to the bottom of the wings and fuselage. The hoop was capable of projecting a magnetic field powerful enough to trigger mines fitted with magnetic fuses. This was an extremely dangerous duty, because in order to successfully explode the mines, the Wellington had to skim the surface of the waterway. Planes that flew too close to the water, or too slow, were damaged by exploding mines.

Ground crews loading bombs onto Vickers Wellington bomber, circa 1943

P-40 WARHAWK

The Curtiss P-40 Warhawk, with its famous shark mouth design on the engine cowling, was the United States' frontline fighter at the start of World War II. Rugged, reliable, and highly maneuverable at low altitude, in the hands of experienced pilots it could hold its own against such higher performance enemy fighters as the Messerschmitt Bf-109 and Mitsubishi Zero. It saw service in all theaters in the squadrons of both the United States and its allies.

The P-40 became operational in 1938. By the time the United States entered World War II in 1941, the P-40 had been in action for almost two years, fighting in North Africa and China. It served in the British and Commonwealth air forces in the North African campaign where it was the primary front line fighter.

Credit for the shark mouth design on the P-40 engine cowling belongs to the American Volunteer Group, or Flying Tigers—three squadrons of American volunteer aviators organized by Brigadier General Claire Chennault—that served in the Chinese Air Force before the United States' entry in the war. Though other aircraft would have similar designs on their cowling, it is most associated with the P-40.

The P-40 was the first fighter flown into action by the 99th Fighter Squadron, part of what would later become known as the Tuskeegee Airmen. The 99th got its baptism of fire supporting the attack of the Italian-held island of Pantelleria in the run-up to Operation Husky, the Allied invasion of Sicily. The 99th performed so well in combat that, in addition to receiving personal commendations from commanders including supreme commander Lieutenant General Dwight Eisenhower, it was awarded the Distinguished Unit Citation.

Almost fourteen thousand P-40s would be built before production was discontinued in 1944. The P-40 would be remembered as a "best second choice" because, while good, it never was the performance equal of more modern adversaries. Even so, countless pilots owe their lives to its ability to absorb tremendous punishment.

Shark-nosed P-40 Warhawks on an air base in China. In the background is a B-24 Liberator

KATYUSHA ROCKET LAUNCHER

Two of the most terrifying conventional weapons used during World War II were the BM-8 and BM-13 multiple rocket launchers used by the Soviet army, nicknamed Katyushas. Though less accurate than tube artillery, Katyushas could provide devastating saturation bombardment with volleys of up to 48 rockets launched from a single truck mount.

Designs for the BM-8 and BM-13 were drawn up in 1939. The first successful tests occurred in March 1941. The first mass production order was signed on June 21, 1941, just one day before Germany launched Operation Barbarossa, the invasion of the Soviet Union. A top secret experimental Katyusha battery was formed by the Soviet NKVD secret police (the predecessor of the KGB) and it saw action in a battle at Orsha in Belarus. The battery destroyed a railroad station and several supply trains, and it caused many casualties before being forced to retire. This success caused the Red Army to organize elite Guards rocket artillery batteries in support of infantry.

The Katyushas were also highly mobile. They could be mounted on platforms and immediately moved after firing a volley, which reduced their vulnerability to attack by counter-battery fire.

It is one of war's many ironies that one of the most fearsome weapons of World War II was christened with a romantic, intimate name of a woman. The Russian language expresses levels of formality, friendship, and intimacy through the use of various diminutives of given names. For instance, the formal form of Katyusha is Ekaterina (Katherine). The diminutive, or nickname, of Ekaterina is "Katya." The tender diminutive, conveying a close romantic or family bond, is Katyusha—"Little Kate." "Katyusha" was also a popular Soviet song composed in 1938 about a girl longing for her beloved, who is serving in the military.

Another, more appropriate, nickname for the rockets was given by the Germans who called the launchers "Stalin's Organ." By the war's end, the Katyusha, along with the T-34 tank, was one of the most famous Soviet weapons of the war. Even though the Russians have since developed different multiple rocket launch systems, the name Katyusha continued to be used, becoming a generic name for all Russian rocket artillery.

A katyusha rocket is fired from the back of an army truck into an a partment complex during the Lebanese Civil War

Combat Knife

Combat knives are large knives designed for military use. Though some, like the Fairbairn-Sykes Fighting Knife, are designed as close combat weapons, most of today's combat knives are used as a utility tool.

The Ka-Bar is an 11 ¾ inch (7 inch blade) fighting and utility Bowie blade style knife that has been standard issue in the U.S. military since 1942. Shortly after the United States entered World War II, the U.S. Marine Corps discovered that the World War I-era trench knives were unsuitable. During their search for a replacement, the Marines discovered the Ka-Bar in a hunting catalog. Military modifications included a slightly longer blade for combat use, the use of non-reflective matte black or gray phosphate finish, and some other small changes to the blade, pommel, and handle. Each branch has features that distinguish it from the other branches, primarily the stamping of the service's initials or symbol. Millions of Ka-Bar knives were manufactured during World War II. Though it is impossible to say for certain how many have been manufactured, it's safe to say that the Ka-Bar is the most ubiquitous of the military knives.

The Fairbairn-Sykes Fighting Knife is a double-edged dagger-style knife with a foil grip. It was created by British officers William Ewart Fairbairn and Eric Anthony Sykes, who designed it while serving in Shanghai before World War II. It was the standard close combat weapon for the British SAS, Marine Raiders, and American special operations troops in the OSS. Fairbairn trained a large share of the soldiers who went through the SAS and OSS training courses, and he was an outstanding instructor in hand-to-hand combat. Though knife use in combat is not emphasized now, Fairbairn wrote in his book, *Get Tough!*, "In close-quarters fighting there is no more deadly weapon than the knife."

A Fairbairn-Sykes Fighting Knife strapped to a commando's boot.

YAK-1

The top Soviet fighter aircraft of World War II was the Yakovlev Yak-I "Krasavy-ets" ("Little Beauty"). That it is not as well-known as such counterparts as Britain's Spitfire, the United States' Mustang, Japan's Zero, or Germany's Bf-I09 is primarily due to the consequences of cold war politics. More than 36,000 Yaks were built during the war, making it one of the most produced fighters of the conflict.

Alexander Sergeevich Yakovlev, one of the great Soviet aircraft designers, created the Yak-I in response to a 1938 Soviet government request for a modern fighter made of wood. Problems occurred because a compressed production schedule forced him to test prototypes at the same time he was tooling up actual production. That Yakolev survived this period without censure—which in the Soviet Union ruled by Josef Stalin usually meant execution, or a long stay in a gulag—is indicative of the regard and affection Stalin had for the designer.

When the Soviet Union was invaded by Germany on June 22, 1941, in Operation Barbarossa, the Soviet air force had only 425 Yak-I fighters on hand. Production was accelerated and by the end of the war about 36,000 Yaks had been built.

The Soviet Union was unique in World War II in that it had women combat pilots. Three all-women air regiments (including all-women ground crews) were formed. Three women pilots would go on to become aces, with five or more aerial victories. The top woman ace of the Soviet Union was Lilya Litvak. Because she painted a white rose on both sides of the fuselage of her Yak-I, she became known as the White Rose of Stalingrad.

Litvak scored her first two victories on her second mission, downing a Messerschmitt Bf-I09 fighter and a Junkers Ju-88 light bomber. According to reports, she loved wildflowers and, when possible, carried a small bouquet in her cockpit. During the summer of 1943, she and the members of her squadron found themselves flying a brutal schedule of four or five missions a day. She shot down at least twelve German planes; some accounts put it as high as twenty. On August 1, 1943, at age 22, she took off on her fourth and final mission. Despite an intense ground search, her body was not found. In 1979, her body was discovered buried beneath the wing of her aircraft. In the official state funeral that followed, President Mikhail Gorbachev awarded her the Hero of the Soviet Union medal, the nation's highest award for valor.

Russian female fighter pilots Lilya Litvyak (left), Katerina Budanova (center), and Mariya Kuznetsova (right), all of the 437th fighter regiment, plot their flight plans on the tail of a Yak-1 fighter plane, Russia, mid 1942

Spitfire

The Supermarine Spitfire, designed by the team led by Reginald Mitchell, is the most famous British warbird of World War II. With its sleek fuselage and distinctive elliptical wings, it is one of the most graceful and beautiful aircraft ever built.

The Spitfire was one of the first all-metal, low-wing, retractable-undercarriage, enclosed canopy monoplane fighters. Remarkably, the Spitfire remained in production for eleven years, from 1938 to 1949.

The Spitfire achieved its fame as one of the fighters flown by "the few"—the pilots that saved Great Britain during the Battle of Britain (1940). During the time of United States neutrality, a handful of Americans fought for England as members of the Eagle Squadron. One of them was Pilot Officer John Gillespie Magee, Jr., who served in the Royal Canadian Air Force. On August 8, 1941, his experience while flying a Spitfire Mk I inspired him to write a sonnet. Tragically, Magee died later that year in a midair collision. But his poem, *High Flight*, would become famous. It is the official poem of the Royal Canadian Air Force and the Royal Air Force. First-year cadets at the United States Air Force Academy are required to memorize it.

High Flight

Oh! I have slipped the surly bonds of Earth
And danced the skies on laughter-silvered wings;
Sunward I've climbed, and joined the tumbling mirth
of sun-split clouds, — and done a hundred things
You have not dreamed of — wheeled and soared and swung
High in the sunlit silence. Hov'ring there,
I've chased the shouting wind along, and flung
My eager craft through footless halls of air . . . .

Up, up the long, delirious, burning blue
I've topped the wind-swept heights with easy grace
Where never lark nor even eagle flew —
And, while with silent lifting mind I've trod
The high untrespassed sanctity of space,
Put out my hand, and touched the face of God.

REGINALD JOSEPH MITCHELL

(1895–1937)

Reginald Joseph Mitchell died of cancer at age forty-two just as his greatest creation, the Spitfire, was going into production. Thus he would never know the remarkable heights it would achieve.

Mitchell was born in Stoke-on-Trent, in the region in the middle of England famous for its ceramics. After an apprenticeship at a locomotive engineering works, he joined the Supermarine Aviation Works in 1917. Two years later, at age twenty-four, he was promoted to chief designer. He became chief engineer in 1920, and in 1927 he was the technical director. By this time, his reputation had so grown that when the arms manufacturer Vickers purchased the company, a condition of the sale was that Mitchell would remain with the company for at least five years.

The top Vickers aircraft designer was Barnes Wallis, who would go on to design the Wellington heavy bomber. He and Mitchell clashed to such an extent that whenever Wallis walked into a room for a meeting, Mitchell would promptly leave. Vickers eventually relented and allowed Mitchell to keep his autonomy. Like fellow aircraft designer Sidney Camm (Hawker Hurricane), he did not suffer fools gladly, but he was not overbearing with his team. He would let even junior drafts-men voice opinions on projects and never allowed others to criticize individuals in the team. If mistakes were made, Mitchell, as the leader, took full responsibility.

Between 1920 and 1936, Mitchell designed twenty-four aircraft ranging from light aircraft to sea planes, fighters, and bombers. His seaplane the S.6b won the prestigious Schneider Trophy in 1931, which prompted the Royal Air Force to ask him to submit designs for a high-speed fighter. In February 1932 he presented the RAF with plans for what would become the Spitfire. It was also in 1932 that he was awarded the Commander British Empire (CBE) for his contribution to high-speed aviation. When told that "Spitfire" was the name chosen for the aircraft, Mitchell is reported to have said it was "just the sort of bloody silly name they would choose."

In 1933, Mitchell was diagnosed with rectal cancer and underwent a colostomy. The cancer returned in 1936 and was forced to give up work on the Spitfire by 1937, though he did observe prototype test flights from his bed. He died in June of that year.

Reginald Joseph Mitchell (right) with a seaplane he designed that won the prestigious Schneider Trophy

F4F WILDCAT

The Grumman F4F Wildcat was the U.S. Navy and Marine Corps' top front-line fighter during the first eighteen months of World War II. Though it was outclassed by its main opponent, the high performance Japanese Zero, the stubby fighter was more rugged and capable of taking much more punishment than its more fragile enemy. Some of the greatest Navy and Marine Corps pilots in aviation history flew the Wildcat in some of the most important battles of the war, making the Wildcat one of the most storied fighters in history.

Leroy Grumman, who had recently founded an aviation company, was hoping to obtain a Navy aircraft contract to boost business. He saw his opportunity in 1935 when the Navy requested bids for a new carrier-based fighter. The F4F was originally designed as a biplane. But when Grumman saw that other companies were submitting monoplane plans, he ordered his design team back to the drawing board. The F4F lost out the first competition to the Brewster Company's Buffalo. The Navy maintained an interest in the F4F and, after trials, the Navy received the first production F4Fs in 1940. It would not get the name "Wildcat" until 1941.

The British Royal Navy was the first to use the F4F in combat when it purchased some in 1940 as an interim fighter until the navy version of the Spitfire was ready. It scored its first aerial victory by downing a Junkers Ju-88 bomber over the Scapa Flow naval base.

The Wildcat had some quirks. One of them was that its undercarriage was not hydraulically operated; it had to be cranked by hand. After takeoff and before landing, ship crews would be greeted with the sight of Wildcats bobbing up and down as the pilot retracted or extended the landing gear.

When the United States entered the war in 1941 after the Japanese sneak attack on December 7, the Wildcat was in the thick of some of the greatest battles in the war, including Wake Island, Coral Sea, Midway, and Guadalcanal. Wildcat pilots Butch O'Hare (for whom Chicago's O'Hare airport is named), Jimmy Thach (creator of the "Thach Weave" defensive maneuver), and Joe Foss (future governor of South Dakota) would receive Medals of Honor for their heroic exploits in the Wildcat.

The Wildcat was replaced as a frontline fighter in 1943 with the F6F Hellcat. But it saw service for the rest of the war flying off escort carriers.

SBD Dauntless

The U.S. Navy Dauntless gained fame as the dive bomber that destroyed four Japanese aircraft carriers in the decisive Battle of Midway (1942). It was the Navy's top dive bomber in World War II until mid-1943 when it was replaced by the Helldiver.

To anyone who asked what the letters "SBD" stood for, Dauntless crews invariably replied, "Slow But Deadly." Its top speed was only 250 miles per hour, and it carried a maximum bomb load of 2,250 pounds. In addition, it was heavily armed with two .50-caliber machine guns in the wings, and the rear gunner had a twin-mount machine gun.

The Dauntless was more successful than its fellow pre-war aircraft, the Devastator torpedo bomber and Buffalo fighter. Though the Devastator and Buffalo were considered innovative in the 1930s, when World War II began they were hopelessly obsolete. Devastator squadrons were annihilated during the Battle of Midway, though their sacrifice enabled the Dauntless to score the decisive victory. When the Buffalo proved unable to fight the Japanese Zero, it was swiftly retired.

The Dauntless was unusual among U.S. Navy aircraft in that it did not have folding wings, which saved space in the cramped hangar of an aircraft carrier. It needed fixed wings to support bomb loads mounted under the wings and to maintain structural integrity during dives.

By 1944, the Dauntless was relegated to a secondary role, flying off the decks of escort carriers. But there was one last moment of glory left for these heroes of Midway. In October 1944, the Imperial Japanese Navy launched Operation Sho-Go, an all-out campaign to destroy the American landing on the Philippine island of Leyte. It was a complex plan involving three fleets and massive deception. Two Japanese fleets had sufficiently drawn away the more powerful American fleets, leaving just a small force of escort carriers, destroyers and destroyer escorts guarding the landings on Leyte. That force was no match for the Japanese central force containing four battleships, six cruisers, and several destroyers. But they defended the beaches with exemplary courage. The Dauntlesses, equipped only with land-attack high explosive bombs instead of naval armor piercing, launched attack after attack—harrying the enemy even after they had dropped their bombs. The force's defense was so spirited that the Japanese admiral broke off the fight and retreated.

EDWARD HEINEMANN
(1908–1991)

Gustave Edward Henry Heinemann designed more than twenty outstanding fighter, bomber, and rocket aircraft for the United States military during his sixty-year career in aviation design. His life spanned the golden age of flight and his accomplishments are all the more remarkable because he was a self-taught engineer.

Like many aircraft engineers, Heinemann had a stubborn streak. Born in Saginaw, Michigan, Heinemann was six years old when he decided that from then on he was going to be called "Edward" because he knew too many friends and family members named Gustave.

The Heinemann family moved to Los Angeles in 1914 and it was there that Heinemann studied aeronautical design. Heinemann's career began in 1926 as a draftsman for Douglas Aircraft. In 1936 he became its chief engineer. Many of the airplanes he and his team designed have become aviation legends. These include the SBD Dauntless dive bomber, for which Heinemann received a personal letter of thanks from Admiral Chester Nimitz, the commander in chief of naval forces in the Pacific during World War II; the Skyraider, a dive bomber that fought in the Korean and Vietnam wars and was considered the greatest close air support aircraft ever designed; the Skyrocket, the first airplane to reach Mach 2; the Skyray, which set numerous flight records in the 1950s; and the Skyhawk, nicknamed "Heinemann's Hot Rod," which served with distinction in the Vietnam War and was used by the Navy's Blue Angels team for many years. The Skyhawk was also used by instructors in the Top Gun training exercises where they took on and defeated pilots flying everything from Phantoms to Tomcats and Hornets.

Heinemann had seventeen basic rules that he followed throughout his career. They included such common sense things as make the best use of each person's ability, don't waste time; avoid lengthy committee meetings, and do unto others as you would have them do unto you. As basic as they were, they helped Heinemann win aviation's prestigious Collier Trophy for his work on the Skyray in 1953, as well as the Guggenheim Medal and the National Medal of Science. In 1983, Heinemann was inducted into the Aviation Hall of Fame. The Naval Air Systems Command annually presents the Edward H. Heinemann Award to the individual or group that makes a significant contribution to aircraft design.

MITSUBISHI ZERO

Japan's greatest fighter, and one of the most outstanding fighters of World War II, was the Mitsubishi Zero, designed by Jiro Horikoshi. Officially designated the Mitsubishi A6M type O, the Zero was used by both the Japanese army and navy as its premier fighter.

The Zero became operational in 1940 and initially it was the best carrier-based fighter in the world. Capable of speeds of 330 miles per hour or more, it was swift, highly maneuverable, and had a very long range. The Zero easily outclassed its slower, less agile opponents. Standard armament was two synchronized machine guns located above the engine and two 20-mm cannons, one on each wing. Production continued throughout the war, with more than eleven thousand built. The main weaknesses of the Zero were that it lacked protective armor and did not contain self-sealing gas tanks.

Pilots flying the slower, heavier, and more rugged Wildcats and Warhawks developed defensive tactics to exploit the few weaknesses of the Zero. Later, when better performance fighters such as the Corsair, Hellcat, and Lightning arrived, the Zero found itself outclassed. During the final weeks of the war, the Zero was converted to carry bomb loads and participated in the kamikaze suicide attacks on the U.S. Navy fleet.

Saburo Sakai, one of Japan's greatest aces with 64 victories, was introduced to the Zero in 1940. He recalled, "On the airfield I saw strange new fighter planes, as different from the familiar Type 96 Claudes as night from day. These were the new Mitsubishi Zero fighters, sleek and modern. The Zero excited me as nothing else had ever done before. Even on the ground it had the cleanest lines I had ever seen in an airplane.... The Zero had almost twice the speed and range of the Claude, and it was a dream to fly. The airplane was the most sensitive I had ever flown, and even slight finger pressure brought instant response. We could hardly wait to meet enemy planes in this remarkable new aircraft." Sakai survived the war, becoming first a printer, and later a motivational speaker. He visited and reconciled with many of his former adversaries and became an advocate for honesty regarding Japanese responsibility in the war.

Zeros preparing to take off from the aircraft carrier *Hiryu* for the raid on Pearl Harbor, December 7, 1941

Jiro Horikoshi
(1903–1982)

Jiro Horikoshi is considered by his peers to be one of the world's greatest aeronautical engineers. He was the chief designer for Japan's first important fighter plane, an open cockpit, fixed landing gear aircraft codenamed Claude, which became operational in 1937. In 1940, his greatest fighter, the Mitsubishi Zero, became operational. Though he designed other aircraft for the Japanese army and navy, he is most famous for being the designer of the Zero.

Horikoshi graduated from Tokyo Imperial University and joined the Nagoya Aircraft Works of Mitsubishi Heavy Industries, Ltd., in 1927. His contributions to Japan's aeronautical industry played a great part in enabling Japan to stake an independent claim of innovation and excellence among the other great powers.

He is the co-author of *Zero!* which was first released in 1956 and has remained in print ever since. It was written with Masatake Okumiya, a Zero squadron commander, and Martin Caidan, who wrote military aviation histories as well as the novel *Cyborg*, which was the basis for the popular television series *The Six Million Dollar Man*. Horikoshi's memoirs were published in Japan in 1970. The University of Washington Press released a translated edition a few years later titled *Eagles of Mitsubishi: The Story of The Zero Fighter.*

The cockpit of a Zero

Aichi D3A "Val" Dive Bomber

Japanese Val Typer 99 bomber replica

The Aichi D3A dive bomber was the top Japanese dive bomber for most of World War II. Allied intelligence, following the pattern of giving Japanese fighters male names (the Zero being the exception) and bombers female names, gave the D3A the code name "Val." It was the first aircraft to drop bombs on American targets during the attack on Pearl Harbor and is credited with sinking more Allied ships than any other Axis bomber.

Designed in 1937 and made operational in 1940, the Val was a fixed wing monoplane capable of a top speed of 267 miles per hour. It carried a crew of two, a pilot and a rear gunner, and had a maximum bomb load of one 500-pound bomb attached beneath its fuselage and two 132-pound bombs, one attached below each wing. Armament on the aircraft included two forward mounted machine guns and one rear mounted machine gun. Aichi had a long relationship with the German airplane manufacturer Heinkel, and the German company passed on to Aichi the designs for its Heinkel He 70, which had lost the competition to the Junkers Ju-87 Stuka. The He-118 designs formed the foundation for what became the Val.

The Val saw action in all the important air battles during the first three months of World War II. Japan's greatest dive-bomber pilot Takashige Egusa flew the Val throughout his career. He was a squadron leader on the aircraft carrier *Soryu*. During the Japanese surprise attack on Pearl Harbor on December 7, 1941, he calmly circled the harbor in his bright red Val before dive-bombing his target. Egusa's squadron was stationed on the *Soryu* during the Battle of Midway (1942). Though the *Soryu* was sunk, Egusa survived. He was killed in action in 1944 and posthumously promoted from lieutenant commander to captain.

During the final months of the war, like other Japanese aircraft, the Val was used as a kamikaze suicide plane against United States ships. It was ineffective, with substantially more Vals being shot down compared to those reaching their targets.

Japanese aerial view of battleship row at Pearl Harbor during torpedo and dive bombing attack

88-mm Cannon

The German 88-mm cannon was the most famous artillery piece of World War II, and one of the great cannons in history. Originally designed as an anti-aircraft gun, German Chancellor Adolf Hitler ordered that its design be expanded to make it an anti-tank weapon as well. As a dual-purpose gun, it was one of the most feared weapons in the German arsenal.

The mobile anti-aircraft FlaK 36 "88" first saw action in the Spanish Civil War (1936–1939) with the German Condor Legion that fought on the side of General Francisco Franco. Later a less mobile variant, the FlaK 37, was developed. It was arranged in battery groups of four near industrial sites under the command of a single controller. Thousands of anti-aircraft batteries were deployed in Germany and occupied territories. The flight path used by Allied bombers over the Netherlands was so thick with batteries of 88s that area became known as "Flak Alley." Similar Flak Alleys were established at other strategic sites, particularly around Me-262 jet fighter fields, which were easily identified because they were significantly longer than regular landing fields.

The 88's role as an anti-tank weapon debuted during the North African campaign. General Erwin Rommel, the "Desert Fox," used them as mobile artillery against British armor with an efficiency that astonished the British commanders.

The 88 took on a more mobile role when it was installed in the Tiger tank and on tracked assault guns in 1942. This was done in response to finding a weapon powerful enough to stop the Russian T-34, one of the great tanks of World War II.

Otto Carius was one of the most successful German tank commanders in the war. He is credited with destroying more than 150 enemy tanks and was awarded the Knight's Cross of the Iron Cross with Oak Leaves. Cairus scored most of his victories in a Tiger tank. In his memoir, *Tigers in the Mud*, he noted that he and his fellow Tiger commanders followed the guideline of shooting first or, if that wasn't possible, then "at least hit first." He added, "The 88 mm cannon was good enough to defeat every tank, assuming that you hit it in the right place."

1940

Eastern front 1944, German 88 mm anti-aircraft battery

T-34

A Soviet T-34/85

The best tank of World War II was the Soviet Union T-34 medium tank. It used a modified suspension originally designed by maverick American inventor J. Walter Christie. The T-34 became operational in 1940. The standard main gun for the T-34 was a 76 mm cannon, with secondary armament being two 7.62 mm machine guns. The T-34 also had wide treads that enabled it to easily travel across muddy terrain that would immobilize other tanks. During the war more than 57,000 T-34s were built. One of the most successful tank designs in history, as late as 1996 it was still in service in the armies of at least twenty-seven nations.

When the Germans invaded the Soviet Union in June 1941, the Soviet Union had only about a thousand T-34s on hand. Even though its effectiveness in the early weeks of the invasion was handicapped by poor tactics as well as a lack of concentration and proper infantry support, its appearance in the battlefield came as a rude shock to the Germans. At ranges over 200 yards, shots from German tanks bounced off its thick armor, while shells from the T-34's cannon easily penetrated German tank armor. One action report spoke of the T-34 as being "a wonder weapon . . . spreading terror and feared wherever it moved."

The tank warfare genius German General Heinz Guderian remarked after one tough tank-versus-tank battle, "The short-barreled 75 mm gun of the Panzer IV was only effective if the T-34 were attacked from the rear; even then a hit had to be scored on the grating above the engine to knock it out. It required very great skill to maneuver into a position from which such a shot was possible."

The T-34 participated in the greatest tank battle of the war, Operation Citadel in July 1943, in which more than 6,600 tanks fought. The Soviet Fifth Guards Tank Army played a prominent role in the battle. Its commander, Lt. General Pavel Rotmistrov, later described one engagement: "The T-34s were knocking out Tigers at extremely close range, since their powerful guns and massive armor no longer gave them advantage in close combat. . . . The shells fired at extremely close range pierced not only the side armor but also the frontal armor. . . . When a tank was hit, its ammunition and fuel blew up, and torn-off turrets were flung through the air over dozens of yards."

Even though the Soviet Red Army lost more than 1,600 tanks, compared to about 250 German tanks lost, it ended in a decisive Soviet victory.

Soviet soldiers walk and drive past a burning T-34 medium tank during the Battle of Kursk, July 1943

Hawker Typhoon

Originally designed as a replacement for the Hawker Hurricane fighter, the Typhoon was reconfigured to provide ground support for advancing troops. It proved to be the most effective Allied ground attack fighter-bomber in World War II.

It was the heaviest and most powerful single-seat, single-engined warplane at the time of its design in 1938. Rushed into production before all the kinks had been worked out, and consequently it initially gained a bad reputation from pilots forced to fly into combat a plane that wasn't fully developed. That situation proved to be a blessing in disguise. During the redesign of the Typhoon, a new role was decided for it, that of a ground attack fighter-bomber. The standard armament package was four 20-mm cannons, two on each wing, and eight sixty-pound rocket projectiles or two thousand-pound bombs. Though the Typhoon gained fame in its ground attack role, with a top speed of 435 miles per hour, it proved itself capable of easily besting top of the line German fighters in a dogfight.

The Typhoon played a major role during the Normandy campaign in France in June 1944. Before June 6, the D-Day landing itself, Typhoons from 2 Tactical Air Force repeatedly swept across the region destroying targets. Once the Allies established a foothold, Typhoons began operating from hastily constructed airfields within sight of the landing beaches. Typhoons found themselves diving across their own runways to fire their rockets and cannons into enemy concentrations only a thousand feet away. From takeoff to landing, a mission could last less than ten minutes. Their deadly effectiveness was acknowledged by Generalleuttnant Heinrich von Lüttwitz commander of the 2nd Panzer Division who lamented, "They came down in hundreds, firing their rockets at the concentrated tanks and vehicles. We could do nothing against them."

Pilots of a Typhoon squadron study maps in front of their Hawker Typhoon fighter plane at a Forward Tactical Air Force Base in France

De Havilland Mosquito

The aphorism "desperate times call for desperate measures" could certainly be applied to the de Havilland Mosquito. Conceived as a bomber, it became one of the greatest, most versatile twin-engined warplanes in the war. Its many roles included fighter, night fighter, low- and high-level attack bomber (day and night), long-range photo-reconnaissance, mine layer, pathfinder, high-speed military transport, and fighter-bomber. All this from an aircraft that, because of a lack of metal, was built out of molded plywood. Perhaps the greatest accolade for the Mosquito came from Reichsmarschall Hermann Göring, the commander in chief of the Luftwaffe. His address commemorating the tenth anniversary of the Nazi party's rise to power on January 30, 1943, was interrupted by an attack by three squadrons of Mosquitos. Göring later said, "It makes me furious when I see the Mosquito. I turn green and yellow with envy. The British, who can afford aluminum better than we can, knock together a beautiful wooden aircraft that every piano factory over there is building, and they give it a speed which they have now increased yet again. What do you make of that?"

The Mosquito had a top speed of 378 miles per hour and a maximum range of almost two thousand miles. It was modified to carry a variety of weapons systems, but the standard armament was four 20-mm cannons located in its nose. By the time it was retired in 1950, 7,781 were built, in 27 variants, with 6,710 seeing service in World War II.

One of the most courageous pilots to fly the Mosquito was Group Captain Geoffrey Leonard Cheshire. The son of an Oxford University professor, he did more than any other pilot to turn the violent art of bombing into a science. He pioneered precise low-level target marking at night. In a Mosquito he would dive to within 200 feet of a factory roof to be sure his marking flares pinpointed the target for the following streams of bombers. Cheshire flew perilous bomber missions over occupied Europe and Germany from 1940 through 1944, surviving more than three normal tours of duty and 100 combat missions. He was awarded Britain's highest medal for valor, the Victoria Cross, for his unparalleled four-year demonstration of stamina, courage, and skill. Other honors included the Order of Merit, a life peerage as Baron Cheshire, and in the 2002 BBC poll to find the 100 Greatest Britons, he was ranked number 31.

British aircraft designer Captain Geoffrey De Havilland is pictured with a model of the Mosquito in his office

Consolidated B-24 Liberator

The B-17 Flying Fortress is the most famous American heavy bomber of World War II. The B-29 Superfortress is famous as the heavy bomber that dropped atomic bombs on Hiroshima and Nagasaki. Even though it participated in some of the greatest air raids of the war, the B-24 Liberator is probably the least known of the three American heavy bombers.

The B-24 carried a heavier bomb load (8,000 pounds), had a longer range (2,200 miles), and more were built (more than 18,000) than the Flying Fortress. The first prototypes flew in 1939, and the Liberator became operational in 1941. B-24 squadrons conducted the famous low-level bombing raid on the Ploesti oil fields in Romania in 1943. Liberators also participated in the disastrous Schweinfurt raids that same year, and, in 1945, the controversial fire-bombing of Dresden. One of the more notable B-24 pilots was Hollywood actor Jimmy Stewart. Major Stewart was group operations officer of the 453rd Bombardment Group and by the end of the war he had received the Distinguished Flying Cross with Oak Leaf Cluster, the French Croix de Guerre with Palm, and the Air Medal with three Oak Leaf Clusters.

The Liberator's greatest contribution to World War II was something that no one could talk about for decades. Its exceptional range, load capacity, and high air speed (more than three hundred miles per hour) made it ideal for special operations missions. Formed into groups code-named "Carpetbaggers," specially modified B-24s were used in top-secret special operations missions conducted by the Office of Strategic Services (OSS), the forerunner of the CIA.

On April 26, 1945, the 492nd Bombardment Group, one of the Carpetbaggers, was awarded the Distinguished Unit Citation (the highest award for valor given to a unit as a whole). Even the citation couldn't reveal mission details, stating, in part, "Although it is impossible at this time to evaluate fully the results of these operations . . . the information already obtained from the agents who were dropped has been of very great value to the Allied armies. . . . It is safe to say that no group of this size has made a greater contribution to the war effort."

B-25 Mitchell Medium Bomber

The North American B-25 Mitchell, designed by John Leland "Lee" Atwood, became operational just before World War II began and participated in every theater of operations. It became the most famous medium bomber in the war as a result of its participation in the Doolittle Raid. In April 1942, sixteen modified B-25s flew off the flight deck of the USS *Hornet* in April 1942 and successfully bombed targets in Japan. The commander of the raid, Lt. Colonel James H. "Jimmy" Doolittle, would be promoted directly to brigadier general and receive the Medal of Honor.

The B-25 Mitchell was named after U.S. military aviation pioneer and advocate Brigadier General William "Billy" Mitchell and is the only American military aircraft named in honor of an individual. By the time production ended, almost 10,000 bombers had been built. Among its variants were the F-10 (photo reconnaissance) and the B-25J (precision bomber). The B-25 would go on to see service for almost 25 nations. The final B-25 squadron, in Indonesia, was retired in 1979.

Operational requirements in the Southwest Pacific theater inspired one of the more unusual field modifications of an American warbird. Major (later Lt. Colonel) Paul I. "Pappy" Gunn (also known as the "Mad Professor") transformed the lightly armed medium bomber into a fighter-bomber gunship bristling with .50-caliber machine guns. He also helped rewrite bombing tactics to take advantage of the Mitchell's new capability. The result was a deadly warbird designed for low-level strafing and skip-bombing missions. Gunn's modifications were formally incorporated into the B-25G and H variants that were equipped with as many as ten .50-caliber machine guns and a specially designed 75 mm cannon.

Captain Ted Lawson, a test pilot for the early model B-25s and later one of the Doolittle Raid pilots, wrote that the Mitchell was "a grand ship, fast, hard-hitting and full of fight." Army Chief of Staff General George Marshall acknowledged the B-25's contribution during the early stages of the war. In a letter dated February 25, 1943, written to North American chairman and chief executive officer James H. "Dutch" Kindelberger, Marshall praised the B-25's combat action in North Africa, concluding, "You certainly have reason to be proud of the splendid record being made by your B-25 bombers."

Martin B-26 Marauder

The B-26 Marauder was a medium bomber whose reputation as a crew-killer overshadowed its contribution to Allied victory in World War II.

This high performance twin-engine warplane had such a short wingspan that it quickly got the nickname "The Flying Prostitute" (because it had "no visible means of support"). This short wingspan made it unstable at low speeds during take-offs and landings. Pilots coming out of flight school without any prior experience in twin-engined airplanes suffered a high rate of accidents, enough of them fatal to inspire another nickname, "Widow-Maker." In fact, the Marauder suffered the lowest attrition rate of any American aircraft in the war.

The Marauder had a top speed of 280 miles per hour and a range of 1,100 miles. A normal bomb load was 3,000 pounds and a maximum bomb load was 4,000 pounds. It carried a crew of five to seven and standard armament included eleven .50-caliber machine guns. Though its ceiling was almost 20,000 feet, the Marauder usually flew much lower in tactical ground support missions. A total of 5,157 were built.

One pilot who went out of his way to disprove the Marauder's deadly reputation was Major General James H. "Jimmy" Doolittle, who in 1942 led the Doolittle Raid flying B-25s off the deck of the USS *Hornet* against Japan.

He offered to show Major Paul Tibbets, a B-17 bomber pilot who was at that time General Dwight Eisenhower's personal pilot, how easy the Marauder was to fly. The skeptical Tibbets agreed to go up with Doolittle. After they had reached 6,000 feet, Doolittle turned off one engine and feathered the propeller. As Tibbets later wrote, "We did some flying on one engine, turning in both directions, climbing, making steep banks. The Marauder was a tame bird with Doolittle at the controls. Suddenly he put the plane into a dive, built up excess speed and put it into a perfect loop—all with one engine dead." Doolittle then restarted the engine and landed the Marauder. When they left the airplane, Tibbets noted, "The pilots and operations people who had been watching us were impressed. The flight was an important start toward convincing them that the B-26 was just another airplane."

Tibbets would later become a B-29 bomber pilot. On August 6, 1945, Colonel Tibbets, flying the *Enola Gay*, dropped the first atomic bomb on Hiroshima.

Formation of Martin B-26Bs

FOCKE-WULF FW 190

The Focke-Wulf 190 was one of the most versatile high-performance war birds of World War II. Kurt Tank, chief designer and technical director at Focke-Wulf, said, "Although conceived as a fighter, it did double duty as an attack bomber and, in fact, throughout most of the war, was the only reliable, light attack bomber we possessed in numbers."

The Fw 190 was fast, maneuverable, and adaptable. Modifications included fighter-bomber, ground attack, reconnaissance fighter, long-range reconnaissance, all weather interceptor, night fighter, tank destroyer, torpedo plane, and two-seat trainer. High-altitude variants included pressurized cabins. In its combat debut in September 1941, the Fw 190A proved superior to the Supermarine Spitfire MkV.

Yet the Fw 190 almost didn't get off the drawing board. The Messerschmitt Me 109 was Germany's top fighter when designs for the Fw 190 were submitted in 1937 to the German Air Ministry (*Reichluftfahrtsministerium*, or RLM). Some senior leaders at the RLM believed the Me 109 so technologically advanced that it didn't need a successor. Also, demand outstripped supply for the popular Daimler-Benz inline 12-cylinder DB601A engine. Prototypes using the 14-cylinder twin row BMW 801 radial engine were flown in 1939. (Later models, starting with the Fw 190D in 1942, used the Junkers Juno 213 twelve-cylinder inverted-V inline engine.) Test pilot reports were enthusiastic and the first production model, the FW-109A-2, emerged in 1941.

Basic armament was two 13 mm MG 131 synchronized machine guns mounted over the engine, and two 20 mm MG151/20 cannon in the wing roots. Modifications included a wide variety of weapons packages. An Fw 190F variant, the Panzerschreck (tank terror), carried three 88 mm projectile launching tubes under each wing.

One important feature of the Fw 190 was its ease of field maintenance. Its sturdy construction housed complex, self-contained subcomponents designed to be replaced rather than repaired, dramatically reducing maintenance downtime.

At war's end, more than 20,000 Fw 190s had been produced and it had served in every theater from the Arctic to North Africa. Oberleutnant Oskar Romm, an ace who survived the war with 92 victories, said, "I could fly the Fw 190 as an armament platform with greater assurance and reliability under any and all conditions than I could the 109."

A Focke-Wulf Fw 190 beneath camouflage in an airfield near Normandy, France, 1944

LOCKHEED P-38 LIGHTNING

The cockpit of a P-38

With its distinctive twin boom configuration, the P-38 Lightning was the most recognizable warplane of World War II. For that reason, the P-38 was the only Allied aircraft authorized to fly over the Normandy landing beaches during D-Day on June 6, 1944, even though all the Allied aircraft had their fuselages and wings painted with identifying alternating black and white stripes. A radical and innovative departure in design, the Lightning was one of the truly great fighter planes ever built. The top two American aces in the war, Major Richard Bong and Major Thomas McGuire, would rack up their respective 40 and 38 victories in Lightnings.

Designed by Lockheed's legendary Clarence "Kelly" Johnson, the Lightning had a top speed of about 400 miles per hour, a service ceiling of 40,000 feet (though pilots suffered terribly from exposure at high altitudes because of inadequate cockpit heating), and a range of about 900 miles. Standard armament was one 2 mm cannon and four .50-caliber cannons mounted on the nose and a maximum bomb load of 4,000 pounds or ten five-inch rockets. The concentrated configuration of the machine gun and cannon gave the Lightning tremendous firepower powerful enough to sink a ship, which it sometimes did. About ten thousand Lightnings were built, making it one of the most-produced American fighters in the war.

The Lightning participated in one of the most important intercept missions of the war. American intelligence had intercepted the flight plans of Japanese Admiral Isoroku Yamamoto, who had planned the attack on Pearl Harbor. On April 18, 1943, sixteen P-38G Lightnings, carrying external wing tanks to extend their range, took off from their base on the island of Guadalcanal. They flew northeast 435 miles at no more that fifty feet above the water. They arrived at Bougainville island just as Admiral Yamamoto's plane was about to land. Lieutenant Rex T. Barber was credited with shooting down Yamamoto's plane and in recognition he received the Navy Cross, a noteworthy gesture of gratitude by the U.S. Navy as Barber was a U.S. Army Air Force officer.

A squadron of Lightnings painted with black and white D-Day stripes on wings and fuselages en route to the Normandy landing beaches

Ilyushin Il-2 Shturmovik

The ground attack Il-2 Shturmovik is regarded as the Soviet Union's most important warplane in World War II. So important was the Shturmovik that Stalin said it was "as essential to the Red Army as bread and water." A total of 36,183 Shturmoviks were built, making it the most produced military aircraft design, and the third-most behind the civilian aircraft Cessna 172 and Polikarpov Po-2.

It was designed as an anti-tank light bomber with a crew of two (pilot and rear gunner) by Sergei Ilyushin in 1939. The Shturmovik had just gone into production in 1941, and 249 were on hand when the German Army attacked the Soviet Union in June. Stalin immediately made production of the Shturmovik a priority, but it initially lagged. By 1942 production would peak at three hundred a month. The Shturmovik had a top speed of 251 miles per hour, a range of 373 miles, and its standard armament included two machine guns, two 30 mm cannons, and a bomb load of 1,321 pounds or rockets. The bottom of the fuselage was armored, protecting the engine and crew, a crucial feature in ground attack operations.

The Shturmovik proved to be an efficient tank killer. To Soviet soldiers it had a variety of nicknames including the diminutive "Ilyusha," as well as the "Hunchback," the "Flying Tank," or the "Flying Infantryman" (an infantryman's greatest compliment). The Germans referred to it as *Der Schwartz Tod* ("The Black Death").

One of the most famous Soviet pilots to fly the Shturmovik was Senior Lieutenant Anna Yegorova, who flew about 270 missions in the attack plane (accounts vary). Initially she flew reconnaissance and delivery missions in the biplane Polikarpov Po-2. After she was shot down, she transferred in 1943 to the 805th Attack Aviation Regiment. She participated in some of the fiercest battles of the war in and around the Crimea and later in Poland. Believed dead after a mission near Warsaw in August 1944, she was posthumously awarded the Soviet Union's highest medal for valor, the Hero of the Soviet Union. Though wounded, she had survived and was discovered in a German prisoner of war camp in 1945. For years afterwards, Yegorova suffered Stalin-era suspicion and persecution that affected all Soviet citizens who were captured by the Germans.

A Soviet aircraft assembly crew standing in front of a Shturmovik

MITSUBISHI G4M BETTY

A counterpart to America's B-25 Mitchell and B-26 Marauder medium bombers, the Mitsubishi G4M was Japan's most important bomber in World War II. It had a top speed of 270 miles per hour, a range of almost 3,000 miles, and a crew of seven. Standard armament was three machine guns and one 20 mm cannon. It was capable of carrying either bombs or torpedoes and had a payload capacity of 1,765 pounds. A total of 2,435 were built. Because its gas tanks were poorly protected (and were not self-sealing), American pilots mockingly referred to them as the "Flying Zippo" and "One-Shot Lighter." Japanese pilots nicknamed it the "Type One Lighter" and *Hamaki* ("Cigar").

The Betty's greatest success occurred on December 10, 1941, just three days after the attack on Pearl Harbor. G4Ms of the Japanese 22nd Air Flotilla were instrumental in the sinking of Force Z composed of the British battleship *Prince of Wales* and battle cruiser *Repulse*. It was the first sinking of capital warships in open water exclusively by aircraft.

Admiral Isoroku Yamamoto, the planner of the attack on Pearl Harbor, was flying in a Betty when he was shot down by long-range P-38 Lightnings on April 18, 1943.

In the last weeks of the war, G4Ms were modified to carry kamikaze Ohka rocket-propelled piloted bombs beneath their wings. Substantially slowed by the extra drag, they became even more vulnerable to counterattack.

CHURCHILL TANK

The Churchill, named after British Prime Minister Winston Churchill, was the last of the British infantry tanks, designed to operate in close support with infantry units. It was commissioned by the British government following the British army's evacuation of Dunkirk (1940) and rushed into production while the prototypes were still being tested because the British army needed an immediate and updated tank to replace armor lost in France. As a result the Churchill was built in haste, and early models suffered from mechanical defects.

The chassis of the Churchill proved amazingly adaptable, and the tank is most notable for the huge number of variants, 22 in all. Some of the more unusual variants were designed by the iconoclastic tank genius Major General Sir Percy Hobart and collectively known as "Hobart's Funnies."

The Funnies were developed as a result of hard lessons learned during an amphibious raid at Dieppe, France, in August 1942 that tested German beach defenses. Standard tanks encountered problems against even the simplest of fortifications. Major General Hobart was a military engineer and tank expert with unconventional ideas that often placed him at odds with superiors. Hobart was appointed commander of the 79th Armoured Division Royal Engineers and, as its leader, conducted a crash program to modify Churchill and Sherman tanks for amphibious assaults.

The Churchill Funnies included the Crocodile, fitted with a flame-thrower; the AVRE (Armoured Vehicle, Royal Engineers) designed for anti-fortification, transportation, and mine-clearing purposes; and the ARK (Armoured Ramp Carrier), a turretless Churchill fitted with extendable ramps used to scale obstacles. "Funnies" was certainly an apt name. One AVRE design, for instance, sported a gigantic reel of ten-foot-wide reinforced canvas cloth that could be unrolled to form an unsinkable path over soft ground. It was called a "Bobbin" because it resembled bobbins found in a sewing kit.

Amphibious Landing Craft

Amphibious operations—large-scale attacks of hostile shores by combined naval and land forces—are among the most challenging of military operations. Amphibious landings have occurred throughout history, notably Julius Caesar's invasions of England in 55 and 54 B.C. Amazingly, vessels specifically designed for amphibious operations were not built until World War II. That quickly changed and a new set of acronyms identifying amphibious vehicles became a part of the military lexicon.

American military leaders recognized the need for amphibious assault vessels capable of carrying artillery, tanks, and assault troops in the 1920s. Two commercial designs emerged in the 1930s with the most promise: the "Eureka," designed by Andrew C. Higgins for work in the Louisiana swamps, and the "Alligator," Donald Roebling's track-laying rescue vehicle for the Florida Everglades. From these came the workhorses of U.S. forces in World War II: the Landing Craft Vehicle Personnel (LCVP) and Landing Craft Mechanized (LCM) based on Higgins' design, and the Landing Vehicle Tracked (LVT) based on Robeling's. The LCVP could carry 36 troops or 8,100 pounds of cargo. The LCM could transport 30 tons of cargo, and the LVT capable of carrying 24 troops. Later models of the LVT were modified into light tanks.

Other amphibious assault ships included the Landing Craft Tank (LCT), capable of landing three tanks on a beach, and the larger Landing Ship Tank (LST), capable of transporting as many as eighteen 30-ton tanks. The largest of them all was the 457-foot Landing Ship Dock (LSD) that was a combination troop transport and floating dry dock capable of transporting the largest landing craft.

The vital importance of these vessels was acknowledged by General Dwight Eisenhower, who said, "Andrew Higgins . . . is the man who won the war for us. . . . If Higgins had not designed and built those LCVPs [Landing Craft, Vehicles and Personnel], we never could have landed over an open beach. The whole strategy of the war would have been different."

Soldiers exiting a landing craft and heading toward the Normandy shore during D-Day

V-1 Flying Bomb

Nicknamed the "buzz bomb" and the "doodlebug" by the British, the *Vergeltungs-swaffen-1*, or "Vengeance Weapon 1" was an early type of cruise missile. It was the first of a new series of secret wonder weapons announced by German Chancellor Adolf Hitler and designed to regain the strategic initiative for Nazi Germany.

The V-1 was a single-wing missile about twenty-five feet long, with a wingspan of 17 1/2 feet. It had a gross weight of 4,750 pounds, and its warhead of Amatol, a mixture of TNT and ammonium nitrate, weighed 1,870 pounds. It had a top speed of 393 miles per hour and a range of 150 miles. Because of the shrill, sputtering sound it made in flight, some Londoners derisively called it the Farting Fury.

The V-1 was designed in the top-secret rocket research station on the Baltic island of Peenemünde. The V-1 did not achieve full-scale production until 1944 and did not become operational until after the Allied landings in Normandy in June of that year. Instead of using them against military targets, Hitler ordered them to be used as a weapon of terror against London. His hope was that the V-1 attacks would so demoralize the citizens that they would force an end to the war.

London Air Raid Warden L. N. Adamson was at his station at Banstead Common in the southern edge of London. At about 3 A.M. on June 16, 1942, he saw a small glow in the eastern sky streaking toward him at a slight angle and guessed it was a German plane on fire. Suddenly the engine spluttered and stopped, and the glow disappeared. A few seconds later there was a large explosion. After phoning in a crashed aircraft report, he and two other air raid wardens set out for the scene of the crash. When they reached the site, an open field, there was nothing to see except a shallow crater, a few bits of wreckage, and three long curious bits of metal. Puzzled, Adamson phoned the Home Guard and alerted them to be on the lookout for a shot down German air crew. Once back at his post, real trouble began. "More and more of these 'crashed aircraft' came over," he wrote later, "and it began to dawn on our feeble intelligence that we were faced with something entirely new."

London had just suffered its first V-1 attack. By the time the war ended, Germany had fired 9,251 V-1s against England. Though at least 25,000 buildings were destroyed, 5,470 people killed, and 15,994 wounded, the V-1 did not succeed in breaking the morale of the English people.

M4 Sherman Tank

The M4 Sherman medium tank, named after the Civil War general William Tecumseh Sherman, was the primary tank of the U.S. Army and Marine Corps in World War II. Its design and performance standards reflected the cavalry philosophy then prevalent in the United States Army that placed an emphasis on speed and maneuverability instead of armor (with its extra weight) and firepower.

According to that school of thought, the Shermans weren't expected to waste their efforts on fighting other tanks. Destruction of enemy armor was the business of antitank guns and tank destroyers. Shermans were designed to tear through enemy defenses and make holes for the armored infantry to come through, while the tanks plunged deeper and deeper into the enemy's rear. As a result, in tank battles, the Sherman with its short-barrel 75-mm cannon was outmatched by its German medium tank counterpart, the PzKw IV, which carried a higher velocity 75-mm cannon. At a distance of a thousand yards, the PzKw IV stood a good chance of knocking out a Sherman, whereas at the same distance, a Sherman stood a poor chance of knocking out the German tank. In addition, if a German anti-tank round hit a Sherman, it also stood a good chance of setting the American tank on fire because the Sherman ran on gasoline instead of diesel. This caused the Sherman to be nicknamed "Ronsons" after the cigarette lighter.

Where the Sherman succeeded was in mass attack tactics. The Sherman tank became operational in 1942 and by war's end more than 48,000 had come off the assembly line. U.S. manufacturers simply outbuilt the German tank manufacturers.

Major Herbert F. Hillenmeyer wrote of his experiences fighting in a Sherman in his privately published memoirs, *The Little Picture: Tales of World War II for My Children*. An ambush by a German anti-tank gun provided a particularly unforgettable memory: "The first shot penetrated the turret of my tank, killing my gunner immediately. That red-hot slug of tungsten steel banged around and came to rest on the floor of the turret spinning on its point like a top. It was bouncing up and down making a terrible racket, and others later told me they could hear it as I talked over my radio. I remember looking down at it and wondering if I would burn my foot if I stepped on it." After a second shot completely disabled the tank, Hillenmeyer and the surviving members of the crew managed to escape.

Snow-covered Sherman tanks in northern Europe during the winter of 1944–1945

FLAME THROWER

Flame throwers have been used throughout history. The most famous are the tubes used during the Byzantine Empire to shoot out Greek Fire. Other objects using flame include catapult projectiles, arrows, and flaming pigs. Early models of the modern flame thrower were first used in World War I. The flame thrower saw extensive use in World War II, particularly in the Pacific theater of operations.

The flame thrower usually consisted of a backpack carrying two or three cylinders, a hose that ran from the cylinders to a long-handled "gun." One cylinder contained a compressed gas propellant (usually nitrogen) and the other two cylinders contained fuel and a fuel thickener. The gun contained a nozzle with an ignition system. Depressing the trigger started the flow over the ignition system. Flame throwers had an effective range of up to 270 feet and were used primarily against such defensive fortifications as bunkers or pillboxes.

The flame thrower was a dangerous, frightening object, almost as terrifying to the man who used it as the men it was used against. Many a soldier received third-degree burns from handling this weapon. A few became human torches. Initially the flame thrower was a specialized tool used only by combat engineers.

Flame throwers were used by all the major combatants in World War II. But the most extensive use was by American troops in the Pacific theater. The Army 7th infantry division in the Battle of Kwajalein (1944) carried 192 flame throwers. When the Marines landed on Okinawa in 1945, each division had almost 250 flame throwers. Basic tactics called for an assault squad, equipped with two flame-throwers, a BAR (Browning Automatic Rifle), and a supply of grenades, to make a three-stage attack on a pillbox or bunker. Covered by the BAR man, the operator of one flamethrower would put a lateral burst across the face of the bunker. This would make the defenders inside jump back from their weapons. The operator of the second flamethrower would advance and hit the embrasure with an oblique burst into the bunker. The grenadier would then throw grenades inside to kill or wound any survivors.

Flame throwers were used in both the Korean War and the Vietnam War. Though they are not banned by international treaty, the Department of the Defense made a unilateral decision in 1978 to stop using them.

GRENADE

Grenades are essentially small bombs. They contain two basic parts: a body and a fuse. Depending on the purpose of the grenade, a hollow container within the body is filled with explosives or other chemical agents. Screwed into the grenade's body is a fuse that burns at a controlled rate, allowing the weapon time to reach its target before exploding. Grenades are used for both lethal and non-lethal purposes. Grenade types include fragmentation, concussion, percussion, chemical, incendiary, stun, and smoke (for camouflage and location marking).

Originally only specially trained troops were allowed to use grenades. Grenadiers, as they were called, made their appearance in 1692. The great military engineer Vauban, who was as skilled in capturing fortresses as he was in erecting them, has a good claim to be also known as the father of grenadiers. His capture of the fortress town of Namur 1692 owed in large part to the training of picked infantrymen in the tactics of the comparatively new weapon. The French used no less than twenty thousand grenades in this operation alone, giving such a convincing demonstration that soon other such battalions were formed. The storm troopers of their day, only the strongest and bravest could qualify, and soon grenadier units came to be known as the elite of every European army.

The stun grenade, also known as the flashbang grenade, is a non-lethal grenade designed to immobilize an enemy. The elite British Special Air Service special operations unit developed it in the 1960s. The flashbang explodes in a simultaneous loud noise and blinding burst of light capable of immobilizing an opponent for about five seconds, enough for the individual to be apprehended. The flashbang grenade is standard equipment for all special operations units as well as law enforcement SWAT teams.

German with a Russian hand grenade

TIGER

The most famous German tank of the war was the fifty-ton monster called the Tiger. Though it was not the most numerous German tank—about six thousand Panther medium tanks were built compared to just 1,355 Tigers—with its thick, impenetrable frontal armor and powerful 88-mm main gun, the Tiger so dominated the battlefield and intimidated its tanker opponents that it caused "Tiger phobia." In extreme cases, Allied tank units would go out of their way to avoid tank-on-tank battle with a Tiger. "Tiger" came to be a term used to describe all German tanks. Its one major weakness was that it was high maintenance—it suffered chronic breakdown problems.

The Tiger became operational on the Eastern Front in 1942. It had a robust design with a powerful engine and eight forward and four reverse gears. But it was a gas-guzzler even by tank standards and its range was only seventy miles. Tiger tank commander Otto Carius recalled his first meeting with the Tiger. In his book, *Tiger in the Mud*, he wrote, "Its outer form was anything but pretty and pleasing. It looked plump." Though it was short on looks, he was happy to discover it was long on performance. "It really drove just like a car."

The most effective tactic against a Tiger was for Allied tank units to "gang up" on one. This usually involved five tanks taking on a Tiger, with one acting as the decoy while the other maneuvered to the sides and rear and then rapidly attacking to fire close-range shots at the thinner side and rear armor. Needless to say, this was a highly risky maneuver.

The overwhelming dominance of the Tiger was brutally demonstrated on June 13, 1944, in the Battle of Villers-Bocage in Normandy. In a fifteen-minute period, one Tiger tank commanded by SS-Obersturmführer [First Lieutenant] Michael Wittmann and operating alone, destroyed eleven Sherman tanks, two anti-tank guns, and thirteen personnel carriers. Other accounts of the action claim Wittman's total was even higher. His action stopped cold the advance of the British 22nd Armoured Brigade. For his achievement he was promoted and awarded the Knight's Cross of the Iron Cross with Oak Leaves and Swords.

General Heinz Guderian (center) stands on top of a Tiger tank to address his men

Avro Lancaster

The Avro Lancaster was the most successful heavy bomber used by the Royal Air Force and the Royal Canadian Air Force in World War II. Though primarily used as a night bomber, the "Lac" or "Lankie" as it was affectionately known, gained fame as the "Dam Buster" in the May 1943 mission to destroy German dams in the Ruhr River Valley.

Powered by four Rolls-Royce Merlin engines (far and away the most important Allied aircraft engine design of the war), the Lancaster had a top speed of 280 miles per hour, a range of three thousand miles, and a ceiling of 23,500 feet. A standard bomb load was fourteen thousand pounds. This could be expanded to accommodate the 22,000-pound Grand Slam bomb. Defensive armament was eight machine guns. A total of 7,377 Lancasters were built.

The Ruhr River Valley in western Germany, with its concentration of war industries, hydroelectric power plants, and waterways, was regarded as a strategic target during the war. Planners decided destroying hydroelectric dams on four tributaries would have the most far-reaching impact. But bombing dams presented special challenges and to ensure their destruction, new bombs and new bombing tactics had to be developed. The results were special dam-busting bombs shaped like gigantic oil drums and a bomb release method called "skip-bombing" where the bombs skipped across the water toward the target.

Code-named Operation Chastise, Wing Commander Guy Gibson led RAF 617 Squadron against the Ruhr dams on May 17, 1943. Despite the frightful cost of suffering 40 percent casualties, the mission succeeded, though not as well as hoped. Thirty-three of the survivors received decorations, including Gibson, who was awarded the Victoria Cross.

After the war, Bomber Command Chief Marshall of the Royal Air Force Sir Arthur T "Bomber" Harris, paid tribute to the Lancaster, saying, in part, "The finest bomber of the war! . . . Above all, the Lancaster won the air war by taking the major part in forcing Germany to concentrate on building and using fighters to defend the Fatherland, thereby depriving their armies of essential air and particularly bomber support."

Lancaster air crews watch as ordnance crews prepare to load the bombers with mines

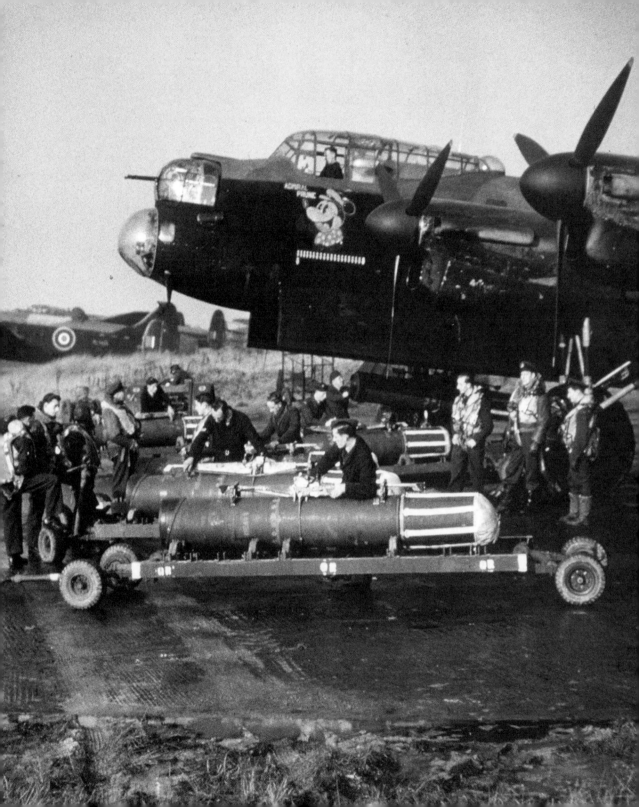

Republic P-47 Thunderbolt

The Republic P-47 Thunderbolt, affectionately nick-named "The Jug" and "The Flying Milk Bottle," was, together with the P-38 Lightning and the P-51 Mustang, one of the "Big Three" American fighters that broke the back of the Luftwaffe in World War II. Of the three fighters, the Thunderbolt was the largest, heaviest, and most rugged. More Thunderbolts were built (15,485) than the Mustang (14,501) or the Lightning (12,655).

Depending on the variant, the Thunderbolt had an average speed of 430 miles per hour, a range of 600 miles and a ceiling of 42,000 feet. Standard armament was eight .50-caliber machine guns. Late model Thunderbolts were capable of carrying bomb loads up to three thousand pounds.

The Thunderbolt began combat operations in the European Theater of Operations on March 1943. Initially, the Thunderbolt's weight was both an asset and a curse. The Thunderbolt had excellent high altitude, roll rate, and dive characteristics. In fact, it outperformed all fighters in diving. But its climb rate and maneuverability were inferior to the top-of-the-line German fighters and the British Spitfire. That changed when the Thunderbolts were equipped with the Curtiss paddle-blade propeller that dramatically increased its climbing performance.

The Thunderbolt's ruggedness saved Captain Robert S. Johnson's life on June 26, 1943. While returning from a mission escorting B-17 bombers over France, Johnson's Thunderbolt was seriously damaged during an attack by FW-190s. As he attempted to fly back to England, he was bounced by another FW-190 that repeatedly attacked his crippled aircraft. The German pilot finally broke off action over the English Channel after running out of ammunition. Though wounded, Johnson safely landed at the RAF airfield at Manston. He then began counting the bullet holes. He later said, "The Thunderbolt was literally a sieve, holes through the wings, nose, fuselage, and tail. Every square foot was covered with holes. There were five holes in the propeller. Three 20-mm cannon shells burst against the armor plate. Five cannon shell holes in the right wing, four in the left wing." Though there were more left to be counted, Johnson gave up after two hundred holes. Johnson ended the war a major and one of the ETO's top aces with twenty-eight confirmed kills.

North American P-51 Mustang

Chuck Yeager

The North American P-51 Mustang is considered by many experts to be the finest American fighter plane in World War II. But that was not the case when the first models rolled off the production line.

The North American P-51 Mustang was originally produced for Great Britain. The Royal Air Force wanted a high-performance, high-altitude long-range fighter. Initially named the Apache, the Mustang went from drawing room to prototype within eight months, an astonishing production feat. These first Mustangs were powered by the Allison V-1710 engine. Though the Mustang had exceptional performance below fifteen thousand feet, it suffered a severe drop-off when flown above that altitude. As a result, the RAF used it for low-level missions, most notably in support of the amphibious raid at Dieppe, France, in August 1942.

Impressed by its low-level performance and maneuverability, the RAF, in an experiment, had Rolls-Royce engineers modify five Mustangs with the Rolls-Royce Merlin 61 engine. The results were astonishing. High-altitude performance literally skyrocketed. Tests showed that these experimental Mustangs reached a speed of 433 miles per hour at 22,000 feet, a rate of climb of 3,300 feet per minute, and a service ceiling of 40,600 feet, making them more than a match against top enemy fighters. Merlin-equipped Mustangs received a high priority production designation and the first production models, P-51B and P-51C, arrived in England in August 1943. Standard armament was six .50-caliber machine guns. Some variants were capable of carrying bomb loads of two thousand pounds, or four half-inch rockets.

Colonel Clarence "Bud" Anderson, a triple ace who flew with Chuck Yeager in World War II, said, "The older twin-engined fighters, Me-110s and Me-410s, were fish in a barrel for a Mustang." And even though the jet-powered Me-262 was about a hundred mph faster than the Mustang, Anderson said that when they slowed to attack bombers, "You could bounce them. . . . They weren't nearly as nimble as the P-51."

When equipped with external fuel tanks to increase its range, the Mustang became the first fighter to provide continuous fighter escort for bombers flying long-range missions deep into Germany. Though it came late into the war, the Mustang is credited with destroying more enemy aircraft than any other fighter in the European theater of operations.

CHANCE VOUGHT F4U CORSAIR

F-4Us in flight

Nicknamed by Japanese ground troops the "Whistling Death" because of the distinctive whistling sound from its wing-mounted air intakes, the F4U Corsair was the top U.S. Marine Corps fighter in World War II. The Corsair was primarily used by the Marines and the Navy and fought in World War II and the Korean War.

The distinctive, bent-wing Corsair became operational at the end of December 1942. A total of 12,571 were built during its twenty-year production lifetime. Variants included fighter, fighter-bomber, and photo-reconnaissance. Depending on the variant, it had a top speed of 425 miles per hour, a range of 1,015 miles, and a ceiling of 36,900 feet. Standard armament was six machine guns. It could also carry four half-inch rockets or a two-thousand-pound bomb load.

The most famous Corsair pilot was Major (later Colonel) Gregory "Pappy" Boyington, the leader of a bunch of Marine cast-off and misfit pilots known as the Black Sheep Squadron. Boyington was a colorful character himself. He enlisted with the Marines in 1935 and left in 1941 to join the Flying Tigers. While flying P-40s he made ace, shooting down six Japanese planes. In 1942, he was reinstated with the Marines and given command of VMF-214, the Black Sheep Squadron. When he was shot down on January 3, 1944, Boyington was the Marine's top ace, with 28 victories. He spent the rest of the war in a Japanese prisoner of war camp.

Shortly after his release he was presented with the Navy's highest award, the Navy Cross, and his nation's highest award for valor, the Medal of Honor. His Medal of Honor citation read, in part: "Consistently outnumbered through successive hazardous flights over heavily defended hostile territory, Major Boyington struck at the enemy with daring and courageous persistence, leading his squadron into combat with devastating results to Japanese shipping, shore installations, and aerial forces."

After the war, Boyington wrote his memoir, *Baa Baa Black Sheep*. Published in 1958, it became a bestseller and has been in print continuously ever since. It later was used as the basis for the popular 1970s television series *Black Sheep Squadron* starring Robert Conrad as Boyington.

Black Sheep Squadron wearing baseball caps given them by the St. Louis Cardinals

SUBMARINE (CONVENTIONAL POWER)

Submarines are boats designed to travel underwater. The submarine was used in warfare during the American Revolution. Patriot David Bushnell designed an egg-shaped submersible vessel operated by one man; he christened it the *Turtle*. On September 7, 1776, Sergeant Ezra Lee piloted the *Turtle* into New York harbor and unsuccessfully attacked the HMS *Eagle*.

In 1800, Robert Fulton created the first practical submarine and tried to sell it to Napoleon. That effort failed. After a similar rejection by the British Royal Navy in 1804, Fulton turned his interest to building a steamboat. Though shelved, Fulton's *Nautilus* was not forgotten. It became the inspiration and namesake of French novelist Jules Verne's submarine in his 1870 epic adventure, *Twenty Thousand Leagues Under the Sea*.

The first successful submarine attack occurred during the Civil War. On February 17, 1864, the CSS *Hunley*, named after its inventor Horace Lawson Hunley, attacked the USS *Houstatonic* with a torpedo-tipped ram. Unfortunately, the *Hunley* was not able to escape and was sunk along with the *Houstatonic*.

Because these early submarines relied on human muscle power when submerged, underwater propulsion remained a problem. It was not solved until the 1890s, when John Holland perfected a method using electric motors. In the first half of the twentieth century, submarines used two power sources: diesel or gasoline engines for surface running, and electricity from batteries or a chemical process when submerged.

One hundred and thirty-eight years after its combat debut, the submarine finally made its strategic impact. Improved designs and the development of self-propelled torpedoes transformed the problem-plagued unconventional vessels into efficient sea-spanning fighting ships. The German U-boats of World War I (1914–1918) were so deadly that they almost won the war for Germany. The U-boats came close to success again in World War II (1939–1945). British Prime Minister Winston Churchill admitted, "The only thing that ever really frightened me during the war was the U-boat peril."

In the Pacific, by the time Japan capitulated in 1945, American submarines had established a cordon around the country so tight it was on the verge of starvation.

Panzerfaust

One of the simplest and most effective weapons of World War II was the German single-shot anti-tank weapon called the *panzerfaust* ("tank fist").

The *panzerfaust* (plural, *panzerfäuste*) consisted of a launch tube with a primitive aiming device and a trigger and a shaped, anti-tank rocket-powered warhead. It was designed for close combat; its ideal range was just sixty yards. Within that range, it was deadly. One American infantryman wrote the *panzerfäuste* "were more powerful than our American bazookas. [They] could penetrate our tanks with impunity, even through the extra armor we'd put in front of the driver and on the ammunition boxes on the side." One post-war study by the U.S. Army noted that American infantrymen were always on the lookout for abandoned *panzerfäuste*, "confirming that battle conditioned soldiers knew a good weapon system when it was used against them." This was confirmed by Brigadier General James M. Gavin, commander of the 82nd Airborne Division, who later said that the division "did not get adequate antitank weapons until it began to capture the first German *panzerfäuste*. By the fall of 1944, we had truckloads of them. . . . They were the best hand-carried antitank weapon of the war."

The *panzerfaust* was cheap, easy to make (by the end of the war, more than six million had been manufactured), and easy to use. Albert Speer, Nazi Germany's minister of production, recorded that 997,000 *panzerfäuste* were manufactured in November 1944, 1.253 million in December, and 1.2 million in January 1945.

In the final weeks of the war, during the Battle of Berlin, small factories throughout the city continued to produce *panzerfäuste*. The finished weapons were carried by wheelbarrow to the front lines, often just yards away from the factory. Typical of the type of people using the *panzerfaust* during the dying days of the Third Reich was Klaus Kützer of Berlin, a member of the paramilitary Hitler Youth organization. By April 1945 he had become an expert in using the *panzerfaust* to knock out Soviet tanks. Kützer was not yet sixteen years old.

After suffering heavy tank losses from the *panzerfäuste*, Soviet tankers ingeniously discovered a surprisingly effective, though visually bizarre, countermeasure: bedsprings. Lashed to the front, sides, and rear of their tanks, the tightly coiled springs successfully broke the impact of the large blunt-nosed *panzerfaust* rockets.

A German army officer instructs a civilian woman in the use of a panzerfaust

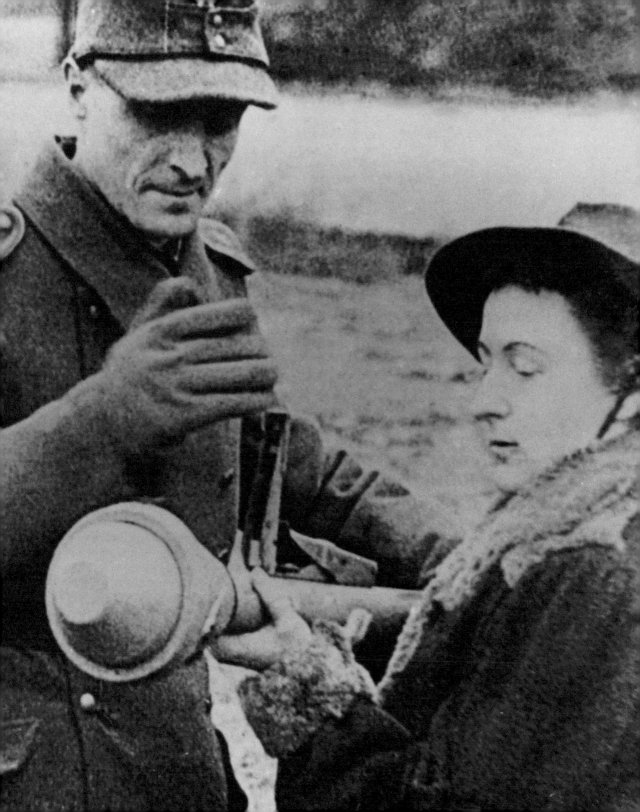

Grumman F6F Hellcat

The Hellcat was the successor to Grumman's F4F Wildcat. It was the most successful fighter in U.S. Navy history, officially credited with shooting down 5,163 enemy aircraft.

Nicknamed the "Wildcat's big brother," the Hellcat's design was heavily influenced by lessons learned from pilots who had fought against Japan's top fighter, the Zero, and by extensive study of a Zero that had been captured intact. When the Hellcat entered combat in September 1943, it could outfly the Zero in every category. The Hellcat had a top speed of 380 miles per hour, a ceiling of 37,300 feet, a combat radius of 945 miles, and was armed with six .50-caliber machine guns. By the time production ended in 1945, 12,275 Hellcats, in all variants, had been produced.

The Hellcat was also easier to operate than its predecessor. It had a larger cockpit and hydraulic systems. No longer would a pilot have to hand-crank the undercarriage 38½ times to raise and lower the landing gear, as he did in the Wildcat.

David McCampbell was the Navy's top ace with 34 victories. In 1944, he was the Air Group Commander (AGC) of Air Group Fifteen, one of the Navy's best units. As AGC, he was supposed to oversee air operations from the aircraft carrier's control room. But on October 24, McCampbell found himself flying into action, and because of on-deck confusion, with only half-full fuel tanks.

The air group encountered a large force of Japanese planes heading toward the American fleet. McCampbell ordered his fighters to attack. McCampbell shot down nine enemy planes; then he remembered he had entered the fray low on fuel. He quickly turned away and returned to the fleet. The engine of his Hellcat quit just after he landed, its tanks bone dry.

By flying on that mission, McCampbell had been insubordinate and was subject to court-martial. Instead, his commander, Admiral Frederick Sherman, gave him a verbal reprimand. For his role on October 24 in stopping the Japanese air attack and for shooting down nine enemy aircraft, McCampbell was awarded the Medal of Honor.

A Hellcat in flames preparing to land on the aircraft carrier *Cowpens*

PANTHER TANK

The Panther (originally designated the Panzer V) was Germany's response to the Soviet Union's T-34 tank. The Panther was the standard tank for panzer divisions from 1943 to the end of World War II.

Even before World War II began in 1939, General Heinz Guderian, the father of the blitzkrieg, had advocated the production of a tank larger than the then-standard medium PzKw III (mounting a 50-mm cannon) and PzKw IV (low velocity 75-mm cannon). But work stalled until after the invasion of the Soviet Union in June 1941 when the German tanks proved inferior to the Soviet T-34. A new design, incorporating some of the features studied in captured damaged T-34s, was swiftly drawn up and crash-production of the Panther commenced in 1942. More than six thousand were built.

The Panther featured improved suspension, a more powerful engine, and a high-velocity 75-mm cannon. Armor was thicker, except in the glacis (front), where the thinner armor was sloped to deflect shots better.

The Panther went into action on the Eastern Front during Operation Citadel, the Battle of Kursk, in July 1943. Because design bugs had not yet been worked out, more Panthers went down due to mechanical failure than enemy gunfire.

The main Allied tank on the Western front was the M4 Sherman medium tank. Earlier models, with a low-velocity 75-mm cannon, were outmatched by the Panther. Modifications were made, up-gunning the Sherman with a higher-velocity 76-mm cannon, with questionable results as this excerpt of an engagement during the Battle of the Bulge (December 1944) reveals: "[The Sherman tank commander] fired the first round from the 76-mm gun and struck the Panther square in the middle of its forward glacis plate. There was a tremendous flash of sparks, like a grinding wheel hitting a piece of steel. When it was over, the tank commander realized that the round had ricocheted. . . . He quickly reloaded, fired the second round, and struck the glacis plate again as the German slowly turned its turret in his direction. . . . [T]he tank commander got off a third round, with equal results. The Panther was finally able to fire its high-velocity 75-mm, which penetrated the M4 tank like a sieve." The Sherman crew survived.

A Panther tank used as a defensive pillbox, destroyed by British troops

NORTHROP P-61 BLACK WIDOW

The Black Widow night fighter was the world's first fighter designed for night operations. It was built in response to British requests for a radar-equipped night fighter capable of flying for long periods of time. Though it was a late participant in the war, not becoming operational until 1944, the Black Widow served in every theater and provided important practical experience in the development of night operations and fighter design. It is unofficially credited with scoring the last Allied air victory in the war. On the night of August 14, 1945, the P-61 *Lady in the Dark* caused a Japanese Oscar fighter to crash into the Pacific after a low-level dogfight.

Because of British requirements, and the size and weight of early radar units, the Black Widow was the largest fighter in World War II—almost the size of the B-25 Mitchell medium bomber. The twin-engine, twin-boomed Black Widow somewhat resembled the smaller Lockheed P-38 Lightning fighter. It carried a crew of two or three, had a top speed of 366 miles per hour, a range of 610 miles, and a ceiling of 33,100 feet. It housed two dorsal turrets, gun combinations varied, with the standard being either four .50-caliber machine guns in each turret, or one turret armed with four 20-mm cannon and another with four .50-caliber machine guns. Only 742 Black Widows were built, and it was retired from service in 1952.

The 426th Night Fighter Squadron, operating in the China-Burma-India theater, was one unit equipped with the Black Widow. One P-61, the *Jing-Bow Joy-Ride*, was crewed by pilot Lieutenant Carl J. Absmeier and radar observer Lt. James R. Smith. They volunteered to be stationed at the remote Chinese airstrip of Laohokow on detached service to the 7th Chinese air force. Conditions were so primitive that the early warning system announcing Japanese night air attacks was called the "Bamboo Telegraph"—peasant farmers literally banged bamboo sticks in relay when they heard approaching Japanese aircraft.

On one evening, Absmeier and Smith got airborne minutes before Japanese bombers attacked the airfield. They needed a close approach before firing, and Smith directed Absmeier to within 250 feet of their first target, a bomber code-named Lily. Once in position, Absmeier opened fire. The Lily erupted into "an enormous fireball." It was their first kill. They would go on to be one of the most successful P-61 crews in the theater.

MESSERSCHMITT ME-262

The Me-262 was the world's first turbo-jet fighter aircraft to see combat. Though it became operational too late—and in too few numbers (only 1,430 were built)—to win the war for Nazi Germany, its debut announced the beginning of the jet age.

Minister of Production Albert Speer regarded the Me-262 as "the most valuable of our 'secret weapons.'" The Me-262 had a top speed of 559 miles per hour, more than 120 mph faster than the P-51 Mustang. In fighter configuration, it had four 30-mm cannon in its nose. The fighter-bomber variant carried a maximum bomb load of just 1,100 pounds. Though the Me-262 was less maneuverable than top Allied fighters, if things got too dangerous, the Me-262 simply outran its opponent. Mustang pilot Chuck Yeager admitted, "Chasing those guys, I was a fat man running uphill to catch a trolley."

The potential of the Me-262 deeply troubled senior Allied commanders. Eighth Air Force commander Lieutenant General James H. Doolittle briefed Secretary of War for Air Robert Patterson, saying, "The speed differential between our fighters and bombers and [the Me-262] was striking. If . . . produced in great numbers, there was no doubt in my mind that [the Me-262] would become a serious threat."

The reason it did not was revealed by the head of the Luftwaffe, Reichsmarschall Hermann Göring. During a post-war interrogation he was asked the reason for the Me-262's delay as a fighter. He replied, "Adolf Hitler's madness." In September 1943, Hitler ordered a halt to Me-262 production. Then, in January 1944, after hearing of British success of its experimental jet plane, he ordered top priority be made of Me-262 production—but as a light bomber! Though no friend of Göring, Speer acknowledged that Hitler's decision made the Me-262 "worthless." He joined forces with his rival to change Hitler's decision. But for months, Hitler remained obdurate. The first Me-262 fighter squadron was not formed until January 1945. The first full-scale Me-262 attack on Allied bomber formations was in March, too late to affect the outcome of the war.

Me-262 at the National Museum of the U.S. Air Force

V-2

The *Vergeltungswaffe* 2 (Reprisal—or Vengeance—Weapon 2) was one of Chancellor Adolf Hitler's miracle weapons designed to win the war for Germany in World War II. It was the world's first supersonic ballistic missile. It was also the first man-made object to attain sub-orbital spaceflight and is the ancestor of both American and Soviet rockets.

Originally designated the A-4, development of the V-2 rocket began in the 1930s in a complex on the Baltic island of Peenemünde under the guidance of Professor Wernher von Braun. The V-2 rocket was 46 feet long and five feet five inches in diameter. It weighed between 13 and 14 tons and had a one-ton warhead. It had a top speed of 3,500 miles per hour and a range of about two hundred miles. About ten thousand V-2s were built, using slave labor.

The V-2 was used only against targets in western Europe. The first attacks occurred on September 8, 1944, when rockets were launched against Paris and London. When the war ended, about 1,300 V-2s had been fired against England, with about five hundred striking London.

Hitler believed that the V-2 would play a decisive role in destroying British civilian morale. Though this belief was inflated, there was a some truth to it. After the war, Donald Ketley, a London East End resident, said, "With the V-2s there was no question of getting into a shelter. If they were near enough you could hear them enter the upper atmosphere but that was no more than a few seconds before they hit the ground, so all you could do was attempt to ignore them." Comparing his experience in 1940 during the Blitz—the German attack on London during the Battle of Britain—he noted, "Before, one had felt always like a participant in a battle, but the lack of antiaircraft fire or fighter planes during the V-2 period gave the rockets an aura of invincibility. People become more on edge, more irritable than they'd ever been. In part this was because the war had been going on for so long, but I think it was also the nature of the V-2s. They were cosmic terrors."

WERNHER VON BRAUN
(1912–1977)

Wernher von Braun, the technical director at the rocket complex on Peenemünde, was the most important engineer in the team that designed and developed the V-2 ballistic rocket. Later he was instrumental in developing America's rocket program.

The son of minor Prussian nobleman, von Braun became interested in space-flight and joined an amateur rocket club while a student at Berlin's Charlottenbug Institute of Technology. Von Braun's efforts attracted the attention of Captain Walter Dornberger of the German army's ordnance department, who hired him to work on rocket artillery in 1932. In 1937, von Braun, then twenty-five years old, was appointed the director of research for the A-4, as the V-2 was originally named. Despite budget cutbacks by Chancellor Adolf Hitler, rocket development continued in fits and starts.

On June 13, 1942, von Braun and his team reached a watershed moment by conducting a launch demonstration before a group of dignitaries that included Hitler, Albert Speer (then a member of the engineering arm known as the Todt Organization), and heads of the three armed forces. The launch abruptly ended when the rocket prematurely exploded after traveling about a mile. Though Hitler remained suspicious, Speer later wrote, "I was thunderstruck at this technical miracle, at its precision and at the way it seemed to abolish the laws of gravity, so that thirteen tons could be hurtled into the air without any mechanical guidance."

Hitler was eventually convinced and ordered mass production of the V-2. Von Braun then found himself a pawn in a Nazi power play when Gestapo chief Heinrich Himmler, in a bold attempt to bring the V-2 program under his control, arrested von Braun on trumped up charges of treason. Hitler personally signed the order freeing him.

In March 1945, with Russian troops just a hundred miles away from Peenemünde, von Braun led several hundred colleagues south to Bavaria where they eventually surrendered to American troops. In America, von Braun worked on intercontinental ballistic rockets for the U.S. military and later rockets capable of launching astronauts into space and to the moon. When he died of cancer in 1977, he was considered the greatest rocket engineer of the twentieth century.

Wernher von Braun, arm in cast, with some members of the V-2 rocket team following their surrender to American troops in 1945

BOEING B-29 SUPERFORTRESS

The crew of the B-29 Waddy's Wagon re-enact their nose art

The B-29 holds a unique place in aviation history. It is the first and only airplane to deliver atomic weapons in war.

The four-engine B-29 was one of the largest airplanes used in World War II. It was also one of the most advanced, with a pressurized cabin, a fire control system, and remote-controlled machine gun turrets. Though designed for high-altitude strategic bombing, most of its missions over Japan were low-level incendiary attacks on Japanese cities. The exceptions were the two high-level atomic attacks that destroyed Hiroshima and Nagasaki in 1945.

The B-29 became operational in 1944. It had a crew of eleven, a maximum speed of 357 miles per hour, a range of 3,250 miles, and a ceiling of 33,600 feet. It carried a bomb load of twenty thousand pounds and defensive armament consisted of ten turrets and a tail position mounting twin .50-caliber machine guns.

The B-29s carrying the atomic devices, *Enola Gay* and *Bock's Car*, flew their missions unarmed. Colonel Paul Tibbets, commander of the *Enola Gay*, had discovered that an unarmed B-29 could fly four thousand feet higher and was faster and more maneuverable, significantly reducing its risk of being attacked by Japanese fighters. This was important, because the B-29s would be flying without fighter protection. When Tibbets ordered mechanics to strip the B-29s of their machine guns, they thought he was crazy and christened the two bombers *Sitting Target One* and *Sitting Target Two*.

On August 6, 1945, at 8:15:17 A.M., *Enola Gay*'s bomb-bay doors snapped open and Little Boy, the world's first atomic bomb, was released over Hiroshima. At 8:16 A.M., the nine-thousand-pound device exploded, dramatically heralding the age of nuclear warfare.

The *Enola Gay* became a subject of anti-nuclear war controversy in 1995 during an exhibition at the National Air and Space Museum, which led to a modification of its display. Tibbets retired from the Air Force with the rank of brigadier general and died in 2007. In his will he said that he did not want a funeral service or headstone because he did not want them to become sites for anti-nuclear demonstrations. He was cremated and his ashes scattered over the English Channel.

CONVENTIONAL BOMB

Few weapons of destruction have as rich a legacy or such variety as the conventional bomb. There's just something about blasting an object to smithereens or blowing it to kingdom come that is inspiring to man's destructive imagination. Conventional bombs run the gamut: the Black Cat, cherry bomb, and M-80 firecrackers; grenades; non-lethal smoke; very lethal fragmentation, incendiary, and cluster bombs; and multi-ton behemoths capable of sinking ships or flattening entire city blocks. They can be "dumb" (unguided) or "smart" (contain guidance devices); dropped by sophisticated aircraft or triggered by an individual wearing a suicide corset. But unlike atomic, chemical, or biological warfare bombs, a virtue (though, admittedly, a dubious one) of conventional bombs is that they have a localized impact of short duration.

Conventional bombs are containers filled with explosive material and a triggering device, called a fuse. When the fuse is activated, it causes a sudden and violent exothermic chemical reaction—in other words, the bomb goes "boom." The area destroyed or damaged by a bomb is called a blast radius. With some exceptions, the bigger the bomb, the larger the blast radius.

Though Allied conventional bomb tonnage was higher in the Vietnam War (7.8 million tons) than World War II (about 3.3 million tons), the destruction bombs wreaked during World War II is more famous.

One of the most famous—and most controversial—bombings during World War II was Operation Thunderclap, the bombing of Dresden, Germany, over February 13–14, 1945. One of the great cultural centers of Europe, Dresden was known as "the German Florence" because of its magnificent rococo art collections and splendid baroque buildings. In an around-the-clock bombing mission beginning on the night of February 13, Royal Air Force and then United States Army Air Force bombers attacked the city. The bombings created a gigantic firestorm in which temperatures reached 1,100 degrees Fahrenheit. When it was over, more than 1,600 square acres had been destroyed and as many as 135,000 were killed.

Author Kurt Vonnegut, Jr., was a prisoner of war and part of a work crew stationed in Dresden at the time. His experience surviving the Dresden bombing formed the basis of his novel *Slaughterhouse Five*.

A production line of 500-pound bombs in a bomb plant

BATTLESHIP

The battleship is the largest and most powerful of the "big gun" warships. By their mere presence—known as "a fleet in being"—they were capable of diffusing tension or changing strategy. They figured in some of the most famous naval battles in history, including Trafalgar (1805), Jutland (1916), and the Battle of Leyte Gulf (1944). Though no nation today maintains any in its navy, the battleship (and its predecessor "line-of-battle ship" from which the term "battleship" derived) was the symbol of maritime dominance and national prestige on the high seas for centuries.

The invention of armor plate in the mid-nineteenth century led to the development of the modern battleship. The most famous of these early steel battleships was the British Royal Navy's *Dreadnought*, launched in 1906. The mightiest ship at the time of its launching, the *Dreadnought* so influenced naval ship design that its name became a generic term for battleships built during that time, and the later, larger super-dreadnaughts.

The Japanese *Yamato* and *Musashi*, both launched in 1940, were the largest battleships ever built. When fully loaded, they each weighed almost 73,000 tons. Their main batteries were nine 18-inch cannon capable of firing a 3,200-pound shell up to 26 miles. The largest and most famous battleships in the U.S. Navy were the *Iowa* class, which included the *Iowa*, *New Jersey*, *Missouri*, and *Wisconsin*.

By the time World War II began, the battleship was being eclipsed by the aircraft carrier as the ultimate symbol of naval power. For the most part, battleships provided artillery support for amphibious landings. On the rare instances when they did fight each other, as the battleships USS *South Dakota* and *Washington* did against the Japanese battleship *Kirishima*, the results were not decisive. In that engagement, the *South Dakota* and *Kirishima* were heavily damaged, the latter so much so that it had to be scuttled.

Perhaps the battleship's finest hour as a symbol occurred on September 2, 1945, when the Japanese delegation boarded the USS *Missouri* to sign the treaty that ended World War II. The *Missouri*, commissioned in 1944 and the last battleship built for the U.S. Navy, would ultimately earn eleven battle stars. It was modernized in 1984 and saw action in the First Gulf War in 1991. It was finally retired from the U.S. Navy in 1995. It is now a museum, anchored in Pearl Harbor, Hawaii.

The USS *Wisconsin* firing a broadside of its 16-inch main guns

CRUISER

They are the descendents of frigates, ships designed in the period before wireless communication and used to quickly deliver messages between ships. Cruisers got their name from their primary function—to cruise in search of enemy merchant ships. Because this role required them to act independently, cruisers had to be fast and powerful enough to defend themselves.

For many years, the size and firepower of cruisers varied considerably. It was not until the Washington Naval Treaty of 1922, the first real international arms control agreement, that some order was established. The five top sea powers of the period—the United States, Great Britain, Japan, France, and Italy—met to establish restrictions on the size and number of ships. The largest were battleships, followed by aircraft carriers, cruisers, and destroyers. The treaty stated that cruisers were limited in size to ten thousand tons of displacement and cannon no larger than 8 inches (the diameter of the shell). The treaty had enormous impact on cruiser design and led to technological innovations that increased speed and overall firepower while keeping down the tonnage.

Cruisers played a pivotal role in the United States' first offensive operation against the Japanese in the Pacific, the battle for Guadalcanal (1942–1943). The naval campaign for the island would be the last time that surface warships had the primary role in battle. In three of the engagements, the Battle of Savo Island, the Battle of Cape Esperance, and the Battle of Tassafaronga, cruisers were the largest warships. And, in a fourth, the Naval Battle of Guadalcanal, five U.S. Navy cruisers fought a superior Japanese fleet built around two battleships. These battles proved to be the last hurrah for cruisers as an independent warship.

Cruisers proved incapable of defending themselves against air attack. As a result, cruisers tactics changed. They began operating as part of an integrated fleet, generally providing defensive support for aircraft carriers or in support of amphibious operations. Cruisers would remain in this subsidiary role until the late twentieth century and the development of guided missiles suitable for naval operations.

Lieutenant Eugene B. Ely flies off a flight deck temporarily attached to the heavy cruiser USS *Pennsylvania* in the first successful U.S. Navy aircraft launch

DESTROYER

With a speed of 40 knots or more, destroyers are known as "greyhounds of the sea." They have also been nicknamed "tin cans" because they lacked the protective armor of the larger battleships and cruisers.

Originally called a "Torpedo Boat Destroyer," the destroyer came into being as a countermeasure against a new type of warship, the high-speed torpedo boat that made a devastating debut in the Chilean Civil War (1891) and the Sino-Japanese War (1894). The torpedo boat was a small vessel capable of dashing in close to large ships, attacking with torpedoes, and speeding away before the slower, less maneuverable cruisers and battleships could respond. By the time World War I began, all the great sea powers had destroyers in their fleets. This turned out to be fortunate for Allies' navies because the destroyer was an effective warship against Germany's U-boat submarine.

Before the late twentieth century, standard main armament for a destroyer was five-inch cannon and torpedoes. Today, they also include missiles. The installation of submarine-tracking sonar during World War II greatly increased the anti-submarine effectiveness of the destroyer.

E.J. Jernigan was a sailor who served on the destroyer USS *Saufley*, named after naval aviation pioneer Lieutenant Richard C. Saufley, during World War II. In 1943, the *Saufley* was providing escort for troop ships in the Solomon Islands of the South Pacific. In his memoir, *Tin Can Man*, he recalled, "Everyone sweated during combat. Sweat during battle had an odor much stronger than regular sweat. . . . It also seemed that the ship's sides sweated more when maneuvering at high speed with all the guns firing. If you were below decks, you could tell when the fight moved in closer by the type of gunfire. First the 5-inch, then the 40-mm, and then the 20-mm would cut loose." One day, curiosity over seeing the fight got the best of him. Just as he opened a hatch and stuck his head out, "every gun on the ship opened up to the starboard side at four dive bombers releasing bombs. . . . The blast of the guns nearly took my eyeballs, eyelids, and ears off. I went back to the lower level faster than a prairie dog can get in a hole." The *Saufley* succeeded in shooting down the four planes, and the ship's captain was decorated with the Silver Star.

A Polish destroyer (foreground) serving with the British Royal Navy during World War II

AIRCRAFT CARRIER

The aircraft carrier is a floating mobile air base that, ever since World War II, has been the preeminent symbol of a nation's sea power.

Aircraft carriers were first used in World War I, but it was not until the second world-spanning conflict that they achieved their preeminence. The supremacy of aircraft carriers over all other warships was brutally demonstrated on December 7, 1941, when the Japanese Imperial Fleet launched a surprise air strike against the U.S. Navy base at Pearl Harbor, Hawaii, and sunk or severely damaged most of the navy's battleships. The Battle of the Coral Sea (1942) was the first naval air-to-air engagement where opposing fleets did not see each other. The Battle of Midway demonstrated that even aging and obsolete aircraft could make a decisive contribution to victory.

Depending on the size, aircraft carriers hold from thirty-four to about a hundred aircraft. The smallest carriers are the escort carriers, nicknamed "jeep carriers." The largest are the nuclear-powered supercarriers that have a crew of five thousand men and (since 1979) women.

Lieutenant (junior grade) Gerald Ford was a gunnery division officer on the escort carrier USS *Monterey* during World War II. The *Monterey* was part of the U.S. Navy Third Fleet when the enormous Typhoon Cobra hit the fleet off the coast of the Philippines in December 1944. Ford was in his cabin when the ship's captain sounded general quarters. In order to get to his post in the bridge, Ford had to first exit onto the flight deck. He had reached the base of the bridge when a gigantic wave broke over the ship, pitching the *Monterey* 25 degrees. The next thing Ford knew, he was skimming across the flight deck "as if I were on a toboggan." He saved himself from falling into the ocean by grabbing onto the deck combing, a two-inch-high steel lip fastened along the entire edge of the flight deck, designed to keep tools from slipping overboard. But his troubles had just begun.

The storm was so severe that lashed-down planes in the hangar deck broke free from their cables and smashed into each other, igniting the gasoline in their tanks. Ford led the team of firefighters into the hangar deck and successfully extinguished the blaze. Years later, as president of the United States, "I remembered that fire at the height of the typhoon, and I considered it a marvelous metaphor for the ship of state."

USS *Theodore Roosevelt* nuclear-powered aircraft carrier with its squadrons on its flight deck

ATOMIC BOMB

Nuclear bombs (atomic, hydrogen, neutron) are the most powerful bombs in the world. They get their explosive force through nuclear reactions that occur when atoms are rapidly split apart (fission) or when atomic nuclei are forcibly joined to form a heavier nucleus (fusion). International treaties have identified atomic bombs as weapons of mass destruction because of their ability to kill large numbers of people and cause immense damage.

Development of the atomic bomb in the United States was prompted by a letter by the theoretical physicist Albert Einstein who wrote to President Franklin Roosevelt, warning him that Nazi Germany was working on building an atomic bomb. This caused Roosevelt to authorize the Manhattan Project, the top-secret program to develop the atomic bomb. Then-Colonel Leslie Groves was the overall administrator of the project and physicist J. Robert Oppenheimer was the director of the scientific teams tasked with creating the device. The Manhattan Project included some of the most brilliant men in science.

The first nuclear test occurred on July 16, 1945, near Alamogordo, New Mexico. No one knew if the device would explode, or if the triggering of the device would lead to a chain reaction that would consume the earth. When the test proved successful, Oppenheimer realized that the world would never be the same again. He later expressed his feelings in part by quoting a verse from the Hindu scripture, the *Bhagavad-Gita*, uttered by the god Vishnu, "Now I am become Death, the destroyer of worlds."

The atomic bomb was used twice, both against Japan. The first bomb, named Little Boy, was dropped on Hiroshima on August 6, 1945. When the Japanese government did not respond, a second bomb was dropped on Nagasaki on August 9. The Japanese government then capitulated, ending World War II.

After the war, the United States (and other nations) conducted above-ground nuclear tests in remote regions. One such test occurred in 1946 near the central Pacific Ocean atoll of Bikini. According to legend, French swimwear Louis Reard was so appalled by the forced evacuation of the Bikini islanders and the subsequent atomic bomb test that he named his new two-piece women's bathing suit the "bikini" in honor of the islanders.

The atomic bomb mushroom cloud over Nagasaki

JULIUS ROBERT OPPENHEIMER

(1904–1967)

The father of the atomic bomb was born in New York City, the son of a successful Jewish businessman. He taught theoretical physics at the University of California, Berkley and the California Institute of Technology, where he established himself as the founder of modern theoretical physics. A cultured man, Oppenheimer had a wide range of interests outside of science, including foreign languages, art, literature, and politics. It was the latter, with his friendships with left-wing and communist sympathizers, that would cause an abrupt end to his career.

Oppenheimer was brought into the top-secret Manhattan Project, the cover name for the atomic bomb program, in 1942. The military commander of the program, then-Colonel Leslie Groves, later chose Oppenheimer to become the leader of all the scientific teams working on the project. It was in this role as director of the project that he earned the title "father of the atomic bomb."

After the war, Oppenheimer became a target for anti-communist hysteria and stripped of his security clearances in 1954, effectively ending his career in nuclear physics. Oppenheimer died of cancer in 1967 at the age of 62. He was cremated and his ashes scattered in the sea off the coast of his beach house on the island of St. John's in the Virgin Islands.

In September 1944, Colonel Paul Tibbets, commander of the B-29 squadron that would drop the atomic bomb, visited Oppenheimer at the Manhattan Project headquarters in Los Alamos, New Mexico. At one point in his tour, Tibbets saw Oppenheimer stop in mid-stride, turn around and enter an office.

Inside was a disheveled and unshaven man staring fixedly at a blackboard filled with equations. Tibbets wondered if the man "might be the building janitor taking an unauthorized rest after a night out."

Oppenheimer stood behind the man and both stared at the equations. Oppenheimer then erased one part of an equation. The seated man remained immobile as Oppenheimer then wrote on the blackboard a new set of symbols. When Oppenheimer added the final symbol, Enrico Fermi, one of the founders of nuclear physics, leaped up and shouted, "I've been looking for that mistake for two days!"

Albert Einstein (left) and J. Robert Oppenheimer (right) in a meeting at Princeton University

CENTURION TANK

The Centurion main battle tank was one of post-World War II's most successful tank designs. It became operational in 1945 and much-modified versions are still in service. Though designed and built in Great Britain, the Centurion is most famous as the main battle tank for the Israeli Defense Forces (IDF). It was instrumental in the Israeli victories in the Six Day War (1967) and the Yom Kippur War (1973).

More than 4,400 Centurions were built, in a wide number of variants. A standard Centurion was a 51-ton tank whose thickest armor was 6 inches. It carried a crew of four and had a maximum speed of 21 miles per hour. Its main gun was a 105-mm cannon, with secondary armament including one heavy and two light machine guns.

The Centurion amply proved its value to the IDF in the Yom Kippur War. Egypt and Syria launched a coordinated offensive on the holiest day in the Jewish calendar, catching the IDF flat-footed. In the north, Syria with 1,500 Soviet model T-54, T-55 and T-62 tanks, was determined to re-capture the Golan Heights that had been in Israel's possession since 1967. They were able to easily seize their initial objectives. Because of the simultaneous Egyptian attack in the southwest, the IDF could deploy only 170 tanks against the Syrians. Even though the Syrian army had a tank superiority ranging from five-to-one to as high as twelve-to-one in some areas, Israeli combined infantry and armor tactics prevented the Syrians from seizing strategic bridges over the Jordan River.

A three-hundred-strong joint Iraqi and Jordanian tank force reinforced the Syrians and a fierce two-day tank battle began on October 12, 1973. Tanks closed to within point-blank range, no more than two hundred yards during the slugging match. In the end, the Syrian, Iraqi, and Jordanian forces had lost 1,150 tanks. Israeli losses were just 250 tanks, with about 150 of those repairable.

AK-47 Assault Rifle

The Kalashnikov AK-47 is the most successful assault rifle in history. Since its introduction in 1947, an estimated 75 million AK-47s have been manufactured. Cheap and often cheaply made, the AK-47 is easy to use, reliable, and powerful. Initially the standard assault rifle for Soviet troops, the AK-47 has since achieved iconographic status as a symbol of anti-Western—specifically anti-American—ideology.

Mikhail Kalashnikov was a World War II Soviet Army tank commander who wanted to build an assault rifle to fight Germans. Instead, it became one of the major weapons in the cold war power struggle between the Soviet Union and the United States.

The AK-47 weighs 9 ½ pounds and fires a 7.62 cartridge. Cartridges are fed into the chamber from a metal "banana clip." It has a high rate of fire capability, up to six hundred rounds per minute. The AK-47's reliability is legendary. With so few moving parts, it is almost impossible to jam. One of the more famous demonstrations involves the dragging of an AK-47 through thick mud and then shooting it.

The AK-47 became the weapon of choice for insurrectionists and terrorists. Terrorist Khalid Islambouli used an AK-47 to assassinate Egyptian president Anwar Sadat in 1981. Osama bin Laden has repeatedly been photographed and videotaped holding an AK-47. And the AK-47 was so important to rebel success in the overthrow of the Mozambique government that its silhouette was incorporated into the design of the Mozambique flag. Its silhouette is also in the Hezbollah flag. In some societies, the AK-47 has so integrated itself into society that possession of it is regarded as a symbol of manhood and a rite of passage.

The AK-47 has even become furniture. The French designer Philippe Starck created the AK-47 Table Light, part of a series of lamp designs that include the Beretta pistol and M-16 assault rifle.

Though Russia no longer manufactures the AK-47, it is being built in twenty other countries. It is the standard assault rifle for the armies of more than a hundred nations.

Iraqi National Guard soldiers equipped with AK-47 assault rifles

MIKHAIL KALASHNIKOV

(1919–)

The designer of the AK-47 was the son of Russian peasants and had little formal weapon design training. Though his assault rifle would become the most successful small arm in history, because Kalashnikov created his weapon in the Communist-era Soviet Union, he never received a dime in royalties.

Kalashnikov was drafted into the Soviet Union's Red Army in 1938 and trained as a tank driver-mechanic. When the Germans invaded the Soviet Union in World War II, he was a T-34 tank commander. He was wounded in the Battle of Bryansk, about two hundred miles southwest of Moscow. It was while he was in a hospital recovering from his wounds that he overheard wounded infantrymen in the ward complaining about the poor quality of their weapons. His own similarly bad experience with the early Soviet rifles caused him to think about designing a reliable automatic weapon.

He completed his first design in 1944, but it was rejected. His next design, the "Mikhtim," was an entry in the assault rifle competition held by the government in 1946. This was approved, and it became the prototype for the Automatic Kalashnikov 1947, shortened to AK-47.

Kalashnikov's concept was a weapon that was so simple to construct that it could be built by unskilled workers and so easy to handle it could be disassembled and used by soldiers fighting in the arctic, wearing thick gloves. Some military experts have called the AK-47 a piece of junk, and it has suffered from poor machining and workmanship. But despite those deficiencies it could still reliably fire under conditions that would cause its western counterpart, the M-16 to jam.

Over the years, Kalashnikov's feelings about the AK-47 and how it has been used have alternated between regret and pride. He has said, "I wish I had invented a lawn mower." And, on other occasions, stated, "I invented it for protection of the motherland. I have no regrets and bear no responsibility for how politicians have used it."

Mikhail Kalashnikov at an event in 2007 celebrating the 60th anniversary of the AK-47

MiG-15

The symbol of Soviet air power in the 1950s was the MiG-15 jet fighter. One of the first post-World War II swept-wing aircraft, the MiG easily outperformed the straight-wing American and British jet fighters of the era, and in some respects was superior to the top American swept-wing fighter of the period, the F-86 Sabre.

Designed by the outstanding Russian design team of Artem Mikoyan and Mikhail Gurevich (the "M" and "G" in MiG), and introduced in 1947, the MiG-15 was created to shoot down B-29 bombers. The MiG-15 was a single-seat fighter with a top speed of 668 miles per hour and a range of about 750 miles. Standard armament consisted of two 23-mm cannon and one 37-mm cannon. It could also carry a bomb or rocket load of up to 220 pounds. The Soviet Union extensively exported the MiG-15 to its communist allies, such as China and North Korea, as well as other anti-American nations such as Egypt.

The MiG-15 became famous during the Korean War. It debuted in combat on November 30, 1950, when a MiG-15 damaged a B-29 during a bombing raid over North Korea. The communist fighter attacked and flew away so fast that escorting F-80 Shooting Stars were only able to get a fleeting glance of it. Though the F-86 Sabre was able to hold its own against the MiG-15, the American Air Force was eager to obtain an undamaged MiG-15 for examination. This led to an unusual psychological warfare effort launched in 1953 codenamed Operation Moolah.

According to General Mark Clark, then commander in chief of United Nations forces in Korea, the idea for Operation Moolah came from United Press correspondent Dick Applegate while he was "communing with a bottle of brandy in the Seoul correspondents' billet." The idea was to offer $100,000 to the first Communist pilot of a MiG-15 who defected with his aircraft and brought it undamaged to South Korea. Any subsequent pilot would receive $50,000. In September 1953, Clark later wrote, "A North Korean pilot zoomed his MiG out of nowhere, landed at Kimpo Airfield near Seoul and asked asylum. He claimed he never had heard of the $100,000 reward offer but was more than happy to accept the money." He added, "The Air Force got its $100,000 worth—and more."

The underside view of an Egyptian MiG-15

A-1 Skyraider

The Douglas A-1 Skyraider was a single-seat attack bomber of the 1950s, 1960s, and early 1970s. A propeller-driven anachronism in the jet age, the Skyraider had a remarkably long and successful career. At the time of the first prototype's flight, in 1945, it was the largest production single-seat aircraft in the world. Though the Skyraider entered production too late for active service in World War II, it made up for it during the Korean War (1950–1953), where it saw extensive service and earned a reputation as the best close-support aircraft of the Korean War. The Skyraider was at the end of its operational life when it fought in the Vietnam War. One of its primary roles in Vietnam was in support of air rescue missions of downed aviators, as its weapon load and ten-hour flying time far surpassed the jets that were then available.

The Skyraider was designed by Ed Heinemann of Douglas Aircraft Company for the U.S. Navy, who requested a long-range high-performance dual-purpose dive and torpedo bomber. By the time production ceased in 1957, 3,180 Skyraiders in 28 variants had been built, making it one of the more successful post-World War II airplane designs. Depending on the variant, the A-1 had a top speed of 320 miles per hour, a range of 1,315 miles, and a ceiling of 28,500 feet. Standard armament included four 20-mm cannon and up to eight thousand pounds of bombs or missiles (a load that was almost half the dry weight of the airplane itself).

Colonel Bernard F. Fisher was an A-1 pilot in the Vietnam War. On March 10, 1966, his Skyraider was one of six supporting friendly troops in a firefight against communist forces in the A Shau Valley. During the engagement, an A-1 piloted by Major Wayne "Jump" Myers was severely damaged, forcing Myers to crash land on an airstrip just two hundred yards away from enemy troops. A-1s were supposed to provide support for rescue helicopters, but the nearest helicopter was thirty minutes away. Ignoring enemy ground fire that struck his aircraft, Fisher landed his A-1 near Myers' wrecked plane. After Myers climbed into the back seat of Fisher's plane, Fisher took off, weaving past shell holes and debris scattered on the damaged airstrip. For this act of rescue, Fisher became the first member of the United States Air Force to receive the Medal of Honor in the Vietnam War.

An ordnance crew fits bombs to the underwing mounts of a Skyraider as the pilot in the cockpit looks on

F-86 Sabre

Triple ace (16 victories) Captain Joseph McConnell in the cockpit of his F-86 "Beauteous Butch II"

The North American F-86 Sabre was the U.S. Air Force's first swept-winged jet fighter and its last true dogfighter. It first flew in 1947, became operational with the Air Force in 1948, and by the time its last squadron was retired in Portugal in 1980, almost ten thousand aircraft in twenty variants had been produced and it had flown in the air forces of twenty-four different countries.

The F-86 benefited from German World War II jet fighter development. The Sabre incorporated many technological and design innovations. It was the first American jet to have a swept-wing configuration. It was the first to feature a "flying tail" that enables the aircraft to maneuver at high altitudes. It also incorporated full-span leading-edge slats to prevent pitch-up. The F-86's identifying feature was the nose of its fuselage: an open nose-inlet that delivered air to the turbojet engine located behind the pilot.

Standard armament was six .50-caliber machine guns, three on each side of the fuselage, near the nose. Variants allowed it to carry two 1,000-pound bombs, sixteen 5-inch rockets, or twenty-four 2.75-inch rockets. It had a maximum speed at sea level of 687 mph, a service ceiling of 49,600 feet, and a rate of climb of 8,100 feet per minute at sea level.

The Sabre was the jet that defined air-to-air combat in the Korean War (1950–1953). Air Force General William Momyer called it "our best fighter. The F-86 was superior to the enemy's best fighter, the MiG-15, in level flight below 30,000 feet and definitely superior at diving speeds greater than mach .95." Sabre pilot Major George A. Davis, Jr., who racked up fourteen victories, was awarded the Medal of Honor when, in 1952, he and his wingman flew to the defense of a group of fighter-bombers being attacked by twelve MiG-15s. Captain Joseph McConnell, with sixteen victories, became the world's first jet triple ace. And America's top ace in the European Theater of Operations in World War II, Colonel Francis S. "Gabby" Gabreski, scored six and a half victories in the F-86 during the Korean War.

Brigadier General Chuck Yeager, USAF (Ret.), a World War II ace and test pilot who was the first man to break the sound barrier, said of the F-86, "I dearly loved the Sabre, almost as much as I enjoyed the P-51 from World War II days. It was a terrific plane to fly."

F-86 airplanes on the flight line getting ready for combat

Napalm

Ground crewmen secure napalm bombs to the wing of an AV-8B Harrier aircraft

Napalm is gasoline thickened to a gel and was one of the U.S. military's primary incendiary weapons in the Korean and Vietnam wars. The term "napalm" is taken from the first syllables of two of the fatty acids contained in coconut oil, <u>naph</u>thenate and <u>palm</u>itate, which were added to gasoline to produce an incendiary gel. Napalm resembles syrup or jelly, and can be translucent, pale, or brownish, and when exposed to air burns between 1,400 and 2,200 degrees Fahrenheit.

Napalm was developed during World War II by a team of scientists led by Harvard Professor Louis Fieser and patented in 1943. It was first used in France in July 1944. It was one of the most effective weapons against Japanese bunker emplacements. Humans caught in napalm attacks have little defense. The jellied mixture sticks to almost everything it touches and is almost impossible to remove. Death occurs by burning and carbon monoxide asphyxiation.

Napalm-based weaponry was used extensively during the Korean War. On the ground, napalm was projected by flamethrowing tanks, portable flamethrowers carried by troops, special land mines and 55-gallon drums triggered by explosives. One particularly effective method was called "golden rain." North Korean and Chinese Communist army tactics called for "human wave" attacks. When the surging mass of troops got within range, a napalm mixture was sprayed into the air above them, showering them with fire.

A new type of napalm was developed during the Vietnam War. Called Napalm-B, it was composed of 50 percent polystyrene thickener, 25 percent benzene, and 25 percent gasoline, and burned hotter and longer (ten minutes as opposed to thirty seconds) than earlier napalm. Napalm-B was manufactured by the Dow Chemical Company, and the brutal effects of napalm led antiwar activists to target the company with boycotts and demonstrations. The company's image, business, and profits were so negatively impacted that in 1969 the company, either deliberately or not, lost the renewal of its napalm contract with the government.

The term "napalm" has become generic for any attack involving flaming liquids. Napalm munitions remain in the arsenals of several nations. Though American forces were accused of using napalm bombs during the Iraq War, strictly speaking the flaming liquids were not napalm.

Bombs with a mixture of napalm and white phosphorus jelly dropped by Vietnamese AF Skyraider bombers during the Vietnam War

AIM-9 Sidewinder Missile

The AIM-9 Sidewinder missile is a supersonic, heat-seeking, air-to-air missile. It received the name "Sidewinder" after the rattlesnake, which finds its quarry through body heat, and the snake-like trajectory of early models. Introduced in 1953, the Sidewinder became operational in 1956. Easily upgraded, it remains in production. About 110,000 Sidewinders have been built.

The Sidewinder is 9 feet 4 inches long, 5 inches wide, and weighs 190 pounds. Depending on the model, it carries a high explosive fragmentation warhead weighing 20.8 or 25 pounds. It is powered by a solid-fuel rocket engine that can reach Mach 2.5 and has a range of ten to eighteen miles. The Sidewinder's guidance system is known as "fire and forget." Once released, the missile's infrared seeker locks onto the exhaust of its target and independently guides the Sidewinder, allowing the pilot to conduct other operations.

The Sidewinder was first used in combat in 1958. During one of these incidents, a Sidewinder smashed into a MiG-17, but failed to explode. The still-intact missile was removed and reverse-engineered by Soviet technicians. That experience, and Sidewinder plans obtained through espionage, enabled the Soviets to produce in 1961 the K-13, a virtual copy of the Sidewinder.

One of the largest air-to-air battles in the Vietnam War occurred on May 10, 1972, the first day of Operation Linebacker, an attack on strategic targets in North Vietnam. Navy Lieutenant Curtis Dosé was a wingman flying a Phantom F-4, part of an air attack on Kep airport north of Hanoi. As the squadron approached Kep, the pilots saw MiGs taking off to attack. Dosé and his leader streaked after two low-flying MiG-21s. Dosé's first Sidewinder shot missed, because the MiG had turned too sharply to effectively trigger the warhead's proximity fuse. Dosé fired a second Sidewinder, which flew up the MiG's exhaust and exploded. By the end of the day, eighteen Sidewinders were credited with shooting down eight out of eleven MiGs, making it one of the most successful air-to-air engagements for U.S. pilots in the war.

A U.S. Navy aviation ordinanceman assigned to
Strike Fighter Squardon 2 waits to arm an AIM-9X Sidewinder missle

SUBMARINE (NUCLEAR POWER)

The Holy Grail of the submarine service was the capability to travel vast distances for long periods of time while totally submerged. That goal was finally reached when, on 1954, the world's first nuclear-powered submarine, the USS *Nautilus*, was christened. Strictly speaking, the *Nautilus* was also the world's first true submarine. All submarines before it had to surface at some point in order to restore power and resupply air. This actually made them submersibles rather than submarines.

In its maiden voyage, the *Nautilus* traveled underwater 1,381 nautical miles from New London, Connecticut, to San Juan, Puerto Rico. Her next voyage was the history-making polar transit from Pearl Harbor, Hawaii, to Portland, England, in which the Nautilus became the first boat to travel over the North Pole.

Design innovations, including such advances as anechoic tiles and a shrouded propulsor drive that replaced the conventional propeller, expanded the parameters of stealth, depth, speed, and armament, ultimately making American-built submarines including the *Ohio*, *Los Angeles*, and *Seawolf* classes the standard by which all others are measured.

Admiral Hyman George Rickover is the father of the nuclear navy. Rickover was introduced to the possibility of developing nuclear power plants for the navy in 1946. By 1949, he had become the director of the Naval Reactors Branch in the Bureau of Ships. In this role he shaped the future of nuclear warships for the U.S. Navy. When he retired in 1982, after 64 years of service, nuclear power plants were not only in submarines, but also in such surface warships as aircraft carriers and cruisers. Tom Allen, one of his biographers, noted, "Rickover was a complex man and genius, and not appreciated by his colleagues in the Navy for leading it away from coal and oil propulsion. Nevertheless, he was a giant in our time, and there may never be another quite like him."

B-52 STRATOFORTRESS

The B-52 Stratofortress, nicknamed "BUFF" for Big Ugly Fat Fellow, is a long-range jet strategic bomber flown only by the United States Air Force. It has been on duty since 1955, making it the longest active duty strategic bomber in the history of military aviation. Originally built to carry nuclear bombs, its primary role is now conventional aerial warfare.

With an average combat radius of 4,480 miles, the B-52 has the longest range of any bomber and carries a heavy strategic or tactical weapons load. Its economy in operation and high sub-sonic performance (maximum speed: 650 mph) compared to the rest of the USAF strategic bomber fleet has enabled it to remain in active service. The B-52 is a monster, with a height of 40 feet 8 inches and a wingspan of 185 feet. The B-52 has a maximum bomb load of sixty thousand pounds and is capable of dropping or launching a wide array of conventional weapons including free-fall gravity bombs, cluster bombs, and precision-guided ordnance. A total of 744 B-52s were built, with the last delivered in October 1962.

When military aircraft are placed on reserve status, they are flown to the Aerospace Maintenance and Regeneration Center at Davis-Monthan Air Force Base in Arizona. Referred to as the Boneyard, this place is usually the last stop for most aircraft. In the last decade of the twentieth century, as part of the 1991 Strategic Arms Reduction Treaty signed by the United States and Russia, 365 B-52s in the Boneyard, after they had been stripped of all usable parts, were destroyed. A 13,000-pound guillotine chopped each B-52 into five pieces, creating 90 tons of junk. The pile sat outside for three months under observance by orbiting Russian satellites and additional verification by on-site inspection.

Presently 94 B-52Hs are on the active roster, with Barksdale Air Force Base in Louisiana supporting 57 and Minot Air Force Base in North Dakota supporting 36 aircraft. The original defense armament of a pod in the tail of four .50-caliber machine guns was changed to one Vulcan 20-mm Gatling cannon for the H model. All operating B-52s have had their tail guns removed.

A B-52 with a bomb load display

LOCKHEED U-2

The cockpit of a U-2

The U-2 is a single-engine aircraft initially used by the Central Intelligence Agency and later by the United States Air Force to conduct high-altitude, long-distance photo reconnaissance.

The U-2 was built in response to growing cold war tensions between the United States and the Soviet Union. When the Soviet Union became a nuclear power in the 1950s and was working on intercontinental capability to deliver nuclear warheads, President Dwight Eisenhower authorized the development of a special aircraft designed to conduct "pre-hostilities reconnaissance" over potential enemy territory. Designed by the legendary Clarence "Kelly" Johnson and built at the Skunk Works, Lockheed's special aircraft design division, the U-2 is one of the most unusual aircraft ever built. With a wingspan of 103 feet, it is essentially a powered glider. It has a ceiling of more than 85,000 feet, can remain in the air for up to twelve hours (much to the discomfort of the pilot's posterior), and has a range of almost 6,500 miles. Overflights of Soviet and Communist China airspace began in 1956. They stopped when, on May 1, 1960, the Soviet Union shot down a U-2 piloted by Francis Gary Powers, who was captured alive. The Soviet Union reaped great international benefit from the incident. Powers was released to the United States in 1962.

Ben Rich, who later became Johnson's successor at the Skunk Works, was a member of the design team working on the U-2. One of the early problems deviling him was an engine condition that caused twenty quarts of oil (out of a total of sixty-four) to be sprayed onto the cockpit windshield. Rich later wrote that, at one point, one of the mechanics on the projects suggested, "Why don't we just stuff Kotex around the oil filter and absorb the mess before it hits the windshield?" With great trepidation, Rich approached Johnson, who had a volatile temper. After hearing Rich out, Johnson raised his eyebrows, then shrugged his shoulders and said, "What the hell, give it a shot." Cartons of industrial-sized sanitary napkins were quickly airlifted to the Skunk Works' headquarters in Burbank, California. "And, by God, it worked!" Rich observed.

SKUNK WORKS

It's rare that a business entity so influences a field that it becomes the definition for the type of work it does. *The New Oxford American Dictionary* defines "skunk works" as: "An experimental laboratory or department of a company or institution, typically smaller than and independent of its main research division." Lockheed-Martin's Skunk Works has an extraordinary reputation in the aerospace industry. The Skunk Works has produced some of the most innovative aircraft in history, including the U-2 (1955), the SR-71 Blackbird (1966), the F-117 Nighthawk stealth ground-attack aircraft (1983), and the F-22 Raptor (2005).

Created during World War II in 1943, the War Department (predecessor to the Department of Defense) asked Lockheed aircraft designer Clarence "Kelly" Johnson to design a jet prototype in 180 days that could combat German jets that were becoming operational. He was ordered to do it under strict secrecy. Johnson, the son of Swedish immigrants and known as "Kelly" because of his Irish-like temper, rented a gigantic circus tent, set it up on a vacant lot in the Lockheed complex that was downwind of a nearby plastics factory, and went to work with his design team. At the same time, "L'l Abner" comic strip creator Al Capp introduced Hairless Joe and Lonesome Polecat who brewed "Kickapoo Joy Juice" in the foul-smelling "Skonk Works." The designers in the tent, working under an equally odoriferous atmospheric environment, soon took to answering the phone, "Hello, Skonk Works." The name stuck. Finally, in 1960, the strip's publisher, United Feature Syndicate, objected to the company's use of the name. Lockheed changed the name to "Skunk Works" and trademarked it. As for that first aircraft the team had to design, they built the prototype of the P-80 Shooting Star in 143 days, 37 days ahead of schedule.

Kelly Johnson was enshrined in the Aviation Hall of Fame in 1974 and is one of the most honored aerospace designers in the world. He twice received the prestigious Collier Trophy (the industry's top award), the Daniel Guggenheim Medal for outstanding "contribution to the advancement of aeronautics," the National Security Medal, and was elected a Fellow of the Royal Aeronatical Society. Hal Hibbard was Johnson's first boss at Lockheed. He was so impressed with Johnson's design skills he later said, "That damned Swede can actually see air!" Of Hibbard's comment, Johnson said that it was the greatest compliment he had ever received.

Kelly Johnson (left) and Francis Gary Powers (right)

Tactical Nuclear Weapons

Tactical nuclear weapons are low-yield nuclear explosives, sometimes called "mini-nukes," designed for use in battlefield situations. The group includes land mines, depth charges, torpedoes, short-range missiles, demolition munitions, and artillery shells.

Most of the development of tactical nuclear weapons occurred at the height of the cold war, during the 1950s. Before that, the nuclear weapons in the United States and Soviet Union arsenals were high-yield strategic weapons designed to destroy large population centers and seriously damage a country's ability to wage war. The first nuclear artillery shell developed by the United States was a 280-mm shell with a fission warhead and codenamed Shot Grable. It was fired as part of Operation Upshot-Knothole on May 25, 1953, at the government's nuclear weapons test reservation known as the Nevada Test Site, about sixty-five miles northwest of Las Vegas. Shot from a cannon nicknamed "Atomic Annie," it produced a yield estimated at fifteen kilotons. One of the smallest tactical nuclear weapons was the M-388 Davy Crocket, a projectile designed to be fired from a recoilless rifle. It weighed about seventy-six pounds and had a yield of between ten and twenty tons. It was tested on July 7, 1962, at the Nevada Test Site. A second test, on July 17, was the last above ground nuclear weapons test conducted at the Nevada Test Site.

The term "tactical" refers to the weapon's military application. But, politically, all nuclear weapons are "strategic" because of the larger public response that would occur upon their use. Tactical nuclear weapons became a source of controversy in the West, particularly in Europe, where most of the weapons were stockpiled in anticipation of a war between the Soviet Union and its Eastern European allies, and the United States and its NATO allies in Western Europe.

After the collapse of the Soviet Union, the United States in 1991 removed about 1,300 nuclear artillery shells from Europe. Russia responded in kind in 1992.

Despite international efforts to limit and eliminate them, tactical nuclear weapons remain in the inventories of all the nations possessing nuclear technology.

A Pershing II tactical nuclear missile, without warhead, in a test launch

Tupolev Tu-95 Bear

A close-up view of the right side of the tail section of a Soviet Tupolev Tu-95 Bear aircraft showing two crewmen inside.

The most successful bomber to be produced by Soviet aerospace designers is the Tupolev Tu-95, which the North Atlantic Treaty Organization (NATO) code-named "Bear." With four distinctive contra-rotating turbo-prop engines, the Bear became operational in 1956 and, like its United States counterpart the B-52, has been in use ever since.

With fifteen variants, including models capable of conducting electronic intelligence gathering missions, more than five hundred Bears have been built. The Bear has a crew of seven, a top speed of 570 miles per hour, and a ceiling of about 39,700 feet. It carries up to 33,000 pounds of air-to-surface missiles. For defense, earlier Bears had as many as six 23-mm cannon. Later variants have either one or two 23-mm cannon located in a tail turret. Unlike the B-52, which is only used by the United States, the Bear is also in the inventories of the Ukrainian and Indian air forces.

Ever since the start of the cold war, the United States and the Soviet Union, now Russia, have conducted missions near or over each other's airspace, gathering aerial intelligence-gathering missions and testing defense warning capability. In June 1999, two Bear bombers took off from their base near Moscow and flew over the Norwegian Sea toward the United States. They were participating in Russia's largest military exercise since the end of the cold war. Four F-15 USAF Eagle fighters and a P-3 Orion patrol aircraft intercepted the bombers near Iceland and escorted them around the island. The Bears then veered off and returned to Moscow.

In September 1999, USAF radar detected a pair of Bears heading toward the Alaska coast. When the bombers got within 90 miles of the Alaskan coast, and before the scrambled air force fighters arrived, the Bears turned around and headed back to base.

Sometimes opposing pilots will get so close to each other that they will wave and carry on hand-signal conversations and take photographs with their personal cameras.

A Soviet TU-95 Bear flying past a United States Navy aircraft carrier

MiG-21 Fishbed

A map showing the radius of a MiG-21 based in Cuba and Nicaragua

The delta-winged MiG-21 is a supersonic attack aircraft that has the distinction of being the most widely manufactured (11,000) jet aircraft. It became operational in 1959. With an airframe service life of up to thirty years, the MiG-21 is also one of the longest serving. More than three thousand MiG-21s are in active service in the air forces of more than forty countires.

Codenamed "Fishbed" by NATO, its nickname in Russia is "balalaika" because of its resemblance to the Russian stringed instrument. The MiG-21 is a single-engine, single-seat supersonic aircraft primarily designed as a fighter. Other variants include aerial reconnaissance and dive-bomb versions capable of delivering tactical nuclear munitions. Armament includes a variety of cannon and air-to-air missile configurations. The MiG-21 is able to reach speeds up to Mach 2. It has a ceiling of 58,400 feet and a range of 751 miles.

The MiG-21 became famous during the Vietnam War where, unofficially, Russian and Chinese Communist pilots together with their North Vietnamese counterparts flew it against United States Air Force and Navy aircraft.

The Soviet Union widely exported the MiG-21, and it was the main fighter in the air forces of Egypt, Syria, and Iraq, fighting in the Six Day War and the Yom Kippur War against Mirage IIIs, F-4 Phantoms, A-4 Skyhawks, and later F-15 Eagles and F-16 Fighting Falcons of the Israeli air force.

The MiG-21 was used extensively by the Indian Air Force. During the Indo-Pakistani War of 1971, the MiG-21 was credited with shooting down four F-104 Starfighters and one MiG-19 of the Pakistani Air Force before hostilities ended.

One distinctive feature of most MiG-21 variants was the lack of sophisticated electronic technology in their airframes. They did not have radar, elaborate navigation equipment, or computer systems. As a result, MiG-21 pilots needed to be particularly skillful in handling their nimble, fast aircraft against enemies whose aircraft had state-of-the-art electronics and guidance packages.

INTERCONTINENTAL BALLISTIC MISSILE

A Minuteman I intercontinental ballistic missle is launched during a test

One of the major symbols of the cold war was the Intercontinental Ballistic Missile (ICBM) first deployed by the United States and the Soviet Union in 1959. ICBMs are capable of delivering large (1,000 kiloton or more) nuclear warheads at supersonic speeds, striking targets up to 6,500 miles away in about thirty minutes. At the height of the cold war, the two big nuclear powers, the United States and the Soviet Union, had so many ICBMs in their arsenal that the two nations had reached what was called the MAD level. MAD stood for Mutually Assured Destruction, meaning that they had the potential to achieve the ultimate Pyrrhic victory—not only would they destroy each other, they'd also take the entire world with them.

ICBMs can be launched from stationary or mobile platforms on land, from aircraft, and from submarines. A technological breakthrough was the development of the multiple independently targetable reentry vehicle, or MIRV. One missile could carry several warheads that would separate from the main rocket and scatter to simultaneously strike targets hundreds of miles away from each other.

Nazi Germany was the first nation to design ICBMs, the A9 and A10, which were intended for use against New York City and other cities in the United States. After its defeat in World War II, the missile designs and the scientists and technicians who created them were rounded up by the United States and the Soviet Union. Most of the team that designed the A9 and A10, as well as the operational V-2 ballistic rocket, led by Wernher von Braun, emigrated to the United States and became the core team that helped the United States develop its missile and rocket programs.

The list of countries that have nuclear ICBMs officially includes the United States, Russia (formerly the Soviet Union), Great Britain, the People's Republic of China, France, India, and Pakistan. Israel refuses to state whether it has nuclear weapons of any type, but suspicion by its hostile neighbors that it does have a nuclear arsenal that includes ICBMs is one reason for its continued existence.

The United States officially has 450 Minuteman nuclear ICBMs located in the Great Plains states. The National Park Service has a Minuteman Missile National Historic Site, complete with a deactivated Minuteman Missile in its underground silo, at Philip in west-central South Dakota.

Two missile maintenance crewmen perform an electrical check on a Minuteman III intercontinental ballistic missile in its silo

BELL UH-1H HUEY

A pilot at the controls of a Huey

The symbol of the Vietnam War was the UH-1H Iroquois, more popularly known as the Huey. The Huey was one of the most versatile helicopters ever manufactured. As troop transports, known as "slicks," the Huey carried troops and supplies. Gunships, known as "cobras," had extra machine guns, cannon, and rockets. "Medivacs" were designed to quickly transport wounded from the battlefield. Command ships had extra communications equipment and were used by commanders flying over a battlefield. Other variants included search and rescue and electronic warfare.

The Huey became operational in 1959. By the time production ended in 1976, more than 16,000 Hueys were manufactured and used by more than seventy countries. Of that amount, about 7,000 saw service in the Vietnam War. Depending on the variant, the Huey had a minimum crew of one and a maximum of four and could carry as many as fourteen passengers. It had a top speed of 135 miles per hour, a range of 315 miles, and a ceiling of about 19,000 feet. Its maximum takeoff weight was 9,500 pounds. Depending on the variant armament included two machine guns of varying firepower and two rocket pods capable of carrying up to nineteen 2.75-inch rockets.

Though helicopters were used in all branches, they were the primary air arm of the army and marines. Air Force Captain Bruce Wallace witnessed the use of gunships against the enemy. Of the incident, he said, "It is always an experience for an air force pilot to watch a gaggle of Hueys attack a target. . . . In [an air force jet squadron] attack, the target is always in front of us. Not so with a Huey. To watch four or eight of them at a time maneuvering up and down and laterally and even backward boggles a fighter pilot's mind. Those guys swarm a target like bees over honey."

U.S. helicopters pour machine gun fire into the tree line to cover the advance of South Vietnamese ground troops in an attack on a Viet Cong camp

Reconaissance Satellites

The Discover III reconnaissance satellite and part of the design and launch team

When the Soviet Union launched Sputnik I, the world's first artificial satellite, on October 4, 1957, it ushered mankind's next great technological achievement, the Space Age.

Initially, satellites were developed by and for the military for reconnaissance. The cold war, under the specter of global annihilation from the world's nuclear superpowers, was a major factor in the development of satellites. Within a year after Sputnik's launch, the United States responded with the top-secret CORONA satellite reconnaissance program. CORONA was a pioneer effort, the technological equivalent of Lewis and Clark's exploration, and its first satellite, the KH-I reached space in 1959. The goal of CORONA was to photograph every inch of the Soviet Union in a search for military installations, particularly nuclear missile sites. CORONA achieved several notable firsts: first photoreconnaissance satellite, first recovery of an object from space, first mapping of the Earth from space, and first program to fly more than a hundred missions in space. When the CORONA program ended, it resulted in the exposure of more than 2.I million feet (almost 400 miles) of film and more than 800,000 photographs, some which have since been declassified. CORONA photographed a total land area of 557 million square miles. And, more importantly, it achieved all its intelligence goals. It resolved the "missile gap" (determining that while there was one, it was actually the United States that had many more missiles than the Soviet Union). It located all Soviet ICBM sites, all intermediate-range ballistic missile sites, all antiballistic missile sites, and all warship and submarine bases, as well as previously unknown military and industrial complexes.

Commercially, satellite imagery of varying resolution is widely available through the Internet through such sites as Google maps. Today, thanks to reconnaissance satellites, it is almost impossible for any major military action to take place without it being observed from the movement of the very first vehicle.

A declassified CORONA satellite image of Washington, D.C. and select sites

Capitol Building

Pentagon

RFK Stadium

Washington Monument

Union Station

White House

Washington, D.C.

CORONA Mission: 1101-2
Pass/Camera: 157D/FWD
Date: September

ED

McDonnel-Douglas
F-4 Phantom

Originally designed as a missile-equipped all-weather supersonic fleet defense fighter for the U.S. Navy, the two-seat, twin-engine F-4 Phantom was adopted by the Marine Corps and the United States Air Force. Its widespread use by all three services in the Vietnam War as an interceptor fighter and fighter-bomber made it a symbol of American airpower during that conflict.

The Phantom became operational in 1960 and would serve in the U.S. air arms as late as 1990, where thirty Phantoms were deployed as Wild Weasels in Operation Desert Storm to conduct the suppression of enemy air defenses in Iraq. Production ended in 1981, with 5,195 Phantoms being built. It was exported to a number of countries including NATO allies, Israel, Egypt, South Korea, Japan, and pre-revolutionary Iran. Depending on the variant, it had a maximum speed of Mach 2.23, a combat radius of 420 miles, and a ceiling of 60,000 feet. The Phantom variants included fighter interceptor, fighter-bomber, and interceptor. It had a crew of two, a pilot and a weapons control officer. As a fighter-bomber, it could carry a wide range of "smart" and "dumb" bombs, missiles, rockets, and nuclear munitions.

Because of the wide variety and number of munitions it can carry, the ordnance load is carefully organized for each mission. Major John Trotti was a Marine fighter pilot in Vietnam. In his book *Phantom Over Vietnam* he wrote, "The Phantom's weapons select panel—called the dog bone because of its distinctive shape—is fairly complex. . . . Bombs are literally kicked off the racks in a set sequence and interval by ejector feet that are actuated by shotgun shells. This positive separation is important not merely for accuracy, but because of the uncertain airflow patterns about the bottom of the airplane, there is the danger that a bomb could get tossed into the aircraft." Trotti served two tours of duty in Vietnam, flying more than six hundred missions. He received the Distinguished Flying Cross for heroism on January 31, 1970, when as section leader of a two-plane flight, he was assigned to provide support for a mission to rescue a trapped six-man Marine reconnaissance team. Despite severe weather and mountainous terrain that limited his movement and enemy suppression opportunities, Trotti silenced the attacking enemy, allowing the rescue helicopters to retrieve the Marine team.

P-15 Termit/SS-N-2 Styx

The Russian P-15 Termit, NATO codename SS-N-2 Styx, is a medium-range anti-ship missile. A cold war-era missile that became operational in 1960, upgraded variants are still in the Russian arsenal today. It has been exported to several countries, and was the basis for the Communist Chinese Silkworm missile.

The Soviet Union confronted a sobering problem during the cold war. NATO ships outnumbered those in its surface navy in every capital category, leaving the nation vulnerable to attack along its coast. The Soviet navy requested an inexpensive ship-launched surface-to-surface missile that was small enough to be carried by its Torpedo Cutters (motor torpedo boats), had the power of a battleship salvo, and could be quickly and easily mass produced. The result was the P-15 Termit designed by A. Y. Berzhnyak of Raduga Design Bureau. The missile was 19 feet long, 2 ½ feet in diameter with folding wings that unfolded upon launch to give a wingspan of almost eight feet. It weighed about five thousand pounds and carried a thousand-pound armor-piercing warhead. It had a speed of Mach .9 and, depending on the variant a range, up to fifty-four nautical miles.

Egypt used export models of the Termit against Israel in the Six Day War (1967). On October 21, 1967, two Egyptian Komar-class missile boats attacked the Israeli *Eilat*, a World War II-era destroyer purchased from Great Britain, in the Red Sea off the coast of the Sinai Peninsula. Four Termits were fired, with three striking the *Eilat*, almost breaking it in two. The *Eilat* sank a couple hours later with forty-seven men killed and another forty-one wounded, out of a crew of 190 sailors. It was the first time a ship-launched missile had sunk a warship and the Termit's success accelerated development of more advanced ship-launched missiles.

During the Indo-Pakistani War of 1971, three Indian missile boats armed with Termits entered Karachi harbor, which housed the headquarters of the Pakistani navy, in a raid codenamed Operation Trident. When the raid concluded, the Indian boats had fired thirteen Termits and sunk the Pakistani destroyer *Khaibar*, the mine sweeper *Muhafiz*, heavily damaged another destroyer, and severely damaged the harbor's petroleum storage facilities.

Upgrades of the Termit were used with varying success by Iran in the Iran-Iraq War (1980–1988).

A Soviet Osa II fast attack ship armed with Styx missiles contained in the large in the center and aft sections of the ship

HERBICIDES

The military use of herbicides is designed to do one of two things: eliminate the lush foliage where an enemy can hide, or deny him food by destroying crops. Herbicides act by inhibiting growth, prematurely removing leaves, drying the foliage, neutralizing plant nutrients in the soil, and by causing chemicals to adhere to the plants.

The first known use of herbicides in warfare was by Rome after the siege of Carthage in 146 B.C. The Romans were so obsessed with destroying their great rival that, after enslaving the city's population and scattering it and leveling the city, they spread salt over the ruins and on the croplands around the wreckage so that nothing would grow.

The most famous use of herbicides in modern times was by the American military during the Vietnam War under a program codenamed Operation Ranch Hand, begun in 1961. About nineteen million gallons of herbicides were sprayed over about ten percent of the landmass of South Vietnam. While some herbicides were dispensed by riverboats, trucks, and men with individual sprayers, most were deployed by specially rigged helicopters or airplanes. The different herbicides were given military code names based on the color-coding of their 55-gallon barrels. These included Agents Blue, Purple, Pink, Green, and White. The most famous herbicide was Agent Orange, which contained dioxin.

Agent Orange was used from mid-1965 through 1970. Soluble in diesel fuel and organic compounds, Agent Orange was used mostly for jungle defoliation. Toxicologically, Orange was less potent than Agents Purple, Pink, and Green. But the extensive use of Agent Orange (about 11.2 million gallons), and its employment at the time when awareness of the toxicity of these herbicides became known, made Orange the most notorious of the group.

After the war, controversy ensued over the extensive use of herbicides and their health affects on the population and the people who dispensed the herbicides. Class-action lawsuits were filed and ultimately multi-million dollar trust funds were established to aid the victims. Though herbicides remain in the arsenals of a number of nations, their use as a weapon in the future is open to question.

A U.S. Air Force plane spraying Agent Orange over a forest in South Vietnam during the Vietnam War

9K11 Malutka/AT-3 Sagger

A Sagger control
unit

THE 9K11 *Malutka* (Russian for "Tiny Baby" or "Little Baby"), NATO codenamed AT-3 Sagger, is a compact wire-guided antitank missile with a shaped-charge HEAT (High Explosive AntiTank) warhead. It is the most long-lived and widespread anti-tank guided missile weapon in the world.

Introduced by the Soviet Union in 1961, more than 200,000 have since been manufactured. Unlicensed, reverse-engineered versions with improved guidance systems have been manufactured by China (Red Arrow 73 and Red Arrow 73C), Iran (Raad and Improved Raad), North Korea, and other countries.

Depending on the variant, the Sagger is either MCLOS (Manual Command-to-Line of Sight) or SACLOS (Semi-Automatic Command-to-Line of Sight) and requires a crew of three to operate it. An operator controls the missile and directs its flight by using a joystick control. The Sagger is light—variants range from twenty-four to twenty-seven pounds, with a warhead weighing either six or eight pounds. The Sagger is about three feet long, six inches wide, and has a 1¼ foot wingspan. It has a range of 9,800 feet and can travel either 377 feet per second or 426 feet per second. Portable versions are packed in a large plastic suitcase that also serves as a launch platform, and a Sagger can be set up within five minutes. Other launching platforms include armored vehicles such as the BMD, BMP, and BRDM armored personnel carriers and the Mi-8 Hip and Mi-24 Hind helicopters.

The Sagger is not especially accurate, and it requires a lot of training (at least 2,300 simulated firings) for an operator to become proficient. Its two biggest negatives are that it has a long minimum range (1,600 to 2,600 feet, depending on variant), and is slow—it can take about thirty seconds for it to reach its maximum range. This risks exposing the operators to counter fire, and a moving target has time to take evasive maneuvers. The latter problem was partially addressed when more recent models included the SACLOS control system.

Egyptian and Syrian armies successfully used the Sagger in the Yom Kippur War (1973). According to reports, about two thousand Saggers were expended, destroying eight hundred Israeli tanks and damaging almost three hundred others.

An overhead view of a Soviet AT-3 Sagger anti-tank missiles mounted on two BDRM-1 amphibious reconnaissance cars

RPG-7

The RPG-7 is a reloadable, portable, antitank rocket-propelled grenade launcher fired from the shoulder. Like its lineal ancestor, the World War II German *panzerfaust*, it is inexpensive, easy to operate, and effective. The RPG-7 was adopted by the Soviet Union army in 1961 and today is included in the arsenals of more than forty countries.

Without a warhead, the RPG-7 weighs fifteen pounds and is thirty-seven inches long. It can fire a variety of antitank and antipersonnel fin-stabilized, oversized grenades ranging in weight from four to fifteen pounds. Its maximum effective range against moving targets is about a thousand feet and against stationary targets about 1,600 feet. After that, its accuracy dramatically declines. The RPG-7's maximum range is about three thousand feet. If the grenade reaches this distance, in about 4.5 seconds, without hitting anything, the warhead self-destructs. The RPG-7 is operated by one person, but RPG-7 gunners are usually accompanied by another individual who provides protective suppression fire.

The RPG-7 was first used in the Vietnam War by Vietcong guerillas and North Vietnamese troops. Like Soviet tankers in World War II who strapped bedsprings to their T-34s to protect their tanks from *panzerfaüste*, American troops jury-rigged barbed wire bundles on their lightly armored M113 personnel carriers for RPG protection. Since then, add-on slat armor, referred to as "birdcage" armor, has been developed as a countermeasure against RPG attack.

The RPG-7 was the anti-armor weapon of choice by the Mujahideen against Soviet armored and unarmored vehicles in the Soviet-Afghan War (1979–1989). Generally gunners would close to within sixty feet before firing, in almost all cases scoring lethal hits.

Though designed for surface-to-surface action, the RPG-7 achieved notable success in surface-to-air attacks against helicopters. On October 3, 1994, in Somalia, Somali militia RPG gunners shot down two Black Hawk helicopters. In Afghanistan, in March 2002 and in June 2005, Taliban and al Qaeda terrorists used RPG-7s to shoot down special operations helicopters. In those two actions they inflicted the worst single-mission losses suffered by special operations troops.

An Iraqi soldier with an RPG-7

NORTH AMERICAN T-28 TROJAN

The North American T-28 Trojan has one of the more unusual histories for a combat aircraft. As its "T" designation indicates, the T-28 Trojan was designed as a trainer. But it also saw service in the Vietnam War as a fighter-bomber, conducting special operations counterinsurgency missions with the Air Commandos in Operation Farm Gate.

The Trojan was America's first post-World War II trainer, the successor to the venerable T-6 Texan. Though it became operational in 1950, the Trojan did not fully replace the Texan until after the Korean War. The Trojan's non-combatant role abruptly changed in 1961 when propeller-driven, piston-engine aircraft were quickly needed to support counterinsurgency operations in South Vietnam. General William W. Momyer, then Air Force Director of Operational Requirements, later wrote, "The Air Staff had conducted a number of technical studies to determine what propeller aircraft could be put in a combat ready condition as quickly as possible. These studies showed that the T-28, a trainer, could be modified as a fighter-bomber. A modification line was established and the aircraft structure was modified for delivery of bombs." The combat variant, designated T-28D and also known as the Nomad, would see active service over South Vietnam and Laos until 1963, when the A-1 Skyraider replaced it.

During its production run from 1950 to 1957, a total of 1,948 Trojans were built. The largest number were the T-28A for the Air Force. The T-28B and T-28C variants were built for the Navy, with the C model equipped with tail hooks for deck landing training. The Trojan carried a two-man crew and had a top speed of 343 mph and a service ceiling of 35,500 feet. The T-28D combat variant had six underwing hard-points making it capable of carrying a variety of weapons, including .50 caliber machine guns, 2.75-inch rockets, and bombs. The Trojan saw service in the air forces of nineteen countries, including the Philippines, Mexico, South Korea, South Vietnam, France, and Japan.

When parked on the ground, the T-28 Trojan is a squat and stubby "ugly duckling." But once in the air, it becomes a thrilling high-performance warbird of beauty with a reputation as one of the more popular airplanes at airshows throughout the country.

Aviation officer candidates march past a T-28 Trojan aircraft while en route to one of their classes

Booby Traps

Booby traps are improvised passive weapon systems that rely on the inattentiveness or cupidity of the victim. They are secondary weapon systems designed to disrupt or impede the advance of an enemy and erode morale. Booby traps first made their appearance in World War I and have been used in both conventional and guerilla warfare ever since. Today, explosive booby traps are referred to as Improvised Explosive Devices (IEDs).

While the term "trap" is self-evident, there are a variety of suggested origins for "booby." One reference is to the sea bird and how it was trapped through trickery. Other origins are extrapolations of a reference to stupidity, the earliest dating back to Roman times, from the Latin word *balbus*.

In conventional warfare, booby traps were employed by retreating troops. The German armies displayed particular ingenuity in setting up booby traps. During the Afrika Korps retreat across North Africa, one German soldier became particularly skillful placing them. The target of his destructive genius was the British officer. Before he set his booby traps, he would examine homes and rooms with an eye to how the usually well-educated officer would apprise them. As he later explained, a British private or noncommissioned officer would not pay attention to a painting hanging askew on a wall. But an officer, particularly a senior officer, would be prone to straighten the painting.

Booby traps do not have to be explosive. During the Vietnam War, Viet Cong communist guerillas would dig pits and imbed sharpened bamboo sticks, called punji stakes, usually coated with feces, in the bottom of the pits. The pits were then covered with brush. Nothing could be more simple, or more dangerous as Colin Powell discovered. In July 1963, Captain Powell was an advisor working with South Vietnamese troops. Late one morning, while on patrol, his right leg went out from under him and he felt a sharp pain. Upon examination, he discovered that he had stumbled into a small pit about a foot deep filled with punji stakes. One had pierced through the sole of his combat boot and into his foot. Within twenty minutes the pain had become excruciating. By the time he reached the forward base, he could no longer walk and his infected foot had become horribly swollen. He was quickly taken by helicopter to a field hospital. Powell was hospitalized for about a week.

Two Vietnamese preparing a booby trap to use against South Vietnamese and American foes, 1967

LOCKHEED SR-71 BLACKBIRD

The Blackbird is an advanced, long-range, supersonic, high altitude reconnaissance aircraft designed and built by Lockheed's Clarence "Kelly" Johnson and the famous Skunk Works.

The Blackbird was made in response to a problem posed by even the best reconnaissance satellites: their predictability. Because the orbital patterns of reconnaissance satellites are easy to calculate, suspicious or threatening activity can be disguised or hidden during the satellite's flyover. The CIA originally used it to conduct deep-penetration reconnaissance missions over the Soviet Union. The CIA conducted covert reconnaissance missions with the Blackbird in 1964. In 1966, the United States Air Force officially took over operation of the SR-71 and its missions.

The Blackbird had a crew of two and a reconnaissance payload of 3,500 pounds. It had a top speed of Mach 3.2, a range of 3,300 miles, a ceiling of 85,000 feet. It could fly higher and faster than any aircraft or missile attacking it.

The SR-71 was retired in 1989 due to budget cutbacks. It was reactivated in 1993 as a result of increased political tensions in the Middle East and North Korea. It was retired again in 1998.

Designing and building the Blackbird presented all kinds of problems for the Skunk Works team. Titanium was the only metal capable of surviving the extreme altitude, temperature, and speed conditions required. But titanium ore is found in very few countries, and the metal itself is very difficult to refine and fashion. The CIA covertly conducted a worldwide search and secretly purchased all the titanium needed from one of the world's biggest suppliers—the Soviet Union.

As for fashioning the metal, the Skunk Work's Ben Rich recalled, "We learned the hard way that titanium was totally incompatible with many other elements, including chlorine, fluorine, and cadmium." When one of the engineers on the project drew a line on a sheet of titanium, the chlorine in the ink acted like acid, and etched the sheet. One of the most baffling problems occurred when spot welds on titanium panels began failing after a month and a half. It took weeks of investigation before the team discovered that the panels had been welded in July and August, when the Burbank water department increased the amount of chlorine in the water, to inhibit algae growth. From that point on, only bottled distilled water was used.

An SR-71 aircraft undergoing maintenance

ZSU-23-4 Shilka

The ZSU-23-4 Shilka is a Self-Propelled Anti-Aircraft Gun (referred to in the military by the acronym SPAAG) built by the Soviet Union and used by about forty countries, primarily third-world nations. "ZSU" stands for *Zenitnaya Samokhodnaya Ustanovka*, or Anti-aircraft Self-Propelled Gun. The 23 refers to the caliber of its weapons, and 4 refers to number of weapons mounted on the turret.

The ZSU-23-4 was developed in the early 1960s to replace the ZSU-57-2. It is lightly armored (maximum half an inch), operated by a crew of four, has a maximum road speed of about twenty-seven miles per hour, and a range of about 280 miles. It became operational in 1965 and when production ended in 1982, about 6,500 had been built.

The four water-cooled 23-mm cannon are mounted on a turret that has full powered traverse through 360 degrees and with an elevation that ranges from −4 degrees to +85 degrees. A folding Gun Dish radar mounted on the rear of the turret tracks targets. Because of its light armor and exposed wheels and tracks, the Shilka is vulnerable to air-to-ground missile and RPG attack.

When the Shilka entered service in the Soviet Union and allied Warsaw Pact nations of Eastern Europe, it was superior to all its NATO counterparts. Though now obsolete, it is still regarded as a dangerous threat to low-flying aircraft. It has proved to be an effective weapon in ground operations, particularly in urban settings where its cannon, capable of firing eight hundred to a thousand rounds per minute, can elevate to reach attackers on upper levels of buildings.

Export models of the Shilka were used by Egypt and Syria against the Israeli air force in the Yom Kippur War (1973). They proved particularly effective in combined operations with the SA-6 surface-to-air missile. Israeli pilots seeking to avoid the SA-6 by flying low found themselves being shot at—and often shot down—by the Shilka.

ZSU-23-4 SP AA GUN

M-16

The M-16 assault rifle is the primary shoulder arm of the United States military. The U.S. Army officially adopted it in 1965. It was the primary rifle of the U.S. military in the Vietnam War where it became the focus of severe controversy because of frequent jamming. After the problems were solved, the M-16 regained popularity among troops. Since then, an estimated eight million M-16s in a variety of models have been manufactured.

The M-16 shoots a 5.56-mm NATO cartridge and is capable of firing in automatic or semi-automatic mode. The M-16 is just under forty inches long, weighs less than nine pounds fully loaded, is fed by a thirty-round magazine, has a rate of fire of approximately eight hundred rounds per minute and a maximum range of almost four thousand yards.

The prototype of the M-16 was the AR-15 developed in the late 1950s. The AR-15 was field tested in 1962 by the South Vietnamese Army (ARVN) who wanted a light, almost recoilless rifle. The ARVN found it ideally suited to mobile combat counterinsurgency operations. Production of M-16s began in 1964 when the Department of Defense placed an order for 104,000 rifles. The following year General William Westmoreland, the top military commander in Vietnam, ordered a hundred thousand M-16 for troops in South Vietnam.

Controversy erupted in 1966 when senior commanders received large numbers of reports of M-16 unreliability related to the rifle jamming during combat. An investigation revealed that the problems essentially were divided into two categories: poor cleaning and maintenance, and bad ammunition. A contributing factor for the former was that the M-16 had been incorrectly advertised as having a "self-cleaning" bore and chamber. They weren't. Better instruction and minor redesign of the rifle soon solved the problems.

As for the ammunition, studies revealed that 81 million cartridges were filled with a propellant, WC-846, that was five times more prone to fouling than cartridges filled with the second-most popular propellant on inventory, IMR (CR) 8136, in 50 million cartridges. The ammunition problem effectively solved itself by the end of 1967 when the cartridges containing WC-846 propellant had either been all fired or taken out of inventory.

A member of the Air National Guard fires his M-16 on the firing range

COMBAT SHOTGUN

The combat shotgun is usually a short-barreled firearm of short range. Unlike a rifle or machine gun that fires a single bullet and so must be aimed to be effective, a shotgun merely has to be pointed in the general direction of a target. The shotgun typically fires a cartridge containing many small beads ("shot") that scatter over a wide area.

Shotgun use dates back to World War I when they were used as "trench guns" and to guard prisoners. Shotgun use subsequently declined and did not come back into widespread use until the Malayan Emergency (1948–1960), the guerilla war for independence between British Commonwealth forces and Malayan nationalists. The special operations SAS troops used them with great effect during jungle patrols where close-quarter fighting with a well-camouflaged enemy was the norm. That success led to U.S. forces using a variety of commercial shotguns modified for military use during the Vietnam War starting in 1965.

The rapid rise of urban terrorism and Counter-Terrorist Warfare operations has led to development of specialized military shotguns. Ithaca, Mossberg, Winchester, Remington, Beretta, Benelli, and Franchi are among the shotgun manufacturers who make combat shotguns for the military.

Shotguns fire a variety of cartridges. The most common shotgun ammunition is "buckshot," small beads of lead. Shotgun cartridges are measured in units called "gauges." Most military shotguns are 12-gauge. Shotguns also fire bullet-like ammunition, called "slugs."

Loading is either hand operated pump action or gas-operated semi-automatic where the gas from the ejected spent shell facilitates the chamber reloading following each trigger pull. Even though semi-automatics have a greater rate of fire, the hand-operated pump action is most favored because it is regarded as having the more accurate loading action.

Members of the weapons division Armed Response Team take up a position during a security drill aboard the nuclear-powered aircraft carrier USS *Dwight D. Eisenhower*

LEOPARD

The Leopard I Main Battle Tank (MBT) was post-World War II Germany's first tank designed and built in what was then West Germany.

When World War II ended, the Allies divided Germany into four military occupation zones. In 1949, the British, French, and American zones were consolidated into the Federal Republic of Germany, commonly called West Germany. The Soviet Union chose to form its zone in the east as the separate German Democratic Republic (a totalitarian communist state democratic in name only), commonly known as East Germany. In October 1990, following the end of the cold war and collapse of the Soviet Union, East and West Germany were reunified. But, during the forty-one years that the country was divided, the border between East and West Germany was the heavily defended front line in case the cold war suddenly became hot.

The Leopard I began as a joint French-German program in 1957 after West Germany had been invited to join the North Atlantic Treaty Organization (NATO) western defensive alliance in 1955. The purpose of the project was to produce a modern European-made tank to replace tanks purchased from the United States. Though the partnership ended in the design stages, West Germany continued work. In 1965, the West German government accepted its first post-World War II tank.

The Leopard I featured few innovations. Its main gun was a British-designed 105-mm cannon manufactured under license in Germany. Secondary armament was two 7.62-mm machine guns. It had a crew of four. Armor thickness ranged from a maximum of 2 ¾ inches to a minimum of 1/3 of an inch. It had a top speed of forty miles per hour and a range of 372 miles on road and 279 cross-country. As a counter to nuclear, chemical, or biological warfare, the crew's compartment is over-pressurized so that outside air cannot seep in. A total of 6,485 Leopard Is were built and were used in West Germany and nine other NATO nations.

In the 1979, West Germany began replacing the Leopard I with the Leopard 2 that had a larger cannon (120 mm), third-generation composite armor, and other improvements. The Leopard 2 first saw combat in support operations during the 1990s as part of Kosovo Force after the collapse of Yugoslavia. Leopards were deployed by NATO nations in Afghanistan as part of Operation Enduring Freedom against the Taliban in 2006.

BMP Armored Personnel Carrier (APC)

The Soviet BMP is the family of amphibious tracked infantry fighting vehicles that is armed and armored. "BMP" stands for *Boyevaya Mashina Pekhoty*, Russian for "fighting vehicle of the infantry." The first model, BMP-1 was the world's first mass-produced armored personnel carrier with fighting capability. The BMP-1 became operational in 1966 and upgraded models and variants are still in service today. Including licensed manufacturing in other countries and export models, more than twenty-seven thousand BMPs have been manufactured.

The BMP has a crew of three and can carry eight troopers. Over the years the turret-mounted primary armament has changed. The BMP-1 carried a 73-mm semi-automatic cannon, the BMP-2 had a 30-mm cannon and a grenade launcher, and the BMP-3 had a 100-mm cannon and a 30-mm cannon. The secondary armament package varied as well, primarily regarding the number of 7.62-mm machine guns, one in the BMP-1 and three in the BMP-3. The BMP is lightly armored, with the maximum being about 1 1/3 inch and the minimum about ¼ inch. Depending on the model, the BMP had a range of 372 miles, a top speed of forty miles per hour on road, twenty-eight miles per hour cross-country, and four miles per hour in the water. The crew is stationed in the front and in the turret, and the passengers are located in the rear. Gun ports in the passenger's compartment enable the soldiers to provide additional fire support.

Iraq was one of many nations that had purchased Soviet tanks and armored personnel carriers. They were among the armored vehicles used by the Iraqi Tawakalna Division against Coalition troops in Operation Desert Storm (1991). The American 2nd Armored Cavalry Regiment was advancing east through foul weather when forward elements in Bradley M2 APCs, the American counterpart to the BMT, surprised Tawakalna troops manning perimeter positions. Fighting between the BMTs and Bradleys ensued. The initial contact quickly turned into a full-scale battle among tanks, APCs, and infantry. Surprise and superior tactics by American troops turned the engagement into a decisive American victory. The 2nd ACR was credited with destroying eighty-five Iraqi tanks and forty armored personnel carriers.

Soviet BMP-1 mechanised infantry combat vehicles move through Afghanistan

Mk 19 Grenade Machine Gun

A closeup of the grips and trigger of an MK 19

The Mk 19 is a machine gun designed to fire 40-mm grenades. The U.S. Navy first used it in the Vietnam War. The U.S. Army later modified the Mk 19 to make it suitable for combat operations in harsh environments, particularly extreme cold weather and desert conditions.

During the Vietnam War, the Navy operated two forces, one ocean-based and the other that patrolled the rivers and canals of South Vietnam. The Navy discovered that their river patrol boats, armed only with .50-caliber machine guns, were inadequately armed for the type of combat situations they were encountering. The patrol boats operated in narrow channels generally in small teams of no more than three boats. They had to make up for their lack of numbers in a restricted space with overwhelming firepower. Their machine guns needed to be augmented with a type of light, rapid-fire artillery that could quickly launch a large amount of projectiles. The Navy's request was answered with the Mk 19.

The Mk 19 fires belt-fed high-velocity 40-mm high explosive grenades. It has a rapid-fire rate of sixty rounds per minute and a sustained rate of forty rounds per minute. Its maximum range is 7,200 feet and a maximum effective range of 5,200 feet. The minimum range is 240 feet. Army variants are either man portable or vehicle mounted. Portable variants are mounted on tripods and weigh 136 pounds without ammunition.

The first land use of the Mk 19 occurred during Operation Desert Storm (1991). They were also used by regular and special operations troops in Operation Iraqi Freedom (2003). In both cases they proved to be an effective against enemy infantry.

1967

US Marine Corps soldiers fire an MK-19 while training at Pohakuloa Training Area on the Big Island of Hawaii

LTV A-7 Corsair II

The Ling-Temco-Vought A-7 Corsair II was a light subsonic attack aircraft designed for the U.S. Navy to conduct search, surveillance, and close air support attack missions. The A-7's stocky design earned the A-7 a number of nicknames, including "Sluff" (short little ugly fat fellow), or the more vulgar "Sluf" which replaced "fat fellow" with an earthier term. It became operational in 1967, and by the time it was retired in 1991, more than 1,500 A-7s had been built.

The A-7 had a crew of one, a top speed of 698 miles per hour, a combat radius of 715 miles, and a ceiling of forty-two thousand feet. Its armament included one 20-mm cannon and two AIM-9 Sidewinder missiles for defense. It could carry a maximum bomb load of twenty thousand pounds.

The A-7 began combat operations in the Vietnam War in December 1967. The A-7 performed a wide variety of missions during the war. Perhaps its most valuable role was as a Combat Search and Rescue escort. The most famous of these missions occurred on November 18, 1972. Air Force Major Colin A. Clarke flying an A-7D conducted a ninehour rescue support mission over the Thanh Hoa "Dragon's Jaw" area of North Vietnam just across the DMZ to rescue a downed Wild Weasel crew. Severe weather and deadly AAA fire made the mission a test of endurance and courage that fortunately ended in success. For his role in leading the mission, Clarke received the Air Force Cross, the service's second highest award for valor.

After that war, A-7s provided close air support in Operation Urgent Fury, the invasion of Grenada, assisted in the enforcement of the international right of passage in the Gulf of Sidra off the Libyan coast, escort duty of shipping in the Persian Gulf during the Iran-Iraq war during the 1980s, and Operation Just Cause, the invasion of Panama in December 1989. In 1990 during Operation Desert Shield/Desert Storm, the last two squadrons to fly A-7s, VA-46 and VA-72 attached to the USS *John F. Kennedy*, participated in the first combat strike against Iraqi targets in Baghdad as well as the last naval aviation combat strike of the war, against Iraqi troops near An Najef.

Its low production cost and sturdy, versatile design made the A-7 Corsair II one of the most efficient and effective jet aircraft used by the Navy and Air Force.

An A-7 Corsair II aircraft preparing to launch from the flight deck of the nuclear-powered aircraft carrier USS *Dwight Eisenhower*

SA-6 Gainful

The SA-6, NATO codename Gainful, is a two-stage, solid-fuel, low-altitude radar guided Surface-to-Air Missile (SAM). It became operational in 1968, and by the time production ended in 1985, it acquired a reputation as one of the most successful Soviet antiaircraft missiles ever built.

The SA-6 is typically mounted on a tracked vehicle that carries three of the SAMs. Initially the SA-6 carrier was accompanied by a tracked vehicle carrying a Long Track target acquisition radar. Later this duty was assumed by vehicles operating Straight Flush target acquisition radars. The SA-6 is nineteen feet long, one foot in diameter, and has a wingspan of four feet. It has a top speed of Mach 2.8, a minimum effective altitude of 330 feet, and a maximum effective altitude of 39,370 feet. It carries a high explosive fragmentation warhead possessing both contact and proximity fuses that weighs 130 pounds. Typical reaction time by a pilot once an SA-6 launch on his aircraft is detected is a maximum of twenty-two seconds. The domestic version of the SA-6 is codenamed Kub ("cube") and the export version is codenamed *Kvadrat* ("square").

The SA-6 was used by both the Egyptian and Syrian armies during the Yom Kippur War (1973) where ninety-five missiles were fired, shooting down sixty-four Israeli aircraft.

Yugoslavia was one of more than a score of nations who imported the SA-6. When that nation fell into civil war in 1991, a large number of SA-6 batteries fell into the hands of the Serbian army. One such battery was used on June 2, 1995, against two U.S. Air Force F-16 Flying Falcons on patrol over Serbia as part of Operation Deny Flight. A volley of two missiles were fired. The first rocketed between the two aircraft. The second exploded beneath one of the F-16s, eviscerating it. The pilot successfully ejected and safely landed in the mountainous countryside. An intense manhunt by friendly American-led NATO forces and hostile Serbian troops commenced. The pilot evaded Serbian searchers for six days. On June 8, 1995, a combined force rescue team led by U.S. Marines successfully extracted Captain Scott O'Grady, ending one of the largest search and rescue operations since the Vietnam War.

SA-7 Grail

The SA-7 *Strela* ("arrow"), NATO codename Grail, was the first generation of Soviet-designed man-portable surface-to-air missiles.

The SA-7 is a fire-and-forget, shoulder-fired, low-altitude SAM similar to the U.S. Army's Redeye. Complete with missile, it weighs twenty-six pounds, is almost five feet long, and has a diameter of 2 ¾ inches. The missile has a speed of 1,900 feet per second, a maximum altitude of 14,760 feet and a minimum altitude of fifty-nine feet. It had an infrared heat-seeking guidance system and a high explosive warhead with a contact fuse that weighs 2½ pounds. Acquisition to fire reaction time is five to ten seconds. Variants include vehicle-mounted launchers containing four, six, or eight tubes.

The Grail was used by the North Vietnamese Army during the Easter Offensive (1972). It made life hell for U.S. Air Force crews flying low-level air to ground and search and rescue operations. Though it proved to be underpowered against jets, it was particularly effective against much slower helicopters. The SA-7 is credited with shooting down about fifty aircraft during the Vietnam War.

Because its guidance system was easily fooled by such heat-intense countermeasures as flares, the SA-7 soon lost effectiveness. Though it is in the arsenals of such terrorists as al Qaeda, it has rarely been used.

Two Mongolian Air Defense Force Staff soldiers shoulder SA-7s during target practice

Harrier

The Harrier is unique among all jets. Designed and originally manufactured by Hawker Siddeley of Great Britain, it officially classified as a Vertical/Short Take-off and Landing (V/STOL) jet, it is the only jet airplane that combines into one airframe the flight features of both a helicopter and an airplane.

The Harrier became operational for the Royal Navy in 1969. It soon came to the attention of the U.S. Marine Corps who were looking for a jet capable of providing close air support for its land operations. Retired Lieutenant General Harry Blot was a captain when the Marine Corps sent him to England to test fly the Harrier. Blot noted in his report that the Harrier "had potential" but "needed more thrust and firepower, plus an experienced pilot in order to handle it." Additional tests were made along with recommendations for design upgrades that led to the Harrier II. To expedite the Marine Corps' acquisition of the Harrier II, a manufacturing license was granted to Boeing.

The AV-8B Harrier II has a crew of one, a top speed of 675 miles per hour, a range of 1,380 miles, and a ceiling of thirty-eight thousand feet. Standard armament includes one GAU-12/U Equalizer 25-mm five-barrel Gatling gun and a maximum load of 13,200 bombs, rockets, missiles, or extra fuel tanks. A total of 815 Harriers of all types have been manufactured.

The Harrier is easily recognized by its distinctive "elephant ears" air intakes located behind and on either side of the cockpit. The large size was needed to accommodate the dual-directional requirements of the forward fans. The Harrier II can operate from a variety of amphibious ships, rapidly constructed expeditionary airfields, forward sites (such as roads), and damaged conventional airfields.

The Harrier's first combat action occurred during the Falklands War (1982) between Great Britain and Argentina over the disputed Falkland Islands, a British territory in the South Atlantic claimed by Argentina. A total of thirty-eight Sea Harriers saw action in the conflict, shooting down twenty-two Argentine aircraft at a loss of six Harriers, only two due to combat.

Aegis Combat Weapons System

The Combat Information Center, the nerve center of an Aegis ship

Originally called the Advanced Surface Missile System, and renamed Aegis (after the name for the Greek god Zeus' shield) in 1969, it is the world's foremost naval combat weapons system. Space-age communications, radar, and weapons technologies are combined as a fully integrated system capable of simultaneously conducting air, surface, subsurface, and strike warfare.

The Aegis is the latest result of Navy studies to protect its ships from air attack that began with the series of Fleet Problems conducted from 1923 to 1940 and experience gained in combat operations during World War II. The sinking of Israeli destroyer *Eilat* in 1967 by Soviet Styx surface-to-surface missiles launched from Egyptian torpedo boats added a new threat dimension. The Aegis system includes AN/SPY-ID phased array radar; MK 41 Vertical Launching System capable of firing a combination of up to ninety Standard surface-to-air and Tomahawk surface-to-surface missiles; and an ANSQQ-89 Antisubmarine Warfare System with a bow-mounted AN/SQS-53C sonar and AN/SQR-19 towed array capable of active and passive submarine tracking and detection.

The Aegis system is used in the U.S. Navy's *Ticonderoga*-class cruisers and *Arleigh Burke*-class destroyers. It is also used in the fleets of the Japanese Maritime Self-Defense Force, the Spanish Navy, Royal Norwegian Navy, Republic of Korea Navy, and Royal Australian Navy.

The Aegis was involved in the controversial shoot-down of Iran Air Flight 655 on July 3, 1988, by the *Vincennes* guided missile cruiser, killing 290 people. The *Vincennes* was involved in a surface action against Iranian patrol ships in the narrow Strait of Hormuz at the mouth of the Persian Gulf when Flight 655 began to fly over the strait. The *Vincennes*'s Aegis system identified and tracked the aircraft, an Airbus A300, and two missiles were fired. Only after Flight 655 was shot down did the crew realize it had attacked a civilian airliner. The event caused enormous controversy and the United States eventually agreed to pay almost $62 million in compensation to the families of the victims. An investigation into the incident concluded that the Aegis system had functioned properly, correctly identifying the aircraft as civilian, and that the shoot down was the result of operator error.

The *Ticonderoga* Class Aegis guided missile cruiser *Vincennes* fires an RUR-5A anti-submarine rocket from the forward Mark 26 missile launcher

AS-6 KINGFISH

The AS-6 Kingfish is a Soviet-era air-to-surface medium range supersonic missile that can be fitted with a nuclear warhead.

The Kingfish is a cruise missile, one that is guided and powered throughout its flight. In comparison, a ballistic missile has a high arcing trajectory and is initially powered and guided, but relies on the pull of gravity to reach its target.

Three versions are known to exist by the West, two of them capable of carrying nuclear warheads. The first of these is the model Kh-26, guided by an inertial navigation system and armed with a 350 kiloton nuclear warhead weighing about 2,200 pounds. The other nuclear version is the Kh-26N, actually a dual-purpose missile that can carry either a nuclear or high explosive, semi-armor piercing warhead. It has an active radar guidance system that becomes functional when the missile closes in on its target. The Kh-26N's nuclear warhead is smaller, weighing 2,050 pounds. The third version is the Kh-26MP, containing an anti-radar guidance system and a high explosive, blast/fragmentation warhead.

All versions had similar fuselage design and performance characteristics. The Kingfish was 34½ feet long, with a diameter of three feet and a wingspan of 8½ feet. Its launch weight was 9,920 pounds. It had a top speed of Mach 3, a ceiling of 65,600 feet, and a range of 250 miles.

The Kingfish entered service in 1969. It is not known how many were produced, though as late as 1990 a hundred missiles reportedly remained in the arsenal of post-Soviet Russia. It is believed the last Kingfish missiles were retired in 1994.

Bottom view of a Soviet Badger C bomber equipped with a Kingfish AS-6 sir-to-surface missile under the wing

MiG-23 Flogger

MiG-23 Flogger K

The Soviet-built MiG-23 Flogger was a point defense fighter flown during the cold war. Point defense fighters were created during a period when radar range was shorter than it is now. Defending fighters has little reaction time between the announcement of a raid and the enemy's arrival. This placed a premium on quick take-off and climb response.

The Flogger was designed as a successor to the MiG-21 and became operational in 1967. When production ceased in 1985, 5,047 MiG-23s in almost twenty variants had been built. In addition to serving in the Soviet, and later Russian, air force, export versions of the Flogger were sold mostly to Warsaw Pact allies. The most important non-Eastern bloc air forces to buy the Flogger were the Iraq, Iran, Indian, and Libyan air forces.

The Flogger had a crew of one. Though primarily a fighter-interceptor, some variants were designed as fighter-bombers. Depending on the variant, it has a top speed of Mach 2.4, a range of 570 miles, a ceiling of 60,695 feet, and a stunning rate of climb of almost nine miles—47,245 feet—a minute. Standard armament included one 23-mm cannon and four missiles capable of carrying up to 6,610 pounds of rockets or missiles. Like the U.S. Air Force's F-III, the Flogger was a swing-wing fighter. When the wings were fully spread, the MiG-23 was able to use shorter distances for take offs and landings. Once airborne, it would fold its wings back. The Flogger had three sweep settings: 16, 45, and 72 degrees.

The engine of the Soviet MiG-23 jet fighter is shown after it was removed from the rubble of the house on which it crashed, killing one man in Brussels, Belgium, July 5, 1989

MiG-25 Foxbat

Another important front-line high-performance interceptor for the Soviet Union was the MiG-25, NATO codename Foxbat. The Foxbat was specifically designed as an interceptor for the United States Air Force's B-70 bomber. But when that bomber was not built, the MiG-25 was modified for other roles.

The Foxbat had a crew of one, a top speed of Mach 3.2, a range of 1,075 miles, a ceiling of almost 68,000 feet, and an astonishing sustained rate of climb—21½ miles in just less than four minutes. It was armed with two radar-guided missiles and two infrared-guided missiles. Later models carried one of the first look-down/shoot down radars as well as an infrared search and track system. It became operational in 1970 and when production ended in 1983, 1,190 Foxbats of all types (interceptor, reconnaissance, trainer, recon with modified radar) had been built. It is still in limited use in some air forces.

When the Foxbat debuted, it created immense consternation among the NATO air forces because of its high performance characteristics. Discounting the pronouncements from Soviet propaganda, the raw data NATO was able to obtain through radar tracking observation and other reconnaissance indicated that the Soviet air force had an interceptor that could match, if not beat, its best fighters. In 1973, Air Force Secretary Robert C. Seamans called the Foxbat "probably the best interceptor in production in the world today." There was concern that it could intercept the SR-71 Blackbird

The United States Air Force got a rare opportunity to get inside one when, on September 6, 1976, Lieutenant Viktor Ivanovich Belenko flew his late-model MiG-25 from a base in Siberia and defected, landing in Japan. The MiG-25 was taken to Wright-Patterson Air Force Base where it was disassembled and studied. Among the many things technicians discovered was that the Soviet Union was still using vacuum tubes instead of transistor circuitry for their electronics. The reason was that tubes were less susceptible to electromagnetic pulse (EMP) interference caused by a nuclear explosion. Its performance was not as great as initially thought and its flight characteristics were severely limited. After sixty-seven days, it was returned, complete but still in pieces, to the Soviet Union. After debriefing and interrogation, Belenko was granted asylum by President Gerald Ford and provided with a trust fund to support him.

Saab 37 Viggen

The Viggen (Swedish for "Thunderbolt") is a single-seat, single-engine, short/medium range attack, fighter, and reconnaissance built for the Swedish Air Force.

Sweden's close proximity to the Soviet Union dictated a defensive strategy that combined diplomatic neutrality with military strength sufficient for defense. In the north, its border was three hundred miles away from the large Soviet base at Murmansk, and in the south, just one hundred miles of Baltic Sea separated the Swedish capital of Stockholm from the Soviet coast (now Estonia).

The goal of the new aircraft, designed to replace the Saab 32 Lansen and Saab 35 Draken in the early 1970s, was to produce attack aircraft that was easy to service and maintain, and a fighter with optimal short-runway performance that included the ability to take off from specially reinforced roads and highways to reduce the vulnerability to attack in the event of war. In addition, the airplane needed to have low-level supersonic capability and at least Mach 2 speed at altitude. Thanks to a 1960 treaty with the United States that allowed Sweden to take advantage of American aeronautic advances, Sweden was able to design the Viggen quickly and cheaply, with more advanced avionics and performance.

The Viggen became operational in 1971 and when production ended in 1990, 329 Viggens of all types had been delivered to the Swedish Air Force. The Viggen remained in operation until 2005, though in its final years the few remaining Viggens were only used for training. The Viggen has a top speed of Mach 2.1, a range of 621 miles, a rate of climb of 7.5 miles per minute, and a ceiling of 59,100 feet. The wing has a double-delta design with a smaller pair of "dogtooth" winglets on each side of the cockpit and higher than the main wings to improve longitudinal stability when carrying bombs or external fuel tanks.

Though the Viggen was a well built, competitively priced, high-performance aircraft, it didn't sell on the export market. The major reason was the restrictions placed by the Swedish government on any foreign sales that precluded sales to undemocratic regimes or unstable governments. A potential sale to India was blocked when the United States refused to issue an export license (also known as an end-user certificate) for the American built jet engine in the Viggen.

BELL AH-1 COBRA AND SUPER COBRA

The AH-1 Cobra was the world's first rotary-winged aircraft to be designed specifically as an armed attack helicopter.

The need for a dedicated attack helicopter became apparent during the early months of the Vietnam War, when many helicopters were lost to ground fire. The AH-1 was fast, heavily armed, and highly maneuverable. Its ability to cover unarmed helicopters made it a powerful combatant in Vietnam and other conflicts. Its precedent-setting design led to numerous variants, including the Super Cobra introduced in 1971. The combined number of Cobras total more than 2,300 manufactured, making it one of the most successful military helicopters. The Cobra entered U.S. military service in 1967. It was replaced in the Army in the 1980s by the AH-64 Apache. However, upgraded versions are still in use with the U.S. Marine Corps, including the new AH-1Z Super Cobra.

The primary missions of the Cobra are helicopter Close Air Support (CAS), escort of transport helicopters and ground convoys, armed reconnaissance, helicopter air-to-air attack, and anti-shipping operations. For many years it was the only western attack helicopter with proven air-to-air and anti-radar missile capability. The Cobra has a maximum speed of 169 miles per hour, a range of 295 miles, and a ceiling of 18,700 feet. Standard armament includes a three-barreled 20-mm Gatling cannon, 2.75 inch rockets, TOW, Hellfire, Sidewinder, and Sidearm missiles. The Super Cobra has a crew of two, and a maximum speed of 218 miles per hour, a range of 365 miles, and a ceiling of 12,200 feet. Its armament includes a three-barreled 20-mm Gatling gun, seven-shot or nineteen-shot Hydra 70-mm anti-personnel rocket pods, eight 127-mm Zuni multi-purpose rockets, and anti-armor TOW, Hellfire, and air-to-air Sidewinder missiles.

MiL Mi-24 Hind

The Mi-24 Hind was the world's first, and basically only, helicopter designed as both a gunship and a troop transport. Heavily armed and armored as well as fast, it was used so extensively during the Soviet-Afghan War (1979–1989) that it became the symbol of the conflict in the same way that the Huey symbolized American involvement in the Vietnam War.

The Hind was designed in the 1960s by a team led by Soviet helicopter designer Mikhail Leont'yevich Mil. Mil saw that advancements in technology made it possible for helicopters to do more on the battlefield, particularly regarding battlefield mobility and firepower.

The Hind became operational in 1972 and has remained in service ever since. More than two thousand Hinds of all types have been built and, depending on the variant, it has a crew of two or three, and a passenger capacity of eight troops or four stretchers. The Hind was designed to be fast, and, with a top speed of 208 miles per hour, it is one of the fastest helicopters ever produced. It has a range of 280 miles and a ceiling of 14,750 feet. The Hind has been described as a flying tank, but the wide array of offensive and defensive weapons it can carry makes the Hind more a flying arsenal. Armament includes flexible, fixed mounted, and turret-mounted single and twin-barrel machine guns, 30-mm turreted cannon, and a munitions package of rockets and bombs weighing up to 3,300 pounds.

During the Soviet-Afghan War, the Hinds established such a fearsome reputation that the Mujahideen called them *Shaitan-Arba* ("Satan's Chariot"). In one incident, a Soviet company was surrounded and in danger of being overwhelmed by Mujahideen militia. A single Hind was so aggressively maneuvered by its pilot that the Mujahideen were forced to break off their attack, even though the Hind was out of ammunition.

Tu-22 Backfire

The Soviet-built Tu-22 Backfire is a long-range supersonic medium bomber capable of performing nuclear and conventional attack, and anti-ship and reconnaissance missions. The Backfires were used in bombing missions during the Soviet-Afghan War.

The Tu-22 has a variable swept-wing design. It became operational in 1972 and remained in production until 1993. A total of 497 Backfires were built. It is believed that Russia's air force presently has 162 Tu-22s in active service with an additional ninety-three on reserve status. The Backfire has a crew of four, a maximum speed of Mach 2.3, a range of almost five thousand miles, and a ceiling of 40,635 feet. Defensive armament is provided by a 23-mm cannon located in a remote controlled turret in the Backfire's tail. It has a munitions capacity (missiles, mines, and bombs) of 46,300 pounds that are carried by a combination of wing mounts and inside the fuselage's weapons bay.

The Backfire became the focus of a hotly contested arms control debate during SALT-2 negotiations. An initial designation of "Tu-22M" by the Soviets caused American intelligence agents to claim this was an act of deception designed to confuse it with the Tu-22 Blinder bomber, a completely different aircraft. More importantly, American negotiators sought to limit the production and number of Backfires because of their strategic threat capability to attack targets deep within American territory using nuclear-tipped cruise missiles. Though SALT-2 and later START-I arms control treaties were never signed, both parties agreed to their terms. It meant that the bomber would not be used for strategic purposes, nuclear or conventional.

T-72 Main Battle Tank

The Soviet T-72 was a main battle tank that was a "low-cost" design compared to the more expensive, and sophisticated T-64.

The T-72 became operational in 1973 and was one of the main Soviet tank exports of the cold war. Upgraded models continue to be produced and more than twenty-five thousand T-72s of all types have been built.

The T-72 weighs forty-five tons (light for a main battle tank), has a crew of three, and a 125-mm main gun. Secondary armament is two machine guns. The T-72 has a top speed of fifty miles per hour and a range of 290 miles.

For years, the American military was concerned that the T-72 would be a dangerous challenge to the American Abrams main battle tanks. Those concerns were dramatically eliminated during Operation Desert Storm (1991) and the Second Gulf War (2003) in Iraq when the Abrams proved to be overwhelmingly superior, even when outnumbered.

Needless to say, the last place a country wants to find out about an enemy nation's new weapon is on the battlefield. The quest to discover whether the main gun of the T-72 was 122 millimeters (then the standard for Soviet tanks) or 125 millimeters (larger cannon mean bigger, heavier shells with more powerful armor penetration) ran the gamut of intelligence experiences. Reportedly $18 million was spent by American intelligence agencies using reconnaissance satellites, radio-listening stations, and code-breaking computers tried—and failed—to obtain an answer to the three millimeter question.

Then, one evening, a British special operations team infiltrated a Soviet tank storage depot in East Germany where T-72s were parked. It succeeded in not only measuring the gun; they also found in the tank a complete operating manual, which they took.

More astonishing was the success of a French military attaché stationed in Moscow. He casually mentioned to his Soviet liaison that he would like to take a look at the new T-72. Not only did his liaison agree, but gave him a personally guided tour and topped it off with a free dinner afterwards.

Aerospatiale SA 341 Gazelle

The SA 341 Gazelle is a light utility helicopter. It was the first helicopter to carry a shrouded tail-rotor fantail, substantially reducing rotor noise. In addition, it was the first helicopter to use rotor blades made of composite materials, now a standard feature on all helicopters.

The Gazelle was created in response to a French Army request for a light, multi-purpose helicopter. Its military missions include attack, antitank, anti-helicopter, reconnaissance, utility, transport, and training. It attracted British Army attention during the design stage, leading to a joint production program between Aerospatiale and Westland Helicopters of Great Britain. The Gazelle became operational in 1973. Exported to more than twenty nations, it has proved a popular design for both the military and law enforcement agencies. Almost two thousand Gazelles have been built.

The Gazelle has a crew of two and can carry up to three passengers. It is a light, strong military helicopter, capable of carrying a payload heavier than its weight, 2,078 pounds and 2,022 pounds respectively. It has a top speed of 193 miles per hour, a range of 416 miles, and a ceiling of 16,405 feet. Military gunship variants can be outfitted with a variety of weapon suites. These include machine guns, 20-mm cannon, and air-to-air and air-to-ground missiles and rockets (on rails or in pods).

An SA-342 Gazelle helicopter bearing the markings of the Egyptian Air Force

FN Minimi

Within a couple of years after its debut in 1974, the Fabrique National Herstal FN Minimi (a contraction of the French term for mini machine gun, *mini mitrailleuse*) has become the most popular portable light machine gun in the world. The American version of the Minimi is the M249 Squad Automatic Weapon, usually referred to as the "SAW."

The air-cooled Minimi has three basic variants, the standard squad or platoon support model, a shorter-barreled Para model used by paratroopers, armored vehicle and helicopter crews, and a vehicle model that is used as secondary armament on armored and unarmored vehicles.

The Minimi ranges in weight from 11.7 to 19 pounds. It is fed by a hundred-round disintegrating belt or a thirty-round magazine. It fires either a 5.56 or 7.62 cartridge, has a rate of fire of 680 to 800 rounds per minute with a muzzle velocity of either 3,035 feet per second or 2,841 feet per second, and a maximum effective range of three thousand yards.

The Minimi and its variants provide small units (under fourteen troopers) filled a void inherent with such units: lack of automatic weapon firepower. It provides accurate fire comparable to that of a rifle, particularly at close range, with the volume of fire typical of a machine gun.

Its firepower proved especially important during the Battle of Mogadishu (October 1993) when American Special Operations troops captured Somali strongman General Mohammed Farrah Adid's foreign minister and top political advisor. Codenamed Operation Gothic Serpent, it was a two-prong attack into the heart of war-torn Mogadishu in which helicopters would drop the capture team and an armed convoy would transport them back to the American base outside the city. The plan began falling apart shortly after the two men were captured. Troops became separated and isolated. The 160 men in the assault found themselves in a desperate fight for survival against overwhelming numbers of unconventional militia in a hostile urban environment. By the time it was over, American troops had suffered 104 casualties, including nineteen killed. Even though helicopters supported the ground troops (two Black Hawks would be shot down by RPGs), casualties would have been higher if the force had not been equipped with SAWs.

ISRAEL AIRCRAFT INDUSTRIES KFIR

The Kfir (Hebrew for "lion cub") is an Israeli-built multi-role fighter that was Israel's primary strike and later fighter-bomber aircraft until the early 1990s.

The Kfir became operational in 1975. When it was retired from the Israeli Air Force in 1996, about 220 Kfirs of all types had been built. The Kfir has a crew of one, a top speed of 1,516 miles per hour, a range of 480 miles and a ceiling of fifty-eight thousand feet. Standard armament includes two 30-mm cannon, and a rocket, missile, and bomb payload weighing a maximum of 13,415 pounds.

The design of the Kfir is based on the French Mirage III with the help of some espionage. The primary aircraft in the Israeli Air Force in the 1960s and 1970s were export models of French Mirage aircraft. Attrition of serviceable aircraft following the Six Day War (1967) had left Israeli squadrons depleted. But an order for fifty new-model Mirage III fighters to replenish the squadrons was embargoed. French President Charles De Gaulle, seeking to advance French interests in the Arab world, had issued a blanket arms embargo to Israel after an Israeli attack against a terrorist base in Lebanon in late December 1968. Because the Israeli Air Force had so heavily invested in Mirage technology and equipment, any switch to a new airframe would be expensive and take time the Israeli government believed it did not have.

Mossad initiated a covert operation to obtain plans for the Mirage III. In what became the biggest espionage operation in history, Mossad agents succeeded in obtaining more than 250,000 blueprints weighing approximately three tons from a Swiss-based corporation that had a license to build the airplane. With plans in hand, the Israelis developed the Kfir, a heavily modified version of the Mirage III that had an improved avionics package and a more powerful jet engine.

The Kfir initially began service as an air superiority aircraft. The role changed to that of strike aircraft after export models of the F-15 Eagle fighters arrived from the United States. Later models of the Kfir were designed to conduct fighter-bomber missions. The Kfir achieved its first, and only, air victory on June 27, 1979, when one shot down a Syrian MiG-21. Thereafter all Kfir recorded successes were against ground targets.

Israeli-built F-21 Kfir aircraft with U.S. Marine Corps paint scheme

MD/Boeing F-15 Eagle/ Strike Eagle

The Eagle's air superiority is achieved through a mixture of unprecedented maneuverability and acceleration, range, weapons, and avionics. It can penetrate enemy defense and outperform and outfight any current enemy aircraft. The F-15 has electronic systems and weaponry to detect, acquire, track, and attack enemy aircraft while operating in friendly or enemy airspace. The weapons and flight control systems are designed so one person can safely and effectively perform air-to-air combat. The F-15's superior maneuverability and acceleration are achieved through high engine-thrust-to-weight ratio and low wing loading. Low wing loading enables the aircraft to turn tightly without losing airspeed. It also has an internally mounted tactical electronic-warfare system, "identification friend or foe" system, electronic countermeasures set, and a central digital computer. The upgraded F-15E Strike Eagle variant is the all-weather long-range strike and ground-attack variant.

It has a crew of two, a top speed of Mach 2.51, a range of 2,400 miles, a ceiling of sixty thousand feet. Armament includes one Vulcan 20-mm multi-barrel internal gun and a combination of Sidewinder, Sparrow, Maverick, AMRAAM, and Slammer missiles and laser-guided bombs. Since it became operational in 1976, more than 800 F-15s of all types, including the Strike Eagle variant (introduced in 1989) have been built.

The first aerial victories in the F-15 were scored not by American pilots, but by the Israelis. In air operations in June 1979 against Syria, an Israeli F-15 shot down a Syrian MiG-21. Then, in February 1981, an Israeli F-15 Eagle shot down a Syrian MiG-125 Foxbat, a fighter the Soviets had built specifically to defeat the F-15. During Operation Desert Storm, American F-15s were credited with shooting down at least thirty-five of the forty-one Iraqi aircraft lost in air-to-air operations.

Closeup of an F-15 showing the cockpit and part of its weapons load

AGM-84 Harpoon

Designed to sink warships in an open-ocean environment, the Harpoon missile system is capable of being fired from submarine, surface ship, or aircraft. It has all-weather, over-the-horizon capability. It is one of only two missiles in the United States military (the Penguin is the other) specifically designed for anti-ship purposes.

The Harpoon was built in response the success of the Soviet Styx anti-ship missile that sunk the Israeli destroyer *Eliat* in 1967. It became operational in 1977 and is still in production. More than seven thousand Harpoons of all types have been built. The variants include sea-launch, air-launch, SLAM (Standoff Land Attack Missile), and SLAM-ER (Standoff Land Attack Missile-Expanded Response). Depending on the model, the Harpoon's length is from 12 feet 7 inches to 15 feet, weight is from 1,145 pounds to 1,470 pounds, and range is from 57 to 196 miles. All have the same diameter (13.5 inches), wingspan (3 feet), and speed (about 530 miles per hour). The guidance system for sea-launch and air-launch variants is sea-skimming cruise with mid-course guidance monitored by radar altimeter with a seeker radar that activates once the Harpoon is near its target. The SLAM and SLAM-ER variants have an inertial navigation system with GPS and infrared terminal guidance.

Export models of the Harpoon are in service in the armed services of several NATO nations as well as Australia, New Zealand, Chile, Singapore, Turkey, Republic of China, Japan, and others.

FAIRCHILD-REPUBLIC A-10 THUNDERBOLT II

The A-10 Thunderbolt II is a sub-sonic single-seat, twin-jet engine aircraft designed for close air support (CAS) and forward air control (FAC) missions.

Officially designated the A-10 Thunderbolt II, it is more commonly referred to by its nickname "Warthog" or "Hog." Shortly after the designs had been approved, an Air Force officer writing in a professional journal speculated on what name would be selected. Referring to earlier aircrafts with colorful nicknames such as the F-84 ("Groundhog" and "Hog") and F-105 ("Super Hog," though more commonly "Thud"), the officer opined that given that this new plane promised to be "the meanest and ugliest plane ever to join the Air Force" that it "should perhaps be called the 'Warthog.'" Senior Air Force commanders were not amused. Fairchild chose Thunderbolt II in homage to the P-47 Thunderbolt fighter-bomber of World War II.

Instead of following the typical pattern of building an airframe or engine and then attaching armament, Dr. Robert Sanitor, head of the A-10's design team, later said, "We literally sat down and designed a plane around the gun that we had to have." That gun was the seven-barreled 30-mm GAU-8/A Avenger Gatling Cannon capable of firing three thousand to four thousand rounds per minute. It has been described as one of the most awe-inspiring weapons ever used by an aircraft. The armor-piercing shells can slice through all but the toughest armor. The A-10 can carry a mixed ordnance load weighing up to sixteen thousand pounds, including smart and dumb bombs, missiles, rockets, and other munitions and electronic warfare pods. It has a crew of one, a top speed of 420 miles per hour, a range of eight hundred miles and a ceiling of forty-five thousand feet. It became operational in 1977 and 715 have been built.

The A-10s participated in Operation Desert Shield/Desert Storm. One dramatic rescue involved a pair of A-10s, flown by Captain Paul Johnson and Captain Randy Goff, on January 21, 1991. A Navy flier had been shot down and was hiding deep within Iraqi territory. The rescue mission ended successfully nine hours later with the A-10s having to strafe Iraqi military vehicles approaching the Navy pilot's location. For their roles in the mission, Johnson received the Air Force Cross and Goff received the Distinguished Flying Cross.

E-3 Sentry (AWACS)

The E-3 Sentry is an Airborne Warning And Control System (AWACS) aircraft that provides all-weather surveillance, command, control, and communications needed by commanders of air defense forces. Battle-tested in Operation Desert Shield/Desert Storm, Operation Enduring Freedom, and Operation Iraqi Freedom and other missions, the E-3 Sentry as proved to be the premier air battle command and control aircraft in the world today.

The E-3 Sentry is a modified Boeing 707/320 commercial airframe with a rotating radar dome. It contains the million-watt Doppler radar system, which permits surveillance from the earth's surface up into the stratosphere and over land or water. The radar has a range of more than two hundred miles for low-flying targets and farther for aerospace vehicles flying at medium to high altitudes. The radar combined with a friend-or-foe identification subsystem can look down to detect, identify, and track enemy and friendly low-flying aircraft by eliminating ground clutter returns that confuse other radar systems.

The Sentry became operational in 1977, and sixty-eight have been built and are in use by the United States Air Force, Great Britain's Royal Air Force, NATO, France, Japan and the Royal Saudi Air Force. It has a top speed of five hundred miles per hour and a range of a thousand miles. It carries a flight crew of four and an AWACS specialist crew of thirteen to nineteen personnel.

The Sentry established its reputation during Operation Desert Shield, providing around-the-clock radar reconnaissance against Iraq during the buildup of Coalition forces in Saudi Arabia. When Operation Desert Storm was launched on January 17, 1991, crews in the E-3 Sentries were able to monitor and control the air battle to such an extent that within a half hour of the attack, Iraqi air defense was all but nullified.

F-16 Fighting Falcon

The F-16 Fighting Falcon is a compact, highly maneuverable multi-role fighter aircraft. The cockpit and its bubble canopy give the pilot unobstructed forward and upward vision, and greatly improved vision over the side and to the rear. The avionics systems include a highly accurate inertial navigation system in which a computer provides steering information to the pilot. It also has a warning system and modular countermeasure pods to be used against airborne or surface electronic threats.

The Fighting Falcon has a crew of one, a top speed of Mach 2, a range of two thousand miles, and a ceiling of fifty-five thousand feet. Its armament includes one 20-mm Gatling gun, and external pylons can carry up to six air-to-air missiles, air-to-surface munitions, and electronic jamming pods. The F-16 became operational in 1978 and to date more than 4,400 have been built for the United States Air Force, and twenty-four other countries.

The F-16 was built under an unusual agreement between NATO member nations the United States, Belgium, Denmark, the Netherlands, Norway, and later Portugal that would provide the all with the first batch of F-16s. Components were manufactured in all the countries with final airframe assembly lines located in Belgium and the Netherlands. This provided such benefits as technology transfer and an increase in the supply and availability of repair parts.

The F-16 has seen extensive combat action throughout the world. Its first air-to-air victories occurred over the Bekaa Valley of Lebanon when Israeli F-16s shot down two Syrian aircraft in April 1981. Later that year they escorted Israeli F-15s in Operation Opera, the mission that severely damaged the Iraqi nuclear reactor, Osiraq, under construction near Baghdad. Pakistan Air Force F-16s shot down at least ten Soviet-built Afghan aircraft during the Soviet-Afghan War when Afghan aircraft intruded into Pakistani airspace. During Operation Desert Storm, 249 F-16s flew 13,340 sorties, the most of any aircraft to participate in the campaign. Only three were lost, all from ground launched rockets or missiles. Air Force Captain Scott O'Grady was flying an F-16 when he was flying over Bosnia in an Operation Deny Flight peace-keeping mission in June 1995. F-16s were also heavily involved in Operation Iraqi Freedom and in air-to-ground attack missions against the Taliban and al-Qaeda in Afghanistan.

Captain Scott O'Grady poses next to a F-16 jet at Hill Air Force Base, Ogden, Utah

Dassault-Breuguet Super Étendard

The Super Étendard (French for "standard" or "battle flag") is a French carrier-based strike fighter.

It is a single engine fighter-bomber that is a highly modified and updated variant of the Étendard that increased its performance and made it capable of delivering nuclear bombs. It became operational in 1978 and seventy-four have been built. Export models were sold to Argentina and Iraq. They remain in active service and are stationed on the French aircraft carriers *Foch* and *Clemenceau*. The Super Étendard is a single seat, single-engine supersonic fighter with a top speed of Mach 1.3, a range of 1,243 miles, and a ceiling of forty-five thousand feet. Conventional armament consists of two 30-mm cannon and a munitions suite of rockets, missiles, and bombs weighing a maximum of 4,600 pounds.

The Super Étendard gained international fame flying in the Argentine Air Force during the Falklands War (1981) against Great Britain. They were used in action against the British fleet in which Super Étendards fired French-built Exocet anti-ship missiles, sinking the HMS *Sheffield* guided missile destroyer and the merchant ship *Atlantic Conveyor*.

A French Navy Super Étendard about to touch down on the
USS *John C. Stennis* as part of a joint exercise in the Arabian Sea in 2007

Panavia Tornado

The Panavia Tornado is a series of "swing wing" strike aircraft developed during the cold war by a three-nation consortium of Great Britain, West Germany, and Italy. It has proven to be a very successful aircraft and has been praised by experts as being "for more than a quarter of a century . . . the most important military aircraft in Western Europe."

The Tornado became operational in 1979 and when production ended in 1999, 992 Tornados had been built. It is in service in the British Royal Air Force, the German Luftwaffe, the Italian Air Force, and the Royal Saudi Air Force. Variants include the Tornado IDS (Interdictor/Strike) fighter-bomber, Tornado ADV (Air Defense Variant) interceptor, and the Tornado ECR (Electronic Combat/Reconnaissance). The Tornado has a crew of two, and depending on the variant a maximum speed of Mach 2.34, a range of 870 miles, and a ceiling of fifty thousand feet. Excluding the Tornado ECR, its standard armament consists of either one or two 27-mm cannon and a munitions package of rockets, missiles, or bombs weighing a total of 19,800 pounds.

Tornado squadrons served as part of the NATO air forces enforcing no-fly zones over Bosnia-Herzegovina in the 1990s during the civil war following the break-up of Yugoslavia. They also saw action during Operation Desert Shield/Desert Storm. Initially Tornados bombed Iraqi airfields and later assisted in medium level strike missions.

UH-60 Black Hawk

The medical evacuation flight of Michael Durant

The UH-60 Black Hawk helicopter is the workhorse helicopter of the United States military and a successor to the successful Huey. The Black Hawk is a medium-lift assault helicopter that can perform a wide variety of missions, including tactical transport of troops, command and control, special operations support, electronic warfare, and medical evacuation.

The most advanced twin-turbine military helicopter in the world, the Black Hawk is equipped with armor protection, self-sealing fuel tanks, and advanced avionics and electronics for increased survivability and capability. It became operational in 1979 and more than 2,600 have been built. They are presently on active duty in the military of twenty nations, including the United States.

The Black Hawk has a crew of two, a maximum speed of 222 miles per hour, a combat radius of 368 miles, and a ceiling of nineteen thousand feet. Standard armament includes two machine guns of varying sizes. It has an external load capacity of up to nine thousand pounds and an internal load capacity of 2,640 pounds, or eleven combat-equipped troops. The Black Hawk is capable of lifting and repositioning a 105-mm howitzer, its crew of six, and up to thirty rounds of ammunition in a single trip. Its rotor blades are able to survive impacts from 23-mm cannon fire.

The Black Hawk debuted in combat in Operation Urgent Fury (1983) the invasion of Grenada and has been involved in every United States military action since. The Black Hawk is arguably most famous for its participation in the Battle of Mogadishu (1993) when two Black Hawks were shot down by RPGs during the assault to capture associates of Somali strongman General Mohammed Farrah Adid. Chief Warrant Officer Michael Durant was a pilot of *Super Six Four*, one of the shot down Black Hawks. He was captured shortly after his helicopter crash-landed and held prisoner for eleven days. He was the only survivor of the helicopter crew. Two Delta Force operatives, Master Sergeant Gary Gordon and Sergeant First Class Randy Shughart, volunteered to rescue Durant when he was still trapped in his helicopter and before the Somali militia captured him. They were killed defending Durant and both would posthumously receive the Medal of Honor for that mission.

U.S. Army soldiers run towards a UH-60 Black Hawk helicopter as they are extracted

Exocet

The Exocet (French for "flying fish") is a French-built multi-platform, subsonic, anti-ship missile capable of being launched from the ground, air, surface warships, or submarines.

The Exocet became operational in 1979 and is still in use today. Widely exported, it is in the arsenals of thirty nations, many in the Middle East. Perhaps the most famous user of the Exocet is Argentina, who successfully used them against British ships in the Falklands War (1982).

The Exocet is about 15½ feet long and 1.14 feet in diameter. Its warhead weighs 364 pounds and total weight is 1,480 pounds. It has a speed of 704 miles per hour.

The Exocet was accorded great respect by military experts throughout the war for its success in sinking the British destroyer *Sheffield* and a merchant ship, and damaging the destroyer *Glamorgan*. The success of the Exocet against these ships defied the belief held by a number of senior Royal Navy officers that its ship-based anti-missile defenses were inadequate. Interestingly, the respect accorded the Exocet by military experts around the world was for something it didn't do in the sinking of those ships—explode. The Exocet that sunk the *Sheffield* did so because of the release of the missile's kinetic energy upon impact and subsequent ignition of unused missile fuel that spread the fire that ultimately doomed the ship. The missile that hit the *Glamorgan* also failed to explode and its unused fuel did ignite. But the *Glamorgan's* damage control system was not wrecked and personnel extinguished the fire.

An Exocet missile is mounted beneath the right wing of this Super Étendard

GENERAL DYNAMICS

An air-to-air view of an F-16 Fighting Falcon aircraft in a vertical climb

The conglomerate General Dynamics is the fifth largest defense contractor in the world. For many years General Dynamics was virtually a "one stop shop" defense contractor. It designed and manufactured everything from man-portable surface-to-air missiles (Stinger), to jets (F-16), to tanks (Abrams), to guided missile destroyers (*Arleigh Burke* class), to nuclear submarines (*Virginia* class). In 1993 it sold its military jet division to Lockheed. But it is still a major supplier of land and sea weapons systems.

General Dynamics began as Electric Boat Company. Electric Boat was founded in 1899 to build submarines for the U.S. Navy designed by Irish immigrant John Holland. Holland, a schoolteacher and tinkerer was fascinated by submarines and had spent decades trying to interest the U.S. Navy in his submarine designs, to no avail. The reason behind their intransigence, Holland scathingly commented that the real reason the Navy rejected his submarines was "because there's no deck to strut on." But President Theodore Roosevelt was fascinated by Holland's submarine, as was the public, and Roosevelt's three-hour underwater trip in and around New York harbor became a front-page sensation.

One of the most important executives for the company was John J. Hopkins who became the company's president in 1947. Following a policy of "grow or die," he began a campaign of acquisition to diversify the company into other defense areas. In 1952, Hopkins oversaw the change of the company's name to General Dynamics. He explained that the new name better described his company's expanding role. But some business wits suggested that the only reason for the name change was that he wanted General Dynamics to appear ahead of General Electric in the telephone book. Hopkins' most important acquisition was the 1954 merger with Convair, a respected military and civilian aircraft manufacturer. The division, subsequently reorganized, would produce in the 1970s the F-16 Fighting Falcon, one of the most successful fighters in the world.

In 1979 it purchased the Chrysler Defense System from the financially-troubled automaker and assumed manufacture of the Abrams tanks. Today General Dynamics concentrates on its land and sea systems and is the foremost builder of armored vehicles, nuclear submarines, and guided missile destroyers in the world.

A bow-on view of the nuclear-powered ballistic missile submarine USS *Ohio*

SHENYANG J-8 FINBACK

The J-8, NATO codename Finback, is the series of Chinese single-seat twin-engine multi-role fighters. Though heavily influenced by Soviet aircraft technology and designs, particularly the MiG-21, it was the first People's Liberation Army Air Force (PLAAF) wholly created by the Chinese.

Designs for the first model in the series were approved in 1964, and a prototype was completed five years later. But civil upheaval caused by the decade-long Cultural Revolution (1966–1976) all but brought development to a screeching halt. Production did not fully resume until the late 1970s, and the J-8 did not become operational until 1980.

The Finback has a crew of one, a top speed of Mach 2.2, a range of 2,486 miles, and a ceiling of 67,256 feet. More than three hundred Finbacks of all types have been built. Depending on the variant, standard armament is either two 30-mm cannon or one 23-mm cannon, and a maximum payload of 9,920 pounds that includes four air-to-air missiles, rocket pods, and bombs.

The J-8 was involved in an international incident on April 1, 2001, whose details are still in dispute. A U.S. Navy EP-3 electronic intelligence aircraft off the coast of Hainan Island over the South China Sea. The United States claimed the EP-3 was in international waters, China claimed that the EP-3 had crossed over into Chinese territorial waters. The EP-3 was intercepted by two J-8s based on Hainan. One of the J-8s made two close passes by the EP-3 in an effort to force the U.S. Navy aircraft to turn away. On the third pass, the J-8 collided with the EP-3. The J-8 crashed and the Chinese pilot was never found. The severely damaged EP-3 landed at the air base on Hainan. A diplomatic row ensued. The crew remained in the aircraft for eleven days before being transported back to the United States. The Chinese returned the EP-3 in July, after completing a thorough examination of it.

ABRAMS MAIN BATTLE TANK

Called the "King of the Killing Zone," Abrams is the name of a series of Main Battle Tanks (MBT) that is the backbone of the armored forces of the United States military, Australia, Egypt, Kuwait, and Saudi Arabia.

The Abrams is named after army Chief of Staff General Creighton W. Abrams, a battalion commander under General George Patton during World War II who lifted the siege of Bastogne during the Battle of the Bulge and who later succeeded General William Westmoreland during the Vietnam War.

The Abrams became operational in 1980 and remains in production; more than eight thousand have been manufactured. There are three variants in service, the MI, MIAI, and MIA2. The MIA2 underwent a modernization program the upgraded its electronic, navigation, and fire control systems. A sub-variant, the MIA2 SEP (System Enhancement Program) adds second-generation thermal sensors and a thermal management system as well as upgrades of the Army's command and control software. It has a crew of four. Depending the variant, the Abrams weighs between sixty and sixty-eight tons, its main gun is either the 105-mm rifled cannon or the 120-mm smoothbore, secondary armament includes one .50-caliber machine gun and two 7.62-mm machine guns. It is powered by a multi-fuel turbine engine and capable of a top speed of up to forty-five miles per hour. The exact composition of the armor is classified, but it includes a combination of steel encased depleted uranium mesh plating, rolled armor, and Chobham ceramic composite armor.

The Abrams entered combat for the first time in Operation Desert Storm (1991). On February 26, 1991, in the Battle of 73 Easting, the Abrams demonstrated its overwhelming superiority. It began when E-Troop of the 2nd Armored Regiment surprised an advance armored unit of Tawalkana Republican Guards containing T-72 tanks. Though outnumbered Captain H. R. McMaster, E-Troop's leader, ordered his command to attack. Within twenty-three minutes, E-Troop's nine Abrams had destroyed twenty-eight T-72s, and, together with support M2 Bradley's destroyed an additional sixteen personnel carriers, and thirty-nine trucks. And that was just the start of the battle. So overwhelming was the victory that, Rick Atkinson, in his account of the conflict, *Crusade*, wrote, "the enemy never had a chance."

An M1A1 Abrams tank participating in field exercises in Louisiana in 2001

Lockheed Martin MC-130 Combat Talon

Looking out toward the rear of the cargo compartment of the MC-130 during a special operations exercise

The MC-130 Combat Talon is the special operations variant of the C-130 Hercules transport. It is designed to provide infiltration, evacuation, and resupply of special operations forces and equipment in hostile or denied territory. Additionally, they can conduct psychological operations and helicopter air refueling.

Variants include the MC-130E Combat Talon I and MC-130H Combat Talon II, MC-130W Combat Spear, and MC-130P Combat Shadow. Differences between them involve the degree of integration of the mission computers and avionics suite, and mission specializations such as search-and-rescue and command-and-control. The Combat Talon I was conceived and developed during the 1960s and though extensively upgraded in the 1980–1990s, it still features analog instrumentation and does not fully integrate the sensors and communications suites.

The Combat Talon II, designed in the 1980s, features an integrated glass flight deck that improves crew coordination and reduces the crew complement by two. The crew for the MC-130E is nine; for the MC-130H, seven. They have a maximum speed of three hundred miles per hour and a range of 3,107 miles. A total of eight-two Combat Talons of all variants have been built.

Invariably MC-130 missions were classified and details on them released only well after the fact—if ever. Some of the missions that have been declassified, beginning in the Vietnam War and continuing up into Operation Iraqi Freedom, reveal that the MC-130s could and did "go anywhere and do anything." Retired Air Force Colonel Thomas Beres was an MC-130E navigator. He described how crews felt about their aircraft and the missions they flew. "If you liked to be a part of a close crew flying unattached around the world doing a neat mission, the MC-130 was for you! We knew we were doing things no one else in the world was doing with C-130s. That was what made us special, not that we were in something called special operations."

M2 Bradley Armored Personnel Carrier

In the words of Tom Clancy, the M2 Bradley is an armed and armored "battle taxi designed to deliver a squad of infantry or a team of scouts to the edge of a battlefield, support that team with fire as necessary, and then reembark the team for movement under armor to the next objective."

It is named after World War II army commander and later Chairman of the Joint Chiefs of Staff General Omar N. Bradley. It was designed to be the American counterpart to the Soviet BMP armored personnel carriers. The Bradley had a much-publicized and troubled developmental history that resulted in an almost complete re-design of the armored vehicle. The M2 became operational in 1981 and since then more than 6,700 have been manufactured. The Bradley has a crew of three and six combat-ready infantrymen, the command variant with its extra communications equipment carries two additional personnel. The Bradley's armor, whose thickness and exact composition is classified, consists of welded aluminum and spaced laminate. Additional armor packages can be added as needed. Its primary armament is a 25-mm chain gun and a TOW ("Tube-launched Optically-tracked Wire-to-command-Link") anti-tank missile launcher and seven TOW missiles. Secondary armament is a 7.62 machine gun. Designed to support and keep pace with the Abrams MBT, the Bradley It has a top speed of 41 miles per hour and a range of 300 miles.

The Bradley's developmental "teething problems" were amply paid off in Operation Desert Storm. Out of the 2,200 Bradleys that fought in the campaign, only three were lost to enemy fire, with an additional twelve damaged.

The situation was less lopsided in favor of the Bradley during the Operation Iraqi Freedom (2003). During the climactic battle of the campaign, the armored assault to capture Baghdad that was called "Thunder Run," Bradley vehicles proved vulnerable to close-quarter RPG attack. But, at that point American troops were facing poorly trained, though fanatic, militia, and losses were lighter than if the defenders had been well-trained regular troops.

Infantrymen exit from an M-2 Bradley infantry fighting vehicle

FIM-92A Stinger

A view of the Stinger missile and a launch tube, a lightweight, portable, shoulder-fired, surface-to-air defense system

The Stinger is a short-range surface-to-air missile (SAM) designed to provide air defense against low-altitude airborne targets.

The Stinger has a crew of two, though it can be operated by one person if necessary. It is five feet long, 5½ inches in diameter. The missile weighs twenty-two pounds and carries a high explosive warhead that weighs about six pounds. Total weight with re-usable tube launcher is 34½ pounds. It is supersonic, has a range from one-half to about five miles, and its guidance system is fire-and-forget passive infrared seeker. Since its introduction in 1981, more than seventy thousand have been manufactured.

The Stinger debuted in combat in a special operations mission conducted by the British Special Air Service (SAS) during the Falklands War (1982) and was credited with shooting down one Argentine attack aircraft.

During the Soviet-Afghan War of the 1980s as part of Operation Cyclone, the CIA supplied the mujahideen with hundreds (some reports claim as many as two thousand) of Stingers for use against Soviet helicopters and airplanes. The mujahideen began receiving the Stingers in 1986. Before that, they had little or no effective anti-aircraft weaponry. Within ten months, according to conservative reports 187 Stingers were fired, shooting down an estimated 140 aircraft. By the end of the conflict, an estimated 269 Soviet aircraft were shot down by Stingers. Though claims were made that the Stingers contributed to the Soviet Union's withdrawal from Afghanistan, the Politburo's decision to draw down forces had actually been made a couple of months earlier.

Firing demonstration of a Stinger surface-to-air missile

MIM-104 Patriot

A Patriot missile is test fired

The Patriot is a surface-to-air missile designed for High to Medium Air Defense (HIMAD). It is also the U.S. Army's anti-ballistic missile (ABM) missile. "Patriot" is the acronym for Phased Array Tracking to Intercept Of Target.

The Patriot became operational in 1981 and since then more than 8,600 missiles have been built. The missile weighs 1,500 pounds, including a two-hundred-pound high explosive blast/fragmentation warhead. It is nineteen feet long, about 1.4 feet in diameter, and has a three-foot wingspan. It has a speed of Mach 5, which it can reach within three seconds after launch. Most missiles in inventory are PAC-2 (Patriot Advanced Capability), a software upgrade to make them more effective in interdicting and destroying incoming missiles. A third upgrade, PAC-3, is gradually being phased in.

Patriot missiles are launched from ground-based Patriot missile batteries. A battery has up to 16 launchers, with each launcher containing four Patriot missiles. A complete launch system contains missiles, launchers, tracking radar, an Engagement Control Station, and a mobile power generator.

During the opening days of Operation Desert Storm (1991), Iraq dictator Saddam Hussein fired Scud tactical ballistic missiles at Israel and Saudi Arabia. On January 17, the Patriot scored its first kill, intercepting a Scud over Bahrain. Then, during the night of January 21–22, in what was called the Battle of Riyadh, Patriot batteries intercepted a number of Scuds aimed at the Saudi capital city, intercepting them all. Meanwhile four Patriot batteries stationed in Israel were kept busy intercepting random Scud attacks. Though Patriot missiles intercepted most of the Scuds fired at Saudi Arabia and Israel, enough Iraqi Scuds did succeed in reaching their targets that an investigation to determine the cause was launched following the end of the campaign. Investigators identified significant software problems and maintenance issues that formed the foundation for latter upgrades.

A pair of Patriot rocket launchers deployed in Kuwait City

OHIO CLASS SSBN

A Trident II missile launch from an *Ohio*-class submarine

Nicknamed "Boomers," the *Ohio* class are fleet ballistic missile submarines (SSBN) are nuclear powered stealth submarines that are ultra-quiet and capable of precision delivery of ballistic missiles. Their mission is strategic deterrence. Quiet, undetectable, and able to park unseen off the shore of a hostile nation, the SSBNs can blindside an enemy with a devastating nuclear strike, silently depart, and repeat the same action within hours hundreds of miles away.

The first boat in the class, *Ohio*, was commissioned in 1981. Other submarines in the class are the *Henry M. Jackson, Alabama, Alaska, Nevada, Tennessee, Pennsylvania, West Virginia, Kentucky, Maryland, Nebraska, Rhode Island, Maine, Wyoming,* and *Louisiana.* The nuclear armament for most of the submarines is the Trident II SLBMs (Submarine Launched Ballistic Missiles).

The *Ohio* class displaces 16,600 tons when surfaced and 8,750 tons when submerged. They are 560 feet long and have a beam of forty-two feet. The exact top speed is classified, but rated at more than twenty knots. They have a crew of fifteen officers and 140 enlisted personnel. In addition to the nuclear missiles, the submarines are equipped with MK48 torpedoes for defense. The *Ohio* is regarded as the quietest submarine in the world. Their hulls are covered with anechoic tiles that eliminate detection by sonar. Because of their nuclear power plants, the *Ohio* class submarines only have to surface and return to port in order to take on supplies and rotate crews. On average, a submarine patrols for 77 days followed by thirty-five days in port for re-supply and maintenance.

Initially the operational lifetime of the submarine was assessed at 30 years. A Navy study in 1995 determined that with overhaul this could be extended to at least 42 years.

The USS *Ohio*, SSBN-726, prior to commissioning ceremonies on April 7, 1981

MiG-31 Foxhound

The MiG-31, NATO codenamed Foxhound, was a supersonic interceptor designed to replace the MiG-25 Foxbat.

The Foxhound was a significant technological leap forward for the Soviet Union. It incorporated advanced digital avionics and was the world's first fighter to have an electronically scanned phased array radar. This gave the Foxhound true look-down, shoot-down capability. The radar could scan approximately 150 miles forward and simultaneously track as many as ten targets. At the same time the radar could also track and engage a target flying behind and below the aircraft. The Foxhound was also the first Soviet interceptor to have a crew of two, a pilot, and a weapon systems officer. This allowed for greater tactical air control by the pilot. Prior to the Foxhound, ground bases closely controlled the interceptors.

The Foxhound became operational in 1982 and about five hundred were built. Initially it was deployed as part of the Soviet Air Defense Force based in Vladivostok. Orders were on the books for upgraded Foxhounds when the Soviet Union collapsed in 1989, causing a temporary delay in new airframes

The Foxhound has a top sped of Mach 2.83, a combat range of 450 miles, and a ceiling of 67,600 feet. Standard armament includes one 23-mm cannon, four air-to-air missiles located in recesses under the fuselage and an additional four wing mounts for additional missiles.

The Foxhound became a Hollywood star in 1982. It is speculated that the Foxhound was the inspiration for the Firefox fictional advanced Soviet stealth aircraft stolen by Clint Eastwood in the movie *Firefox*.

AGM-114 Hellfire

The AGM-114 Hellfire is a multi-platform, multi-target missile system designed to defeat tanks and other individual targets while minimizing the exposure of the launcher to enemy fire. Its name is derived from its original purpose (HELicopter FIRE-and-forget). It is the principal weapon used by U.S. Army helicopters against heavily armored vehicles and reinforced fortifications. Since becoming operational, models also include ground and sea-launched variants.

The Hellfire was developed in 1972 and went into production in 1982. When problems with the initial TV-based guidance system proved insurmountable, the decision was made to switch to laser guidance. The guidance system in the Hellfire models AGM-114A through AGM-114M requires the launcher to illuminate or "paint" the target from launch to impact. The exception is the recent AGM-114L model, which is a true "fire-and-forget" missile.

It is sixty-four inches long, has a diameter of seven inches, and weighs ninety-nine pounds. The conventional warhead is a shaped charge high explosive antitank warhead that weighs eighteen pounds. It has a speed of 1,400 feet per second and a range of 8,750 yards. Its guidance system is semi-active laser homing.

The Hellfire AGM-114N variant fires a thermobaric warhead. Sometimes called "vacuum bombs," thermobaric warheads were designed against enemy forces fighting or seeking refuge in caves or buildings. The warhead is filled with flourinated aluminum powder wrapped around a small explosive trigger. When the missile hits its target, the explosive disperses the powder throughout the enclosed space. This aluminum cloud then ignites, causing a secondary blast that creates a vacuum that sucks in surrounding air and debris with a pressure, depending on the size of the enclosure and strength of the walls, of up to 430 pounds per square inch.

They have proved particularly lethal against Taliban insurgents hiding in caves and buildings in Afghanistan. Human rights groups have condemned the warheads as being "brutal." This has lead to very strict rules of engagement regarding its use.

A SH-60 Seahawk fires an AGM-114B Hellfire missile

FV4030/4 Challenger I

The British Army's Challenger I Main Battle Tank is the world's first tank to use Chobham armor, a classified, bonded composite of ceramics and metal matrices that provide superior protection without significantly adding weight.

The Challenger I became operational in 1983 and by the time that it was replaced with the Challenger 2, 420 had been built. It weighs sixty-two tons (the American Abrams tank weighs about sixty-eight tons) and has a crew of four. Its main gun is a 120 mm rifled cannon and secondary armament are two 7.62-mm machine guns. It has a range of 370 miles and a top speed of thirty-seven miles per hour.

The Challenger was originally built for service in the army of the Shah of Iran, but when he was deposed in 1979 and an anti-West revolutionary government was installed, the British Ministry of Defense blocked delivery of the order. The tanks were then modified and upgraded for use in the British Army. Thus, the British Army wound up with a state-of-the-art tank ten years before a replacement for the present MBT, the Chieftain, was scheduled.

Though the Challenger I was faster, better armed and armored than the Chieftain, it initially suffered by having a poor fire control system. This was corrected and upgraded Challengers were part of the British forces that participated in Operation Desert Shield/Desert Storm.

British participation in the campaign was codenamed Operation Granby, which included the involvement of 180 Challenger I tanks. They accounted for the destruction of 300 Iraqi tanks and armored vehicles without suffering any losses. In addition, a Challenger I is credited with making the longest kill for a tank, when a Challenger I shot and destroyed an Iraqi tank 2½ miles away.

McDonnell Douglas-Boeing F/A-18 Hornet

A member of the flight operations crew signals to prepare another F/A-18 for a catapult launch

The supersonic, twin-engine Hornet is an all-weather multirole fighter used by the U.S. Navy and Marine Corps and a half-dozed other nations. It is the aircraft used by the U.S. Navy's Blue Angels Flight Demonstration Squadron.

The Hornet became operational in 1983 and to date more than 1,500 have been built, including the Super Hornet variant. The Hornet and Super Hornet are among the group of "fourth generation jet fighters" that include the F-16 Fighting Falcon, MiG-29 Fulcrum, and other fighters that became operational in the 1980s. Fourth generation designs place an emphasis on multiple roles and maneuverability and allow for easy upgrades of avionics systems. Depending on the model, the Hornet has a crew of one (F/A-18A and C) or two (F/A-18B and D). It has a maximum speed of Mach 1.8, a combat radius of 330 miles, and a ceiling of fifty thousand feet. Armament includes one 20-mm Gatling gun and a munitions suite of missiles, bombs, and electronic warfare pods with a maximum weight of 13,700 pounds.

The Super Hornet F/A-18E has a crew of one, the F/A-18F has a crew of two. It has a top speed of more than Mach 1.8, a combat radius of 449 miles, and a ceiling of more than fifty thousand feet. Standard armament includes one 20-mm Gatling gun and a munitions package of missiles, bombs and electronic warfare pods weighing as much as 17,750 pounds.

The F/A-18's first combat action was in Operation El Dorado Canyon, an attack on Libyan air defenses in April 1986. The Hornets saw extensive action during Operation Desert Storm in 1991. In one of the sorties flown on January 17, the first day of the offensive, two U.S. Navy F/A-18 pilots were tasked with a bombing mission on H-3, the major military base in western Iraq. For it they were each armed with four two-thousand-pound bombs. As they approached H-3, they received a threat warning. Two MiG-21s were making a head-on attack. With just a flick of a switch, the Hornet pilots went from air-to-ground radar tracking to air-to-air, selected and locked onto their targets. Each fired one missile. Both hit. Once the MiG shoot downs were confirmed, they switched back to their original mission and successfully bombed their target from an altitude of 18,850 feet. Within a week, sixteen Iraqi aircraft had been shot down, causing the survivors to refuse to give battle.

LOCKHEED F-117A NIGHTHAWK

The F-117A Nighthawk is the world's first operational aircraft completely designed around stealth technology.

Designed and manufactured by Lockheed's famous Skunk Works, the Nighthawk created a revolution in military warfare by incorporating low-observable technology into operational aircraft. It is equipped with sophisticated navigation and attack systems integrated into a digital avionics suite. It carries no radar, which lowers emissions and cross-section. It navigates primarily by GPS and high-accuracy inertial navigation. Missions are coordinated by an automated planning system that can perform all aspects of a strike mission, including weapons release. Targets are acquired by a thermal-imaging infrared system, slaved to a laser that determines the range and designates targets for laser-guided bombs.

It has a crew of one, a maximum speed of seven hundred miles per hour. Its armament consists of two internal weapons bays capable of carrying a munitions combination of Paveway and GBU laser-guided bombs or Maverick and HARM air-to-surface missiles. It became operational in 1983. A total of sixty-four were built, and the Nighthawk was retired from the Air Force in 2008.

The Nighthawk's first combat action was in Operation Desert Storm. One of the most vivid images of an F-117A attack during that campaign showed a Nighthawk deliver a precision-guided bomb down the airshaft of the Iraqi defense ministry. Air Force Colonel Barry Horne was an F-117A pilot during the campaign. He had confirmation from an unexpected source about the Nighthawk's stealth capability. He recalled, "The Saudis provided us with a first-class fighter base with reinforced hangars, and at night the bats would come out and feed off insects. In the mornings we'd find bat corpses littered around out airplanes inside the open hangars. They were crashing blindly into our low-radar-cross-section tails."

MiG-29 Fulcrum

The MiG-29, NATO codename Fulcrum, is a highly maneuverable, supersonic multiple-role fighter built by the Soviet Union and one of the most successful export fighters in the world.

The Fulcrum became operational in 1983. More than 1,300 have been built and remain in service in the Russian air force and 28 other nations.

The MiG-29 has a crew of one, a maximum speed of Mach 2.25, a range of 430 miles, and a ceiling of 59,100 feet. Standard armament includes one 30-mm cannon and an air-to-air missile package weighing up to 7,720 pounds. The Fulcrum's avionics package comparable to some of its Western counterparts including the Mirage 2000. Though not as advanced in electronics as the Hornet or Fighting Falcon, the superiority of the American aircraft diminishes the closer the adversaries come to each other. In such dogfight situations, the Fulcrum is more maneuverable and its helmet-mounted missile guidance system, in which the missile goes where the pilot is looking, provides a clear advantage.

Under the terms of the Cooperative Threat Reduction accord of June 23, 1997, the United States purchased 21 Fulcrums from the Republic of Moldova. The treaty is designed to prevent the purchase by rogue states systems capable of delivering weapons of mass destruction. American military intelligence had discovered that representatives from Iran had inspected the jets and were planning to make an offer to buy them. Fourteen of the Fulcrums bought by the United States proved to be advanced models capable of delivering nuclear bombs. The Fulcrums were delivered for study to the National Air Intelligence Center at Wright-Patterson Air Force Base near Dayton, Ohio.

MiG-29 fighter flown by German Luftwaffe pilot

1999 GAFTIC / Red Flag 00-1
2000 Maple Flag   422nd TES
2001 Maple Flag   422nd TES
2002 422nd TES   Twintail 02
2003 Sniper   422nd TES

29✚10

Global Positioning System (GPS)

A U.S. Air Force airman uses a GPS unit in Iraq during a survey

Developed by the United States Department of Defense and originally only used by the military, the Global Positioning System (almost always referred to as "GPS") is one of the great technological achievements in navigation. The heart of the system is an array of about twenty-four navigation satellites (the exact number varies) orbiting Earth. These satellites constantly transmit precise microwave signals to the planet. An individual possessing a GPS receiver can use these signals to determine his location with extraordinary exactness.

When Korean Air Lines Flight 007 was shot down in 1983 as the result of faulty navigation that caused it to accidentally enter Soviet airspace, President Ronald Reagan directed the system be made available free for civilian use. In addition to navigation, it has become an important tool in other fields where accuracy is a premium, particularly map-making, surveying, telecommunications, and science.

Location is determined by the triangulated reception of signals from at least three satellites. The GPS receiver analyses the data from these satellites and then computes both location and time.

For the military, GPS has been particularly useful on the battlefield, where it allows commanders to know constantly the locations of his units down to the individual soldier or vehicle. This has the additional application of helping reduce incidences of casualties as a result of so-called "friendly fire." GPS has also proved valuable in search and rescue operations. One of the more famous uses of GPS was in the rescue of Air Force captain Scott O'Grady in 1995. O'Grady was shot down over Bosnia and trapped in hostile territory. A rescue force was able to extract O'Grady in a minimum amount of time thanks to location information provided by O'Grady's portable GPS receiver.

Artist's global concept of the NAVSTAR Global Positioning System Satellite

AH-64 APACHE

The AH-64 Apache is the U.S. Army's principal attack helicopter. The Apache can operate during the day or night and in adverse weather conditions using the integrated helmet and display sight system. It is equipped with the latest avionics and electronics systems, including target acquisition and designation, pilot night vision, black hole passive infrared countermeasures, surface-of-the-earth navigation, and GPS.

It has a crew of two, a top speed of 182 miles per hour, a ceiling of twenty-one thousand feet, and a combat radius of three hundred miles. Armament consists of one M230 30 mm chain gun, and Hellfire and Stinger missiles, and Sidewinder and Hydra rockets.

The Apache became operational in 1984, and since then more than a thousand Apaches of all types have been built. The AH-64D model is equipped with the AN/APG-78 Longbow Fire Control Radar (FCR) target acquisition system, installed over the main rotor. In addition, a radio modem integrated with the sensor suite allows the D-model Apache to share targeting data with other AH-64Ds that may not have a line of sight to the target. This allows a group of Apaches at different locations to engage multiple targets, with only one Apache revealing its location.

This latter point was a key feature that made possible Operation Eager Anvil, the opening attack against two important Iraqi air defense radar sites prior to the launching of Operation Desert Storm. The Apache-equipped 1st Battalion, 101st Aviation Regiment (Attack) led by Lieutenant Colonel Dick Cody was picked for the operation. It required a simultaneous and coordinated attack on two sites located sixty-nine miles apart. On January 17, 1991, at 12:56 a.m., Cody's Apaches attacked. Flying at night, without navigation lights, and below radar detection at just fifty feet off the ground, the Apaches reached their targets within an hour and a half. The coordinated attack commenced at 2:38 a.m. Within four minutes and before any warning could be issued, both sites complete with antiaircraft artillery defenses, had been annihilated by a combination of Hellfire missiles, Hydra 70 rockets with flechette warheads, and 30-mm chain gun cannon rounds. The "electronic door" into Iraqi airspace was now open. Air Force squadrons quickly flew in and, before dawn, had knocked out almost all of Iraq's air defenses.

American troops head to their barracks following a mission in Afghanistan. In the rear is an Apache helicopter

DASSAULT-BREGUET MIRAGE 2000

Closeup of a pilot in the cockpit of his Mirage 2000 fighter

The Mirage 2000 is a French multi-role supersonic fighter. Though outwardly similar to the Mirage III, which it replaced, it is actually a new design, incorporating advanced interceptor controls.

In addition to its role in the French Air Force, the Mirage 2000 was designed to be a low-cost alternative to General Dynamics F-16 Fighting Falcon. The Mirage 2000 became operational in 1984 and is still in use by the French Air Force, as are export versions in India, Egypt, Brazil, Taiwan, United Arab Emirates, and five other nations. Depending on the variant, the Mirage 2000 has a crew of one or two. It has a maximum speed of Mach 2.2, a range of 963 miles, and a ceiling of fifty-nine thousand feet. Armament includes two 30-mm cannon and a munitions package of missiles, rockets, and bombs with a maximum weight of 13,900 pounds. Production of the Mirage 2000 was concluded in 2007 after 611 had been built, including export models. The French Air Force has begun phasing out the Mirage 2000, replacing it with the Rafael which became operational in 2006.

Mirage 2000 squadrons from France and other countries have served in combat in Operation Desert Storm, in support of NATO operations over the former Yugoslavia in 1995, and in a handful of local conflicts. During the Kargil War between India and Pakistan (1999), India made extensive use of its Mirage 2000 squadrons. The war erupted as a result of Pakistani incursions into the Kargil region of Kashmir claimed by India. If the conflict had escalated modified Mirage 2000s were assigned a nuclear strike role. As both countries had nuclear weapons and other weapons of mass destruction, the international community, led by the United States worked to achieve a diplomatic settlement. This was reached two months after the outbreak of fighting, in July 1999.

Two French military Mirage 2000 aircraft turn on their after burners during a combat patrol over Afghanistan

END USER CERTIFICATE

An End User Certificate issued by Jordan

In the world of international arms sales, nothing is more important than a document known as an End User Certificate. Without one, no country can buy from another even the most basic of weapons. End User Certificate requirements extend to other products, particularly advanced technologies such as electronics and computer hardware and software.

An End Use Certificate is a legal document signed by an authorized official from the buyer nation stating that the buyer confirms that the weapons purchased will only be used by that nation (the "end-use") and will not be resold or shipped to another nation. The purpose of such a document is to prevent weapons going to terrorist organizations or to governments on an arms embargo list. Each country has individual requirements and restrictions that reflect their political history, though all share the intent of regulating the use of what's been sold.

Though the forms themselves are simple, the process of purchasing the weapons, particularly sophisticated ones, is rarely so. As the U.S. Department of Commerce's Bureau of Industry and Security states, "Military end users . . . undergo closer scrutiny than most other end users."

Yet, the record of compliance and enforcement by selling nations has been, well, checkered. The reasons are simple: politics and money. During the cold war, intelligence agencies on both sides became adept at manipulating—even sidestepping—the system. The most notorious example in recent times is the "arms for hostages" Iran-Contra affair of 1985, in which a complicated international arms transaction was arranged in order to free six Americans held by the terrorist group Hezbollah.

Occasionally, transactions would be made through second parties. Arms dealer Sam Cummings, with his CIA connections, was the most famous and successful of these. In other cases, shell corporations would be established as authorized agents. And mineral or oil-rich nations on the embargoed list, such as apartheid-era South Africa and Iraq were sometimes (not always) able to barter their way with poorer nations not on the list to ultimately get what they needed.

An Iraqi soldier holds his new rifle provided by U.S. forces

Ground Mobility Vehicle

The Ground Mobility Vehicle (GMV) is a HMMWV (high-mobility multipurpose wheeled vehicle) manufactured by AM General and customized for Special Operations by Letterkenny Army Depot.

Production of the GMV began in 1985 and more than five hundred have been built in eleven variants, excluding the models built specifically for Special Operations. Actual GMV specifications are classified, but it can be stated that the vehicles feature protective armor; heavy duty and reinforced chassis, suspension, engine, transmission, tires.

It's also a rolling arsenal providing the squad that uses it with a "soup to nuts" inventory of weaponry to fight anything.

It was this aspect that was much on the mind of Special Forces Captain Eric Wright in the days leading up to the launching of Operation Iraqi Freedom. His unit, ODA 391 had not been assigned a role in the upcoming attack, and he believed that one reason was that his commander, Colonel Charles Cleveland, was unfamiliar with the capability of the GMV. When the colonel informed Wright that he planned to conduct a quick inspection of the unit, Wright saw this as an opportunity to show his commander what sort of firepower was in the GMV.

The partial list in a GMV included: one .50-caliber machine gun and three thousand rounds of ammunition or one Mk 19 40-mm grenade launcher; one 7.62-mm machine gun with two thousand rounds; three different types of sniper rifles with up to two hundred match rounds; one shotgun with fifty rounds or a Squad Automatic Rifle with a thousand rounds; eight AT-4 antitank rockets; two Singer surface-to-air missiles; eighty pounds of plastic explosives with detonators, a laser rangefinder/target marker; a minefield-clearing unit; a satellite communications radio; a telescope, thermal imaging gear; a combat medical kit; and food, water and fuel sufficient for operations lasing ten days and over a distance of eight hundred miles. The only thing missing were eight new Javelin antitank missiles, which were en route.

Colonel Cleveland was impressed. On April 6, 2003, at a road junction in Debecka Pass in Iraq, ODA 391 was part of 31 Special Forces troops that decisively defeated a superior Iraqi combined force of tanks, artillery, and mechanized infantry; an action that changed Special Operations doctrine.

CHEMICAL WEAPONS

Classified as a weapon of mass destruction by the United Nations, chemical weapons use the toxic properties of chemical compounds to kill or incapacitate.

More than seventy chemicals have been used or developed for weapons purposes. The most famous of these agents is poison gas, particularly mustard, chlorine, and phosgene. Poison gas was first used in the Second Battle of Ypres (April 22, 1915) during World War I. Using prevailing winds to disperse the agent, German troops released canisters of chorine gas that drifted over French lines, killing and incapacitating thousands. Within weeks the Allies responded with their own poison gas weapons.

The "father of chemical warfare" was Professor Fritz Haber of Germany. Haber developed the chlorine gas bombs used at Ypres and was at the battlefield, supervising their use. His wife, Clara, distraught because he refused her entreaties to end his work on chemical weapons, committed suicide a few weeks later. In 1918, Haber was awarded the Nobel Prize in Chemistry for his work on the synthesis of ammonia. The announcement caused enormous outrage and controversy. In his acceptance speech, Haber made this prediction, "In no future war will the military be able to ignore poison gas. It is a higher form of killing."

After the war, revulsion over the use of poison gas led to the Geneva Protocol of 1925 prohibiting the use of chemical and biological weapons. Two additional treaties, the 1972 Biological Weapons Convention and the 1993 Chemical Weapons Convention, expanded the prohibitions to cover production, storage, and transfer of the chemical warfare agents.

Compliance was not initially universal. During World War II, both the Allies and Axis powers had chemical weapons, though they were never deliberately used, the sole exception being Nazi Germany's use of poison gas in concentration camps.

Poison gas was used by Saddam Hussein's regime during the Iran-Iraq War (1980–1988). On March 16, 1988, Iraqi aircraft began dropping bombs containing mustard gas, hydrogen cyanide, and nerve gases sarin, soman, tabun, and VX on the Kurdish town of Halabja occupied by Iranian troops. Thousands of soldiers and civilians were killed outright. Estimates of the total death toll eventually reached fifteen thousand, with an untold number of people suffering injuries.

Utilitiesmen participate in a chemical biological and radiological warfare drill at the Naval Construction Battalion Center in Gulfport, Mississippi

Biological Weapons

Biological warfare, also known as germ warfare, uses toxins and living organisms, specifically the pathogens of diseases, to incapacitate or kill. Anthrax and smallpox are the two most common diseases associated with biological warfare. Biological weapons are categorized as weapons of mass destruction, and their use has been prohibited by international treaty. The four types of biological warfare agents are bacteria, viruses, fungi, and rickettsii.

The first modern use of biological weapons is believed to have occurred during World War I. The Allies accused Germany of infecting livestock with anthrax and glanders bacteria and sending them into enemy territory, but conclusive evidence to support this claim was never found.

Great Britain and the United States had signed the Geneva Protocol of 1925 that prohibited the use of chemical and biological weapons. But, to borrow the legal term *tu quoque* ("I did it, but you did it, too."), the countries began amassing their own stockpiles of biological weapons after they discovered that Germany and Japan were doing so. By the end of World War II, the United States had almost four thousand people working at four top-secret germ warfare facilities.

For two decades after World War II, the United States conducted more than two hundred biological experiments, using benign bacteria. Their purpose was to estimate levels of infection and establish effective countermeasures. The most famous of these tests were conducted on the New York City subway system. Researchers discovered that wind turbulence caused by the subway cars could distribute the bacteria throughout the system within hours.

Iraq had created substantial stockpiles of anthrax, botulism, and other biological weapons under Saddam Hussein. In addition to chemical weapons, Iraq also used biological weapons containing rotavirus, a disease fatal to children, against the Kurds from 1987 to 1989. Concerned that he might use biological weapons against Coalition forces, thousands of troops were inoculated prior to Operation Desert Storm. Though Iraq deployed the weapons, they were never used.

U.S. Air Force firefighter dressed in Nuclear, Biological, and Chemical gear

AMPHIBIOUS ASSAULT SHIP

Amphibious assault ships are warships superficially resembling aircraft carriers that contain in one vessel everything needed to conduct landing operations: troops, amphibious assault craft, transport helicopters, and fixed- and rotary- winged aircraft capable of providing close combat air support.

Amphibious assault ships are the primary warships in an Assault Ready Group (ARG), a fleet specifically dedicated to littoral (coastal) operations. The ARG's capability to launch an amphibious operation and remain for extended periods of time in support of the landing, sometimes referred to as "bite and hold," with alligator-like ferocity has caused ARGs to be nicknamed the "'Gator Navy."

The United States has two classifications of amphibious assault ships, *Tarawa* class Landing Helicopter Assault (LHA) and *Wasp* class Landing Helicopter Dock (LHD). The *Tarawa* class has five ships, *Tarawa*, *Saipan*, *Belleau Wood*, *Nassau*, and *Peleliu*. They displace 39,967 tons, are 834 feet long, have a beam of 131.9 feet, and a draft of 25.9 feet. They have a top speed of 24 knots and a range of ten thousand miles at a cruising speed of twenty knots. They have a crew of 82 officers and 882 enlisted personnel and berths for 1,900 Marines. Ship armament includes a mix of surface-to-air missiles, 20-mm cannon, and .50-caliber machine guns. They can carry up to thirty-five aircraft. The aircraft component includes Harrier attack aircraft, Super Cobra attack helicopters, and transport helicopters. The larger *Wasp* class, which became operational in 1989, includes the *Wasp*, *Essex*, *Kearsarge*, *Bataan*, and *Bonhomme Richard*. They displace 40,500 tons, are 844 feet long and a draft of twenty-seven feet. They have a top speed of twenty-two knots and a range of 9,500 miles at a cruising speed of eighteen knots. They have a crew of 104 officers and 1,004 enlisted personnel and berths for about 1,900 Marines. Ship armament includes a mix of surface-to-air missiles, 20-mm cannon, and .50-caliber machine guns. Depending on the mission profile, they can hold more than fifty fixed- and rotary-winged aircraft.

The *Kearsarge* became famous in 1995 when, on June 6, a Marine rescue team stationed on the *Kearsarge* rescued Air Force pilot Captain Scott O'Grady. O'Grady had been hiding for almost a week in the mountains of Bosnia after his F-16 had been shot down by Bosnian troops in defiance of NATO peace-keeping operations.

The amphibious assault ship USS *Kearsarge* while off the coast of Port au Prince, Haiti, in 2008

MILITARY ROBOTS

An Owl MKII Unmanned Surface Vehicle (USV) capable of conducting marine reconnaissance

Military robots are machines capable of independent or remote-controlled action that are designed for a variety of military purposes.

The earliest military robots appeared on the battlefields of World War II. Perhaps the most famous of these was Germany's remote-controlled Goliath, a small, explosive-filled tracked vehicle used in Normandy. But it was not until 2001 when military operations commenced in Afghanistan that robots began playing anything more than minor, ancillary roles in campaigns. Today, military robots are used in the air (Predator UAV and UCAVs), on the ground (Unmanned Ground Vehicles, or UGVs), on the water (Unmanned Surface Vehicles, or USVs), and under the water (Unmanned Undersea Vehicles, or UUVs).

The big push for the widespread use of military robots began when, in 1990, the Department of Defense consolidated a number of separate development projects related to ground vehicle robotics under the Joint Robotics Program (JRP). The JRP prepared a master plan to develop a wide array of UGVs. Organized into light, medium, heavy, and large categories, they range in size from the small TALON bomb detection robots to the gigantic Panther II that uses a modified Abrams tank chassis and is designed for mine clearing operations.

The U.S. Navy's robotics program is building a variety of surface and undersea vessels capable of conducting mine countermeasures, anti-submarine warfare, maritime security, surface warfare, electronic warfare, maritime interdiction operations, and provide mission support for Special Operations units. The Navy has organized their robots into four hull classes. The smallest is the X-Class, generally inexpensive man-portable vessels. The Harbor Class (surface), and Snorkeler Class (underwater) are both the same size (about 21 feet). The Fleet Class is the largest, about thirty-five feet, and is designed for sophisticated missions from mine sweeping to anti-submarine warfare. Plans are for them to have a top speed of about thirty-five knots and be capable of operating for at least forty hours.

An Explosive Ordnance Disposal Technician in special full body armor conducting a suspicious package exercise, supported by an explosive ordnance disposal robot—note the robot's shotgun attached to the robot's far left arm.

PRECISION GUIDED MUNITIONS

So-called "smart bombs," Precision Guided Munitions (PGMs) are missiles, bombs, or artillery shells equipped with electrical guidance systems that enable them to accurately home in on a target just before impact.

During World War II, U.S. Army Air Force bombardiers using the optical Norden bombsight that supposedly enabled them to "drop bombs into pickle barrels." But, a study comparing delivery accuracies revealed that in World War II 108 B-17s had to drop 648 bombs to destroy a target. In the Vietnam War, when early generation munition guidance systems became available, that number dropped to 176 bombs. Today's guidance systems have reduced that number, depending on the size of target and munition, to as few as one.

Guidance systems include radio beam, radar, infrared, electro-optical, laser, and, most recently, GPS. GPS has become particularly favored because in addition to being inexpensive and extremely accurate, it is not affected by adverse weather conditions such as fog or sandstorms, which can significantly degrade munitions equipped with laser-guided systems.

And, as guidance systems have become more sophisticated and varied, so to have the warheads. No longer do munitions simply go "boom." Some are designed to disable rather than destroy, as was demonstrated on January 17, 1991, the first day of Operation Desert Storm. U.S. Navy ships fired a number of Tomahawk Land Attack Missiles (TLAMs) at Iraq's Taji and Dawrah electric power plants that "short-circuited" the electrical network. These TLAMs contained then-secret special warheads filled with thousands of small, ¾- by ½-inch rolls of long, fine carbon fibers. When they arrived at their target, the missiles scattered spools of carbon that unrolled over the outdoor portion of the switching system that transferred electricity from generators to the power lines. When automatic circuit breakers detected power surges in the switching yard, they shut down the generators. Plant employees noted that within a day, wind blew the rolls and fibers from surrounding fields back over whatever portion of the outside electrical facilities that had been cleared.

The use of the carbon fibers enabled the Coalition to put the Iraqi electrical system out of action for military purposes without so damaging it that it could not be speedily repaired in postwar reconstruction.

Members of a Precision Guided Munitions shop pose behind an
EGBU-15 2,000 pound bomb

COMMUNICATION DEVICES

In warfare, information is as much a weapon as is the rifle, tank, warship, or warplane. Since the dawn of organized warfare, one of the most persistent and vexing problems faced by commanders at all levels is that of getting the right information to the right people at the right moment, in what the military calls real time. To overcome that problem, they need communications devices.

Before the harnessing of electricity, communications devices included smoke, flaming arrows, polished metal plates, mirrors, semaphore flags, bugles, trumpets, drums, and messages delivered by human or animal (pigeon) courier. And with the exception of the latter, their utility was limited to line-of-sight.

The development of the telegraph in the 1850s opened a new vista in communications devices. Now, leaders half a world away could direct the battlefield actions of subordinates, a fact that almost led to a rebellion by French generals during the Crimean War (1853–1856). They objected over meddlesome orders issued by Emperor Napoleon III from his headquarters in Paris.

Wireless communication began in the 1880s when Heinrich Hertz demonstrated the existence of electromagnetic radiation ("hertz" became the name for the system used to measure radio waves). Technological advances in the years following the war led to the rapid integration of wireless communication into the military. A milestone in radio communication was reached with the International Radio Convention of 1927, which adopted the U.S. Navy's plan for worldwide frequency allocation. The transistor revolutionized radio telecommunications. Radios became smaller, lighter, could communicate greater distances, and utilize more frequencies. Radio transmissions of hundreds of miles or more became possible with the development of troposcatter propagation radios. Using special antennas, these transceivers bounced radio waves off clouds of ionized particles in the higher ionosphere.

Satellites and SATCOMs, radios and cell phones capable of communicating via satellites, have led to further advances. The extraordinary close coordination of Coalition forces during Operation Desert Storm (1991) was in large part due to sophisticated communications and tracking devices. Today for example, a soldier in a remote location in Afghanistan can, by using a device no bigger than his hand, talk and transmit images to superiors sitting in the Pentagon.

A marine from a reconnaissance battalion headquarters sets up a SATCOM for operation

Public Opinion

If religious faith is one side of the spiritual coin that inspires a people to embark on the destructive path of war, then the temporal side of that coin is public opinion.

Though government officials can, and have, invoked divine assistance, they more rely on deeds such as battlefield victories and assorted civilian-front programs to sustain citizen support. Army Chief of Staff General George C. Marshall noted that challenge. In a post–World War II interview, he recalled that President Franklin Roosevelt was insistent that the United States launch an offensive against Germany in 1942, even though the country was still in the midst of rearming. Marshall said, "We failed to see that the leader in a democracy has to keep the people entertained. The people demanded action. We couldn't wait to be completely ready." This led the Allies to stage Operation Torch, the Allied landing in North Africa in November 1942, just eleven months after America's entry into the war.

Dictators generally have it easier once they assume power as they control all forms of communications as well as security forces, thus insulating them from organized public opprobrium that would otherwise vote them out of office.

Iraqi dictator Saddam Hussein demonstrated this in 1991. The Bush administration believed that Hussein would not survive the defeat his regime suffered in Operation Desert Storm. Though Iraq was driven out of Kuwait and its army decimated. Instead, days after the end of hostilities, Baghdad Radio announced, "The allies of Satan and its accursed leader have been taught a lesson." One year later, Saddam Hussein's hold on power had increased, whereas the real victor of Operation Desert Storm, President George Herbert Walker Bush, had lost his bid for re-election.

A lone figure sits outside the Houses of Parliament among crosses and mock gravestones during a Persian Gulf anti-war demonstration

PREDATOR

The Predator is the most well known of a new generation of aircraft known as Unmanned Aerial Vehicles (UAVs) and Unmanned Combat Aerial Vehicles (UCAVs). The term "Predator" officially refers not to the aircraft itself, but to a weapons system package that includes not one, but four aircraft (with assorted sensor packages); a ground control station; a secure satellite communications link; an operations crew composed of a pilot and one or two sensor operators; and a maintenance and support crew containing as many as fifty-two mechanics and technicians.

The Predator has a number of advantages over similarly equipped, manned combat aircraft. Because they don't carry a pilot and life support systems, they're substantially smaller, lighter, and cheaper. As the Predator is controlled by the pilot and operators from consoles in the ground control station, risk of death, injury, or capture of the crew is minimal.

UAVs, per se, are not new. The first record of UAV use occurred in the American Civil War, when both sides briefly floated explosive-laden balloons over enemy lines. In World War II the Allies used radio-guided B-17 bombers filled with explosives to destroy U-boat pens during Operation Aphrodite. The operation was canceled after several crew fatalities, including the death of Lieutenant Joseph Kennedy, Jr., the elder brother of president John F. Kennedy. During the Vietnam War, the United States used with uneven success Buffalo Hunter remote control airplanes for reconnaissance.

Predator success over the skies of war-torn Bosnia in 1995 demonstrated that the day of the UAV had finally come. Lessons learned from those missions led to improvements in foul weather and armament-carrying capability. Improved Predators saw service during Operation Enduring Freedom in Afghanistan. In March 2002, an armed Predator conducted the first Close Air Support mission by a UAV when it destroyed an al Qaeda machine gun bunker in the Battle for Robert's Ridge during Operation Anaconda. Success in Afghanistan led to Predator use in Operation Iraqi Freedom (2003), and against terrorist sites in Pakistan and Yemen.

As more new Predators, UAVs, and UCAVs come into service, they stand to do something once thought impossible—sweep the skies clear of piloted warplanes.

Non-lethal Bullets

As the term indicates, non-lethal bullets are designed to disable and not kill. The projectiles are made of soft compounds, or are gas filled, and fired at low velocity. Only in extreme cases involving short range do they penetrate the skin or cause serious injury. Rubber bullets are the most widely known non-lethal bullet.

One of the first non-lethal "bullets" was rock salt. The exact date of their first use is unknown. During the era of muzzle loaders, the firearm would be loaded with a smaller powder charge, so that the rock salt wouldn't be pulverized by the blast, followed by a handful of rock salt chunks. Shot at relatively close range, the rock salt would puncture the skin and cause extreme irritation. It was usually used in rural areas to drive away varmints (occasionally of the two-legged variety).

Rubber bullets first came in use during the 1960s. British law enforcement officials used them to control rioters in Hong Kong, then a British territory, and Northern Ireland. They were soon adopted by law enforcement agencies around the world. Over the years, new types of non-lethal bullets have been developed and the military has added some new types to the arsenal.

Non-lethal bullets include: blunt-force rounds, stinger rounds, and pepperball rounds.

Blunt force rounds include wood baton, rubber baton, flexible baton, and foam (bean bag and sponge) baton. These look like shotgun shells and are filled with small discs resembling the shapes of hockey pucks made of the appropriate material. As soon as the round exits the barrel, it separates in order to strike multiple targets. The rounds are usually fired on the ground near the targets, causing the rounds to ricochet and strike the legs.

Stinger rounds are loaded with very small rubber pellets and pepperball rounds contain small plastic balls filled with pepper gas that release the gas on impact.

One new type of round under development is a taser-style bullet that sends a small electric charge that causes muscle spasms. Another is a "tunable" non-lethal bullet, one that can actually be adjusted in the field to be "hard" or "soft" depending on the situation. Using a Star Trek analogy, one of the developers said, "It's the difference between 'Set phasers on stun' and 'Set phasers on kill.'"

Spent rubber bullet cartridges

JAVELIN

The Javelin is a fire-and-forget missile with lock-on before launch and automatic self-guidance. It is capable of taking either a top-attack flight profile against armored vehicles, impacting the generally thinner top layer, or a direct-attack mode against fortifications. The warhead is fitted with two shaped charges, a precursor warhead to detonate any explosive reactive armor, and a primary warhead designed to penetrate base armor. The missile is ejected in a "soft launch arrangement" reaching a safe distance away from the operator before the main rocket motors ignite. The disposable Javelin launch tube is attached to a reusable command launch unit (CLU) which aims and launches the Javelin.

The launch tube is 47.25 inches long and the missile is forty-three inches long. The launch tube's diameter is 5.6 inches and the missile's diameter is five inches. The total weight of the Javelin is just over forty pounds, the missile weighing twenty-six pounds. The warhead weighs 18.5 pounds. It has a maximum range of 8,200 feet. The missile has an infrared guidance system.

The Javelin got its first real test in battle during Operation Iraqi Freedom (2003). ODA 392 was the lead unit in an assault team of about 30 Special Forces troops assisted by Kurdish militia in northern Iraq. At a crossroads at Debecka Pass, the group came under attack by roughly a battalion-sized Iraqi unit comprised of four tanks; artillery including a multi-barreled anti-aircraft gun used to support the infantry, a 122-mm rocket launcher, and a 152-mm howitzer, and eight armored personnel carriers containing more than 150 troops. A frantic radio call asking for air support received the response that it would be thirty minutes before any aircraft arrived. The team didn't have three minutes, let alone thirty. Their only chance for survival was the anti-tank Javelin missile, which had never before been tested in battle. While some laid down machine gun and grenade launcher cover fire, others broke out the Javelins. The men fired as soon as the guidance system locked in on a target. In less than ten minutes, seven enemy armored vehicles had been destroyed or disabled. Thanks to the Javelin, the Special Forces team stopped the Iraqi counterattack and, as it turned out, held them at bay without air support for two hours. And did so without suffering a single casualty.

Two US Marine Corps members fire a Javelin anti-tank missile

B-2 Spirit

Northrop Grumman B-2 Spirit is a multi-role stealth heavy bomber capable of delivering conventional and nuclear weapons. With descriptions calling it "boomerang shaped" and a "flying triangle" or "flying wedge," the B-2 is one of the more unusually shaped airplanes in service.

The B-2 became operational in 1997, and twenty-one are presently in service with the United States Air Force. Most of the information about the B-2 remains classified. The first time it was put on public display, tarps of various sizes were positioned over some sections of the airplane in order to hide sections of it. The B-2 has a crew of two, a top speed of Mach 0.95, a range of 6,900 miles, and a ceiling of fifty thousand feet. It has two internal bomb bays that can hold up to fifty thousand pounds of bombs and missiles. Even though it is big (sixty-nine feet long with a 172-foot wingspan), its use of advance stealth technologies makes it almost invisible to radar.

In a departure from tradition and like the U.S. Navy's naming of ships, each B-2 has an individual name. The first B-2 is *Spirit of America*. Other names include *Spirit of Ohio*, *Spirit of New York*, *Spirit of California*, and *Spirit of Washington*. The only other B-2 not named after a state is *Spirit of Kitty Hawk*.

The B-2's first combat action occurred in 1999 when it destroyed Serbian targets in the Kosovo War. B-2s have flown missions in support of ground operations in Iraq and Afghanistan. The home base for the B-2s is Whiteman Air Force Base, Missouri. Because of the advanced technologies in the B-2, forward basing of them is highly restricted. This resulted in some of the longest bombing missions in history, with a number of missions lasting more than thirty hours and one marathon mission topping fifty hours.

Modern Armor

World War I French soldiers wearing body armor that was tested for pistol, rifle, and machine gun fire

Armor-makers faced two growing challenges during the twentieth century. Lethal weapons were becoming more powerful and sophisticated at a pace of unprecedented swiftness. No longer would adding an extra inch of steel plate suffice. In addition to protection against bullets and explosives, troops and vehicles would also have to be protected against nuclear, chemical, and biological weapons.

Two basic types of armor were developed for individuals: ballistic armor and MOPP (Mission Oriented Protective Posture) gear. Ballistic armor composed of ceramic plates and synthetic fabrics and woven into computer-designed thicknesses and patterns to achieve optimum protection went into widespread production in 1998. It includes a gas mask and outer garments that filter out and are impermeable to toxic agents. MOPP suits also have sensor strips that monitor radiation levels.

The principle of vehicle armor is the same as that for the body, to protect the most vulnerable parts of the vehicle. In ships, this means the area of the hull at the water line and compartments necessary for the protection and command of the ship. In aircraft and land vehicles, such as tanks, this includes the engine and transmission area as well as the workspace for the crew and ammunition storage space.

One recent improvement in vehicle armor is Chobham armor, created in the 1960s and named after the British tank research center that developed it. Chobham armor is a classified design of ceramic tiles and metal plates in elastic layers designed to exploit the kinetic energy of an impacting projectile. Chobham armor literally uses the force of the projectile against it. Chobham armor is lighter than traditional steel plates, and more effective against modern weapons. New types of vehicle armor based on the principle of Chobham armor have since been perfected; all are classified.

U.S. Army soldiers on an M1114 Up-Armored Humvee, note the extra side-panel armor on the right

Night Vision Device

Historically, combat operations suffer a significant drop-off in effectiveness once the sun sets. The reason, of course, is that soldiers can't see in darkness. Over the centuries, commanders tried various methods to increase individual effectiveness during night-time operations. It was not until the 1950s that technology had advanced sufficiently to provide man-portable optical devices to turn night into day.

Modern Night Vision Devices (NVDs), sometimes also known as Night Vision Goggles or NVGs, are sufficiently sophisticated that night fighters have the ability to see, maneuver, and shoot at night or during periods of reduced visibility. Night Vision Goggles are electro-optical devices that intensify ambient light in both the visible and infrared spectrum thousands of times by electronic means. Users do not look through NVGs as they would binoculars. Instead, the viewer looks at an amplified electronic image projected on a phosphor screen.

The first generation of NVDs that became available in the early 1960s were able to amplify ambient light a thousand times. The second generation of NVDs that appeared in the early 1970s had increased the amplification level to twenty thousand times. Current NVDs, that started becoming available in 1999, have an amplification range from thirty thousand to fifty thousand times.

Though NVDs have enhanced a soldier's ability to conduct night operations, they are not the same as human eyesight in daylight. Images are monochromatic, either shades of electric green or gray. Field of view in NVDs is just forty degrees (normal eyesight is almost 190 degrees), so the effect is like looking down a tunnel. Image sharpness is degraded, causing even objects nearby to look out of focus. Depth of field is hampered. Normal human vision is stereoscopic, or two-eyed. NVG vision is essentially monocular, or one-eye, vision. This creates problems in judging distances of objects, particularly if they overlap or are beside each other and one is significantly larger.

Yet, even with these limitations, Special Operations troops have become so proficient in the use of NVDs and NVGs that they prefer to conduct all their operations in the hours of darkness and have adopted the motto: "We own the night."

A soldier using a pair of Night Vision Goggles

BAE Systems

Founded in 1999 through a merger of British Aerospace and Marconi Electronic Systems, BAE Systems is the world's third largest defense contractor. The international conglomerate's lineage can be traced back to 1560 and the Royal Gunpowder Factory. Its divisions include some of the most famous names in European arms, including Vickers-Armstrong, Bofors, Supermarine, Avro, de Havilland, and Marconi.

BAE was formed in the wake of a consolidation of the arms industry that reached its peak in the 1990s when, in 1995, Lockheed and Martin Marietta merged to create the world's largest defense contractor and, in 1997, Boeing and McDonnell Douglas merged to create the world's second largest contractor. BAE's corporate structure reflects intra-national security concerns, particularly with regards to its biggest customer, the United States. For example, its American subsidiary, BAE Systems, Inc., is led by American managers and it is subject to American government export arms restrictions.

BAE Systems, either alone or in partnership with other defense contractors, designs and builds weapons systems for use in the air, on land, and on and under the sea. It is a partner with Lockheed-Martin and Northrup Grumman on producing the F-35 Lightning II stealth multi-role fighter, a partner with Alenia Aeronautica and EADS in manufacturing the Typhoon F2 Eurofighter, a multi-role fighter for NATO and other nations, and is building the *Queen Elisabeth* class carriers, *Queen Elizabeth* and *Prince of Wales*, scheduled to replace the aging *Invincible* class carriers beginning in 2014. These new carriers are designed to remain in service for fifty years.

While the high-tech weapons systems grab the headlines (and bring in the big profits), BAE Systems has also been a leader in less complex sytems. It is also the contractor for the adaptable combat equipment vests officially known as Modular Lightweight Load Carrying Equipment (MOLLE) Core Rifleman sets, and other supply and storage luggage and containers.

The first *Astute* class nuclear submarine is brought out of the Devonshire Dick Hall at the BAE Systems production plant

DASSAULT RAFALE

The delta wing Rafale is a supersonic twin-engine multi-role fighter designed for both land- and carrier-based operations.

The Rafale became operational in 2000 and remains in production. Three variants are in service, the Rafale C (*Chasseur*) a single-seat fighter for the French Air Force, the Rafale B (*Biplace*) a two-seat version with enhanced avionics for strike and reconnaissance missions, and the Rafale M (*Marine*) a single-seat carrier fighter. Though not a true stealth aircraft, the Rafale does incorporate some stealth technology, giving it a reduced radar signature. Depending on the variant, it has a crew of one or two, a top speed of Mach 2, a combat radius of 1,150 miles, and a ceiling of 55,200 feet. Standard armament includes one 30-mm cannon and a thirteen-missile package that includes air-to-air and air-to-ground missiles. The Rafale is also capable of firing nuclear missiles.

The Rafale is the latest in a line of military aircraft built by the French aviation company, Dassault Aviation. Marcel Bloch founded the company in 1930 and, though the French government nationalized it in 1936, he remained in charge. During World War II, Bloch was imprisoned by the Vichy government in 1940 and, in 1944, deported to the Buchenwald concentration camp. After the war, Bloch changed his name to Boch-Dassault and began rebuilding his company.

Dassault's most famous aircraft is the Mirage. He later said, "I called it Mirage, because like a desert mirage, the enemy will see it but never reach it." During the Six Day War (1967), the Israeli Air Force, flying Mirages decisively overwhelmed the larger Egyptian Air Force, equipped with Soviet MiGs.

Dassault is the lead contractor for the nEUROn, a stealth Unmanned Combat Air Vehicle that is one of the next generation of combat drones.

Suicide Bomber

Iraqi firefighters atempt to extinguish burning vehicles following a suicide bombing

Suicide bombers seek to inflict the maximum amount of damage knowing that they will die in the process.

Suicide attacks have occurred throughout history. The earliest example is Samson, who died when he caused the collapse of a temple containing Philistines. During the final months of World War II, the Japanese military organized kamikaze ("divine wind") attacks in which pilots flew aircraft with the intent of crashing them into enemy warships.

In the latter part of the twentieth century, Islamic extremists began using suicide attacks as a tactic of terror against targets in Israel and, later, against civilian and military targets in the West. These suicide bomb attacks come in many forms. The most common is with a person carrying explosives under clothing who triggers the explosives at the desired moment. Attackers also use cars or trucks packed with explosives. In 1983, terrorists drove a truck bomb into a barracks building in Beirut, Lebanon, killing three hundred Marines. The largest suicide attack in history was the September 11, 2001, attacks launched by the terrorist group al-Qaeda when members hijacked four airliners. Two struck and destroyed the twin towers of the World Trade Center in New York City, a third smashed into the Pentagon. Passengers in the fourth airliner managed to reach the cockpit after the terrorists had hijacked the airplane. During the struggle for control that airliner crashed near Shanksville, Pennsylvania.

The most common motivations for suicide bombers include religion (incorporating a desire of martyrdom) and nationalism. Though Westerners continue to be a target, after 2003 the two Muslim sects, Sunni and Shiite, began deploying suicide bombers on each other. The use of suicide bombers by Islamic extremists has occurred so often and for so long that it has become the archetype symbol of Muslim violence.

2001

The World Trade Center after a suicide bomber attack

Sniper Rifle

Military sniper rifles, officially designated Long Range Sniper Weapon (LRSW), are semi-automatic or bolt-action rifles equipped with telescopic sights designed for accurate long-range shooting (from a thousand feet to about a mile).

Sniping emerged as a tactic of warfare during the eighteenth century when rifled shoulder arms became widely available. Rifling the barrels with grooves imparted a spin on the bullet, dramatically improving its accuracy. While sniper rifles are built to more exacting standards than standard-issue firearms such as the M-16, they are not customized to the exacting standards necessary for match competition rifles. The target marksman, firing in controlled circumstances, simply seeks the perfect strike on his target with total reliability. Though the military certainly places a priority on accuracy, it must also consider the logistic challenges, durability, and performance of shooter and equipment under the stress of shooting to kill. The best target rifles are simply too delicate for battlefield use.

Most sniper rifles are chambered for the 7.62-mm cartridge. In the late twentieth century, some services began developing larger-caliber sniper rifles that had greater range. One of the most popular of the larger caliber models is the .50-caliber Barrett M82 family of sniper rifles manufactured by the Barrett Firearms Company. Depending on the model, the M82 weighs about thirty pounds, is fifty-seven inches long, with a short barrel length of twenty inches and a long barrel length of twenty-nine inches. It has an effective range of about six thousand feet (more than a mile) and a maximum range of 22,300 feet (or just over four miles). It fires a .50 BMG (Browning Machine Gun) (12.7x99 mm NATO) cartridge. Like all sniper rifles, it can be fitted with different high power telescopes depending on the mission requirements.

Another popular .50-caliber LRSW is the McMillan Tac-50 built by the McMillan Brothers Rifle Company. Canadian Army Corporal Rob Furlong used a Tac-50 to record the longest-distance kill by a sniper in combat. In March 2002 as part of Operation Anaconda in Afghanistan, he shot and killed an al-Qaeda militant carrying a Soviet-built RPK machine gun. The distance was 1.509 miles. Corporal Furlong's shot broke the previous record of 1.42 miles held for 35 years by Marine Corps Gunnery Sergeant Carlos Hathcock.

A United States Marine conducting target practice on a firing range in Iraq with his M82 Barrett sniper rifle

Dolphins and Sea Lions

A sea lion swims to the ocean floor to hook up a retrieving line to practice ordnance

Unlike a millennia-long history of employment of birds and land animals, practical military use of sea creatures is less than sixty years old. It began in the 1950s during the Cold War when the U.S. Navy initiated a study of the hydrodynamics of dolphins and other mammals and fish to improve ship, submarine, and torpedo designs. This study expanded and, in 1960, officially became the classified Marine Mammal Program. Simultaneously, and also under a cloak of secrecy, the Soviet Union created a similar program.

The purpose of the Marine Mammal Program was to train dolphins and sea lions to detect and mark sea mines and swimmers, locate and retrieve lost objects, guard boats and submarines, and conduct underwater surveillance using special cameras. Despite later charges by animal activists, the Navy maintained that, unlike its Soviet counterparts, it never trained their sea mammals to kill people.

During the Vietnam War, five dolphins were deployed to conduct surveillance in the waters of the large U.S. naval base at Cam Ranh Bay in South Vietnam. At the height of the Cold War, the U.S. Navy had more than a hundred dolphins, as well as sea lions and beluga whales.

When the Soviet Union collapsed in 1991, Russia eliminated its marine mammal program. It is reported that some dolphins trained to kill people were subsequently sold to Iran. Other dolphins were put to use in therapy programs for autistic and emotionally disturbed children in Ukraine.

The U.S. Navy declassified the Marine Mammal Program in 1992 and though reduced from its Cold War level, it continues to this day. Dolphins were deployed to the Persian Gulf during the time of Operation Iraqi Freedom in 2003 and remain in the region. Long distance transport of dolphins is conducted under the supervision of a veterinarian. Dolphins are placed in fleece-lined stretchers suspended in water filled fiberglass containers. Sea lions are placed in specially designed enclosures that keep them cool and wet.

A US Navy trained bottle nose dolphin leaps out of the water during a training exercise in the Persian Gulf

EUROFIGHTER TYPHOON

The Eurofighter Typhoon is a twin-engine, canard-delta wing multi-role stealth aircraft. Designed and manufactured by a consortium of three European defense contractors, it was designed for use by NATO and as an alternative to high-performance aircraft from the United States and Russia.

The Typhoon became operational in 2003 and it is in the air forces of Great Britain, Germany, Italy, and Spain. Two variants have been built, a two-seat model for training and a single-seat model for combat. The combat Typhoon has a crew of one, a maximum speed of Mach 2, a range of 1,840 miles, a combat radius of 345 miles, and a ceiling of sixty-five thousand feet. Standard armament includes a 27-mm cannon and a combination of thirteen air-to-air and air-to-ground missiles and bombs. The Eurofighter has "supercruise" capability which means it can fly at sustained speeds of more than Mach I without the use of afterburner.

While it is not a stealth aircraft per se, the Typhoon incorporates stealth technology. It is constructed of carbon-fiber composites, glass-reinforced plastic, aluminum lithium, titanium, and aluminum casting, and it has a state-of-the art avionics package. Its airframe is designed to easily accommodate avionics upgrades as they become available.

The Typhoon has a "glass cockpit" design that does not have conventional instrumentation. It includes full color Multi-function Head Down Displays (MHDDs) and wide-angle Heads Up Display (HUD) with Forward Looking Infra Red (FLIR). It is the first military aircraft to use DVI voice controls. This provides the pilot with speech command and control of up to thirty non-critical cockpit functions and helps reduce pilot workload.

When it was introduced, the Typhoon elicited a wide variety of comments comparing it to Lockheed-Martin's F-22 Raptor. On March 23, 2005, Air Force Chief of Staff John P. Jumper, then the only person to personally fly both the F-22 and the Typhoon, said that comparisons do an injustice to both aircraft. Calling the Typhoon "impressive," he said, "It's like asking us to compare a NASCAR car with a Formula I car. They are both exciting in different ways, but they are designed for different levels of performance."

Eurofighter Typhoons from the German Luftwaffe

High Speed Vessel (HSV)

The High Speed Vessel (HSV) is a high-speed, sealift catamaran, designed for use by Special Operations units. The HSV was built to resolve inter-theater mobility and forward basing problems. It is capable of carrying troops, vehicles and cargo, operating boats and helicopters, and sustaining operations for extended periods.

The program began in 1998 when the U.S. Navy leased a commercial catamaran ferry and had it redesigned to military specifications. This first ship, HSV XI *Joint Venture*, was used in Operation Iraqi Freedom as a staging platform for anti-terrorism and SEAL operations off the coast of Iraq. The success in this HSV in supporting the SEALs led the navy to authorize the construction of thirty-two HSVs of different classifications. The first ship in this program, the HSV 2 *Swift*, was delivered to the Navy in 2003. The *Swift* is one of three vessels in its class. It is 321½ feet long, has a beam of 88.6 feet, and displaces 1,464 tons. It has a top speed of more than fifty three miles per hour and a range of more than four thousand miles. It has a twenty-eight-thousand-square-foot mission deck, a heavy vehicle ramp, a four-thousand-square-foot flight deck, and a boat crane. Depending on the mission, it can carry a crew of forty-two and almost two hundred troops. Other ships will be designed to carry even more troops and equipment.

One of the most important features of the HSV is its ability to quickly transport large numbers of troops and their vehicles and equipment over long distances. For example, normal transit time in a ferry or amphibious shipping for a Marine battalion based in Okinawa ordered to travel to South Korea is two to three days. By air, the battalion would need to have fourteen to seventeen lifts by C-17 transport aircraft. An HSV can make the trip in twenty-four to thirty hours.

Amphibious Assault Vehicle

The Amphibious Assault Vehicle (AAV) is the primary amphibious troop transport used by the United States Marine Corps. In addition to landing troops on beaches, the tracked AAV is capable of conducting mechanized operations on land.

Designed during the Vietnam War and made operational in 1972, the AAV's amphibious capability makes it unique among Department of Defense land vehicle systems. Depending on the variant, it has a crew of three or four, is armed with a turret-mounted Mk 19 40-mm automatic grenade launcher and an M2 .50-caliber machine gun, and is able to transport as many as twenty-seven troops. The inch-and-a-half armor plate is strong enough to protect against small arms fire, but not against RPGs or larger caliber weapons. It has a land cruising speed of thirty miles per hour, a water cruising speed of eight miles per hour, and a land range of about three hundred miles and a water range of about forty miles.

During Operation Iraqi Freedom, AAVs played a key role in the capture of two strategic bridges in An Nasiriya in March 2003 by the 2nd Marine Expeditionary Brigade, designated Task Force Tarawa. The southern bridge was quickly captured. But to reach the northern bridge, Task Force Tarawa had to drive through the city up a route that was dubbed "Ambush Alley."

At first, luck was with the company of Marines assigned the northern bridge's capture. The column of four AAVs raced at top speed through the city, running the Ambush Alley gauntlet of AK-47 and RPG fire. With the Marine passengers providing additional support by firing through the gun ports, the company managed to reach the northern bridge. The element of surprise worked for the first AAV, it reached the bridge intact. But the next three were hit by RPGs and suffered casualties. The company barely had time to form a defensive perimeter on both sides of the bridge when it came under intense fire. Though isolated, the outnumbered Marines succeeded in beating back numerous Iraqi attacks before being relieved the next day by the rest of the task force.

With the bridges in Marine hands, the road was now clear for the 1st Marine Division's advance to Baghdad.

NON-LETHAL WEAPON SYSTEMS

The role of the United States military has expanded from its original mandate and now includes what it calls Military Operations Other Than War (MOOTW). These include peacekeeping, humanitarian assistance, and non-combat evacuations, among other duties. To assist the military in the performance of these new duties, as well as appropriate defense, a new range of non-lethal weapon systems designed to use minimum force were developed.

These weapon systems go far beyond the rubber bullets and include things that could come straight out of *Star Trek* or *Star Wars*. They include energy weapons, heat and pulsating light rays, anti-traction sprays that have been called "liquid ball bearings," and acoustic devices that emit painfully loud sounds. Less futuristic sounding is the Running Gear Entanglement System (RGES), introduced by the U.S. Coast Guard in 2004. Designed for port use, it is an entanglement device that fouls the propeller of unauthorized vessels that approach restricted areas, stopping them.

Non-lethal weapon systems also include robots and sensors. The Boomerang Mobile Shooter Detection System is designed to alert troops of incoming sniper fire who would not hear the sound of incoming bullets because of vehicle traffic or other background noise. Robots are used to search for Improvised Explosive Devices, perform sentry duties, carry communications equipment, and non-lethal weapons.

One of the more versatile robots now available is the LandShark, a low-cost robot platform capable of being outfitted with a variety of systems. One platform contains a dazzler device. This dazzler, created by Boeing, is a bright strobe-like laser. The system also has a detection device used to locate and identify a threat. Once the unit has a fix on its target, it shoots out a high-intensity flashing laser capable of incapacitating the target for about ten minutes. Another non-lethal platform mounts a high-power acoustic system capable of projecting sounds up to a mile away. A third non-lethal platform under development uses thermal beams, or "heat rays," that have a maximum range of a half mile.

A security agent demonstrates the use of a non-lethal spray on a mannequin

F-22 Raptor

The F-22 is the fifth generation of combat aircraft, and the most sophisticated fighter ever built. Its primary mission is air superiority—controlling the skies. But it has multiple capabilities and can perform ground attack, electronic warfare, and signals intelligence.

Designed by Lockheed's Skunk Works and built through a consortium that includes Boeing, the F-22 incorporates a wealth of state-of-the art features. Its sensor system is so sophisticated it can simultaneously track, identify, shoot, and kill several air and ground threats. Instead of a welded skeleton for the airframe, most of the fuselage is cut from solid blocks of titanium. An extraordinarily complicated and expensive process, it provides a level of structural integrity impossible to achieve by the traditional method. The Raptor has a crew of one, a maximum speed of Mach 2.25, the capability to supercruise at Mach 1.82, a range of 1,840 miles, a combat radius of 471 miles, and a ceiling of sixty-give thousand feet. Armament includes one 20-mm Gatling gun cannon. In the air-to-air combat configuration, the Raptor carries eight air-to-air missiles. In air-to-ground combat configuration, it carries four air-to-air missiles and up to three thousand pounds of bombs.

Its outstanding performance was repeatedly demonstrated in mock combat exercises. In June 2006, twelve F-22s from the 94th Fighter Squadron participating in Exercise Northern Edge over Alaska, downed in two weeks of simulated combat exercises a total of 241 "enemy" aircraft against just two Raptors "lost," an unprecedented kill/loss ratio. Later, during the aerial combat training exercise codenamed Red Flag, a regular exercise considered one of the most combat realistic and challenging training exercises, Blue Force F-22s established overwhelming air superiority over the larger Red Force composed of F-15s and F-16s.

Design and production of the Raptor has taken three decades, its high cost (upwards of $137 million per aircraft), and criticism that it is a weapon built to combat a strategic enemy that no longer exists, has made it a subject of controversy. In 2009, Defense Secretary Robert Gates proposed to cap the original order of 750 to less than one hundred.

M777 Howitzer

The M777 is the designation for a series of lightweight 155-mm towed howitzers. The M777 ("Triple Seven") series is lighter, smaller, has better ergonomics and has a lower profile than the M198 155-mm howitzer it is designed to replace. This makes the M777 one of the most mobile pieces of heavy artillery in use today.

The M777 is manufactured by BAE Systems. More than nine hundred have been ordered for the Marine Corps and U.S. Army. All models use titanium, a light but strong metal, in its major structures, making them about six thousand pounds lighter than the M198. Combined with the digital fire control system, the M777's average gross weight is about 9,800 pounds. The M777 is operated by a crew of five, can be set up to fire in less than three minutes, and depending on the model and type of ammunition used, has a maximum range of twenty-five miles, a maximum rate of fire of four rounds per minute, and a sustained rate of fire of two rounds per minute.

The digital fire control system uses Joint Variable Message Formatting (JVMF) software that gives the M777 the ability to actively communicate back and forth with its controlling Fire Direction Center, compared to prior systems which were only capable of receiving data. In addition, the M777 is able to use GPS-guided Excalibur shells which are able to land within thirty feet of a target.

Even though the M777 is still going through the trials stage, performance statistics were so encouraging that eighteen M777 guns were shipped to Afghanistan in 2005. Twelve were immediately deployed to locations Forward Operating Bases (FOBs) throughout the country.

The M777's enhanced capability was demonstrated one day when an M777 crew received an urgent message from an FOB under attack by a large Taliban force. The insurgents had gotten so near the troops' positions that the troops would risk suffering casualties from friendly fire. The cannon's computer guidance system and precision munitions enabled the crew to deliver two hours of nonstop fire onto the Taliban ranks and save the men in the FOB. Soon, intelligence reports revealed that the insurgents had given the M777 a nickname: "Dragon."

U.S. Marines fire a round from an M777 155 mm lightweight towed Howitzer during a training mission

M982 Excalibur

The Excalibur weapon system is the next generation of artillery ammunition, a family of 155-mm GPS-guided, fire-and-forget projectiles. It is designed to be fired by either the self-propelled M109A6 Paladin or the towed M777A2 howitzer.

In the past, artillery fire would bracket a target, firing initial rounds around the target, having the location of the hits radioed back by a forward observer, and then, with after the range was corrected, the artillery battery would fire the main salvos. The Excalibur guidance and navigation unit eliminates the need for bracketing. Equally important, its GPS system provides extraordinary accuracy, substantially reducing the risk of collateral damage and "friendly fire" casualties.

Developed by Raytheon and BAE Systems Bofors, the Excalibur is a 155-mm round with extended range capability. With conventional rounds, the farther the cannon is from its target, the more significant the drop-off in accuracy. The Excalibur is presently accurate to about twenty-four miles, meaning that it will fall within thirty feet of its target; and tests are being conducted to increase the distance. Accuracy is provided by a specially designed rotating fin for roll stabilization, a GPS guidance system that executes course corrections during the shell's trajectory, and four canard fins that execute the guidance and control commands issued by the GPS system. The Excalibur can be fitted with a variety of different warheads and fuses, allowing it to respond to battlefield contingencies.

The Excalibur became operational in 2007, where it was sent to Iraq. On July 2007, two Excalibur rounds were used to destroy a house where a senior al Qaeda leader was meeting. Because it was in an urban area south of Baghdad, the possibility of collateral damage would have made such an attack impossible.

Excalibur shells were used in Operation Arrowhead Ripper, also known as the Battle of Baqubah. The purpose of the operation was to wrest control of the city and Diyala province away from insurgents. The campaign began in March. The first Excalibur rounds arrived in Iraq in May. One neighborhood-clearing mission was conducted during weather so bad, all aircraft were grounded. The only heavy firepower available to assist the troops was the Excalibur. Captain Victor Scharstein who commanded the M777 battery that supported the troops later said, "Had we not had Excalibur, we wouldn't have been able [to help]."

An Excalibur round being prepared for firing from an M777 A2 Lightweight Howitzer

Dogs

"Cry havoc, and let slip the dogs of war." This statement uttered by Marc Antony in William Shakespeare's *Julius Caesar* was not simply an expression of literary eloquence. The use of dogs in war has a history reaching back to the time of Ancient Egypt. Perhaps the most famous dog in ancient history is Sorter, a guard dog in Corinth during the Peloponnesian Wars (432–404 B.C.). Sorter was the only one of fifty guard dogs to survive a surprise night attack on the outpost where he was stationed. Sorter escaped and reached the city where his barking woke the sleeping garrison. Thus warned, the Corinthian troops succeeded in fighting off the attack. The grateful Corinthians presented Sorter with a collar bearing the inscription "Defender and Savior of Corinth." In addition, the city erected a monument engraved with the name of Sorter and the forty-nine dogs that died in the city's defense.

Dog companies composed of mastiffs were an official Roman legion unit. Attila the Hun used war dogs, as did Napoleon I. During the American Civil War, dogs were unit mascots and played no official front line role.

The most famous, and most decorated, war dog of World War I was Sgt. Stubby, a bull terrier mix belonging to John Robert Conroy of the 102nd Infantry Regiment, 26th Division. Sgt. Stubby alerted troops of incoming artillery barrages and gas attacks, located wounded soldiers, and even captured a German spy. Ultimately he received ten medals including the Purple Heart. He became a postwar celebrity, meeting presidents and leading parades. When Conroy entered Georgetown University law Center, Sgt. Stubby became the Hoyas' mascot.

War dogs, designated K-9s (for "canine") were used extensively in World War II and Vietnam. Today they are officially known as military working dogs and are trained for a variety of duties including sentry, tracking, search and rescue, and scouting. One hundred and eighteen Military Dog Teams were deployed for Operation Desert Shield/Desert Storm. On March 18, 2009, in Quantico, Virginia, a Marine Security Battalion held a memorial service in tribute to Keve, a Military War Dog who had served two tours in Iraq and discovered more than twenty-two weapons caches. Colonel Richard A. Anderson, the commanding officer noted, "It's important that we memorialize and honor these dogs, because they are Marines, too."

A military working dog and his handler take a break during a search of buildings near Jurf Nadaf, Iraq

F-35 Lightning II

Interior view of an F-35 fuselage under construction

The F-35 is a fifth-generation multi-role stealth fighter designed to replace four fighters in the U.S. military: the F-16 Hornet, the A-10 Thunderbolt II, The F/A 18 Super Hornet, and the AV-8B Harrier.

A product of the Joint Strike Fighter program which was established to provide an affordable next-generation combat aircraft from all U.S. military branches and American allies, the F-35 is designed and built by an aerospace consortium led by Lockheed-Martin and includes many major defense contractors, domestic and foreign. The F-35 is undergoing trials and is scheduled to become operational in 2011. Three variants are presently being developed: F-35A conventional takeoff and landing, F-35B short-takeoff and vertical landing, and F-35C carrier takeoff and landing. General specifications are a crew of one, a maximum speed of more than Mach 1.6, a range up to 1,380 miles, a combat radius up to seven hundred miles, and a ceiling of sixty thousand feet. Armament includes an internally mounted 25-mm cannon, and a missile and bomb load capacity of fifteen thousand pounds.

The F-35 has a more conventional design than the ground breaking F-22. This, and the fact that it is piggy-backing on technologies first used in the F-22 has enabled it to be produced at a lower unit cost than the F-22. This has helped the F-35 avoid much of the controversy that dogs the F-22.

Among the many features in the F35 is the Distributed Aperture System (DAS). This consists of numerous electronic sensors strategically located all over the aircraft. DAS sensors provide infrared long-range detection and precision targeting all around the aircraft. In other airplanes, the information from these sensors would then be projected onto the canopy, a process known as Heads Up Display (HUD). But the F-35 does not use HUD. Instead, all the information will be transmitted to the pilot's helmet and he will see the images on his visor in a Helmet Mounted Display. When the system is active, the pilot will have 360-degree viewing capability around the aircraft. In effect, if the pilot looks down at his feet, or to either side at the wings, because of DAS he will essentially "see through" the plane at any target below.

Expeditionary Fighting Vehicle

The Expeditionary Fighting Vehicle (EFV) is a tracked, armored personnel carrier designed for the U.S. Marine Corps for amphibious and land operations.

The EFV is scheduled to become operational in 2015 and replace the aging AAV that has been in service, with upgrades, since the Vietnam War. The EFV has a crew of three and can carry up to seventeen fully armed troops. Instead of metal, the EFV's armor is a ceramic composite that is lighter and stronger, making the vehicle better able to withstand larger projectiles such as RPG rounds or 155-mm fragments. It is also capable of defending crew and passengers against attacks by nuclear, biological, and chemical weapons. Primary armament is one 30 mm cannon and secondary armament is one 7.62 machine gun. It has a top land speed of forty-five miles per hour and a top water speed of twenty-nine miles per hour. Its land operational range is 325 miles and water operational range is seventy-four miles.

The Marine Corps' performance specifications presented incredible design challenges—no previous amphibious vehicle had to travel so fast in or out of water, for so long, and be so well armored. Design innovations of the engine almost doubled its basic 1,500 horsepower to 2,700 horsepower. One of the most important breakthroughs was with the armor. Lightweight composite armor panels composed of ceramics, S2 fiberglass, and a Kevlar-like woven fabric called Spectra protect the EFV. This armor weighs less than twenty pounds per square foot, compared to fifty-six pounds per square foot for regular steel armor.

The EFV has had early troubles. The original prototypes experienced several mission failures throughout the vehicle. The problems were so acute that a complete redesign under a new contractor was instituted. Seven new prototypes were subsequently built and are undergoing tests.

Index

A

A-1 Skyraider, combat aircraft, 302-303, 340

A-4 Skyhawks, combat aircraft, 322

A-10 Thunderbolt II, combat aircraft, 178, 394-395, 498

aborigines
atlatls and, 24
boomerangs and, 26-27

Abrams, Creighton W., 412

Abrams Main Battle Tank, 412-413

Absmeier, Carl J., 270

Adamson, L. N., 244

Adid, Mohammed Farrah, 386, 404

Aegis Combat Weapons System, 366-367

Aerospace Maintenance and Regeneration Center, 312

Aerospatiale SA 341 Gazelle, 384-385

AF Skyraider, 306-307

Agent Orange, herbicides, 334-335

Age of Sail, 100

AGM-84 Harpoon, 392-393

AGM-114 Hellfire, missile system, 426-427

AH-64 Apache, 438-439

Aichi D3A "Val" dive bomber, 216-217

AIM-9 Sidewinder missiles, 308-309, 358

aircraft carriers, 208, 284, 288-289, 312, 400

air rifles, 92

AK-47 assault rifle, 296-299

Albatros D. III, 148-149, 154

Albuquerque Tribune, gunpowder and, 64

Alden, James, 102

Alexander the Great
Battle of Gaugamela, 44
Bucephalus and, 104
incendiaries and, 34
sarissa and, 18
siege of Megara and, 46
slings and, 20

Allen, Tom, 310

al Qaeda
F-16s and, 398

rocket-propelled grenade launchers, 338

sniper attack and, 478

suicide attacks and, 476-477

surface-to-air missiles, 362

UAV Close Air Support mission and, 460

American Revolution, submarines, 262

amphibious assault ships, 450-451

Amphibious Assault Vehicles (AAVs), 486-487

amphibious landing craft, 242-243

AN/APG-78 Longbow Fire Control Radar (FCR), target acquisition system, 438

ancient armor, 28-29

Anderson, Clarence "Bud", 258

Anderson, Richard A., 496

Anglo-Mysore Wars, 96

antitank missile
9K11 Malutka, 336
AT-3 Sagger, 336
Javelin, 444

Antony, Marc, 496

Applegate, Dick, 300

archers, 32
crossbows and, 40-41
incendiaries and, 34-35

Archimedes, 48-49

ARK (Armoured Ramp Carrier), 240

Arleigh Burke-class destroyers, 366

armor
ancient armor, 28-29
Chobham armor, 468
modern armor and, 468
samurai armor and, 68-69
World War I, 468

arms manufacturing
BAE Systems, 472-473, 492, 494
Boeing, 278, 364, 390, 396, 430, 472
Dassault-Breguet, 400, 440, 474
Douglas Aircraft Company, 302
Dow Chemical Company, 306
Eli Whitney and, 90
General Dynamics, 408, 440
Israel Aircraft Industries, 388

Krupps family and, 130, 136, 138

Lockheed Martin, 270, 314, 316, 344, 408, 414, 432, 472, 482, 488, 490, 498

McDonnell Douglas, 430, 472

Merchants of Death and, 130

Nagoya Aircraft Works of Mitsubishi Heavy Industries, Ltd., 214

Northrup Grumman, 466, 472

Samuel Cummings and, 130, 166-167, 442

Skunk Works, 314, 316, 344, 432, 488, 490

Société Pour L'Aviation et ses Dérivés (SPAD), 152

arquebus, firearms and, 78-79

artillery
88-mm cannon, 218-219
ballista and, 42-43
Big Bertha, 136-137
Excalibur weapon system, 494-495
Katyusha rocket launcher, 196-197
M777A2 howitzers, 494-495
M777 howitzers, 492-493
pots de fer, 76-77
slings and, 20

AS-6 Kingfish, missiles and, 368-369

ASDIC, underwater sound detection device, 144-145

A Shau Valley, 302

Assault Ready Group (ARG), 450

Assyrian bas-relief, King Ashurbanipal firing bow and, 32-33

Assyrian walls, earliest depictions of slings, 20

Astute class nuclear submarine, 472

AT-3 Sagger, antitank missile, 336

AT-6 Texan, combat aircraft, 340

Atkinson, Rick, 412

Atlantic Conveyor, merchant ship, 400

atlatl, 24-25

atomic bombs, 278, 288, 290-291, 310, 318, 322, 324, 328, 330, 352, 368, 372, 380, 400, 422, 434, 440, 466, 468, 474

Attila the Hun, war dogs and, 496

Atwood, John Leland "Lee", 228

AV-8B Harrier, combat aircraft, 306,
365, 450, 498

AVRE (Armoured Vehicle, Royal
Engineers), 240

Avro Lancaster, 254-255

axes, 30-31

B

B-2 Spirit, 466-467

B-17 bombers, 454, 460

B-17 Flying Fortress, 190-191, 226

B-24 Liberator, 194-195, 226-227

B-25 Mitchell, 228-229, 270

B-52 Stratofortress, 312-313

Baa Baa Black Sheep (Boyington), 260

Bacon, Roger, gunpowder and, 64-65

BAE Systems, arms manufacturing,
472-473, 492, 494

ballista, siege engines, 42-43, 66-67

Barber, Rex T., 234

Barnes, Harry Elmer, 130

Barrett Firearms Company, 478

Barrow, Clyde, 164

Batista, Fulgencio, 166

The Battle of San Romano, painting of,
62-63

Battle for Guadalcanal, 284

Battle for Robert's Ridge, 460

Battle of Auray (1364), illustration of,
76-77

Battle of Balaclava, 104-105

Battle of Baqubah, 494

Battle of Berlin, 264

Battle of Bovine (1214), 62

Battle of Britain (1940), 178, 186,
188, 202

Battle of Cabra (1079), 56

Battle of Cape Esperance, 284

Battle of Cerignola (1503), 78

Battle of Courtrai (1302), 70

Battle of Crecy, engraving of, 64-65

Battle of Eurymedon (190 B.C.), 74

Battle of France (1940), 186

Battle of Gaugamela, 44

Battle of Gettysburg (1863), 84

Battle of Gibeah, 20

Battle of Jutland (1916), 130, 282

Battle of Kursk, 220-221, 268

Battle of Kwajalein (1944), 248

Battle of Leipzig (1807), 96

Battle of Leyte Gulf (1944), 282

Battle of Midway (1942), 208, 216, 288

Battle of Mobile Bay, 118-119

Battle of Mogadishu (1993), 386, 404

Battle of Morgarten (1315), 72

Battle of Pavia (1525), 72

Battle of Salamis, 36

Battle of Savo Island, 284

Battle of Taranto, 170

Battle of Tassafaronga, 284

Battle of the Coral Sea (1942), 288

Battle of the Golden Spurs, 70-71

Battle of the Little Big Horn (1876), 104

Battle of Thymbra, 38

Battle of Trafalgar (1805), 100-101, 282

Battle of Villers-Bocage, 252

Battle of Westrozebeke, 70

Battle of Zama, painting of, 44-45

battleships, 100, 170, 208, 282-284,
286, 288

bayonets, 84-85

bazookas, 264

BDRM-1 amphibious reconnaissance
cars, 336-337

Belenko, Viktor Ivanovich, 372

Bell AH-1 Cobra, 376

Belloc, Hilaire, 128

Bell UH-1H Huey, 326-327

Berdan, Hiram, 110

Beres, Thomas, 414

Beretta, Bartolomeo, weapons builder, 80

Berzhnyak, A. Y., 332

Big Bertha, 136-137

bin Laden, Osama, jihads and, 54

biological weapons, weapons of mass
destruction, 74, 448-449, 500

birds, 158

Bismarck, sinking of, 170

Black Sheep Squadron, 260-261

Bloch, Marcel, 474

Blot, Harry, 364

blowguns, 22-23

Blue Angels, 210, 430

BMP Armored Personnel Carrier
(APC), 354-355

bo, 82-83

Boeing, arms manufacturing, 278,
364, 390, 396, 430, 472

Boeing B-29 Superfortress, 226, 230,
278-279, 292-300

Boelcke, Oswald, 142

Bofors 40-mm anti-aircraft gun,
168-169

Bonaparte, Napoleon
abolishment of the guild system,
80
leadership and, 94-95
propaganda and, 98-99

Bong, Richard, 234

booby traps, 342-343

Boomerang Mobile Shooter Detection
System, 488

boomerangs, 26-27

Bosquet, Pierre, 104

bows, 32-33, crossbows and, 40-41

Boxer Rebellion, Mauser bolt-action
rifle and, 126

Boyington, Gregory "Pappy", 260

Boyle, Robert William, 144

Bradley, Omar N., 416

British Land Pattern Musket, 88-89

Bronze Age
arrival of, 14
development of metallurgy in, 58
spears and, 18

Brown, Arthur "Roy", 150, 154

Brown Bess Musket, 88-89

Browning Automatic Rifle (BAR),
164-165, 248

Browning, John Moses, 134-135, 162,
164-165

Budanova, Katerina, 200-201

bullets
non-lethal bullets, 462-463
rubber bullets, 462

Burnside, Ambrose, leadership and, 94

Bush, George Herbert Walker, 458

Business Week, Adnan Khashoggi, 172

Butler, Benjamin, Gatling guns, 112

Byrd, Richard E., 156

Byzantine Empire, Greek fire and, 248

C

CC-130 Hercules transport, 414

Caesar, Julius
carrier pigeons and, 158

Cleopatra and, 146
invasions of England and, 242
slings and, 20
Callinicus, invention of Greek fire, 52
camels, 38-39
Camm, Sidney, 188, 204
cannons
88-mm cannon, 218-219
Big Bertha, 136-137
Dahlgren gun and, 102-103
decline of trebuchets and, 66
ships-of-the-line, 100
The Capture of Constantinople (Tintoretto), 40-41
Carius, Otto, 218, 252
Carpathian Mountains, boomerangs and, 26-27
carrier pigeons, 158
Castro, Fidel, 166
catapults, 42-43, 48, 66-67
cavalry
ancient armor, 28-29
camels and, 38-39
elephants and, 44-45
flails, 60-61
horses and, 104-105
mail armor and, 62
morning stars and, 70
The Cavalry Charge at Balaclava, 104-105
Central Intelligence Agency, 166, 226, 314, 344, 418, 442
Centurion tanks, 294-295
Challenger I Main Battle Tank, 428-429
Chamberlain, Joshua Lawrence, Battle of Gettysburg (1863), 84
Chance Vought F4U Corsair, 260-261
Charge of the Light Brigade, 104
Charlemagne
ancient armor, 28-29
Durer portrait of, 56-57
chemical weapons, weapons of mass destruction, 446-448, 500
Cher Ami, carrier pigeons and, 158
Cheshire, Geoffrey Leonard, 224
Chilean Civil War (1891), 286
Chobham armor, 468
Choctaw, blowguns and, 22
Church, Alfred J., Siege of Jotapata and, 50

Churchill tank, 240-241
Churchill, Winston, 186, 240, 262
Civil War
Colt percussion revolver, 106-108
Dahlgren gun and, 102
firearms of, 110-111
first record of UAV use, 460
Gatling gun and, 112, 114
ironclads and, 116-117
Clancy, Tom, 416
Clarke, Colin A., 358
Clark, Mark, 300
Clemenceau, French aircraft carriers, 400
Cleopatra, 146
Cleveland, Charles, 444
Cody, Dick, 438
Colt Model 1911, 134-135
Colt percussion revolver, 106-107
Colt, Samuel, 108-109
combat aircraft
A-1 Skyraider, 302-303, 340
A-4 Skyhawks, 322
A-10 Thunderbolt II, 178, 394-395, 498
AF Skyraider, 306-307
Aichi D3A "Val" dive bomber, 216-217
Albatros D. III, 148-149, 154
AS-6 Kingfish, 368-369
AT-6 Texan, 340
AV-8B Harrier, 306, 498
Avro Lancaster, 254-255
B-2 Spirit, 466-467
B-17 Flying Fortress, 190-191, 226, 460
B-24 Liberator, 194-195, 226-227
B-25 Mitchell, 228-229, 270
B-52 Stratofortress, 312-313
Boeing B-29 Superfortress, 278-279
Chance Vought F4U Corsair, 260-261
de Havilland Mosquito, 224-225
E-3 Sentry (AWACS), 396-397
Eurofighter Typhoon, 482-483
F4F Wildcat, 206-207
F-4 Phantom, 322, 330-331
F-15 Eagle, 320, 322, 388, 390-391
F-16 Fighting Falcon, 322, 360, 398-399, 408, 410, 430, 440

F-16 Hornet, 498
F-22 Raptor, 316, 482, 490-491, 488, 490, 498
F-35 Lightning II, 472, 498-499
F-86 Sabre, 300, 304-305
F-117A Nighthawk, 316, 432-433
F/A-18 Hornet, 410, 430-431
Focke-Wulf 190, 232-233
Fokker Dr. I Dreidecker, 154-155
Fokker Eindecker, 142-143
Grumman F4F Wildcat, 266-267
Harrier, 306, 364-365, 450, 498
Hawker Hurricane and, 186-189
Hawker Typhoon, 222-223
Ilyushin Il-2 Shturmovik, 236-237
JU-87 Stuka and, 178-179
Kfir, 388-389
Lockheed P-38 Lightning, 234-235, 270
Lockheed SR-71 Blackbird, 344-345
Lockheed U-2, 314-316
LTV A-7 Corsair II, 358-359
Martin B-26 Marauder, 230-231
Messerschmitt Bf-109, 182-183
Messerschmitt Me 109, 232, 262, 272-273
MiG-15, 300-301, 304
MiG-17, 308
MiG-21 Fishbed, 308, 322-323, 410
MiG-23 Flogger, 370-371
MiG-25 Foxbat, 372-373
MiG-29 Fulcrum, 430, 434-435
MiG-31 Foxhound, 424-425
Mirage 2000, 410, 440-441
Mirage III, 322, 388
Mitsubishi G4M Betty, 238-239
Mitsubishi Zero, 180, 194, 200, 206, 208, 212-215, 266
North American T-28 Trojan, 340-341
Northrop P-61 Black Widow, 270-271
P-38 Lightning, 238, 256
P-40 Warhawk, 194-195
P-51 Mustang, 188, 190, 256, 258-259, 272
Panavia Tornado, 402-403
Predator, 460-461
Rafale, 474-475

504

Republic P-47 Thunderbolt, 256-257
Saab 37 Viggen, 374-375
SBD Dauntless, 208-210
Shenyang J-8 Finback, 410-411
Sopwith Camel, 150-151, 154
SPAD S.XIII, 152-153
Spitfire, 202-203
SR-71 Blackbird, 316, 372
Strike Eagle, 390
Super Étendard, 400-401, 406-407
Super Hornet, 430
T-6 Texan, 180-181
Tu-22 Backfire, 380-381
Tupolev Tu-95 Bear, 320-321
Typhoon F2 Eurofighter, 472
Vickers Wellington, 192-193
Yak-I, 200-201
combat shotguns, 350-351
communications devices, 366, 436, 444, 456-457
Congreve rocket, 96
Congreve, William, 96
A Connecticut Yankee in King Arthur's Court (Twain), 62
Conquistadors
atlatls and, 24
horses and, 104
plate armor, 62
warrior groups and, 32
Conrad II, use of crossbows, 40-41
Conrad, Robert, 260
Conroy, John Robert, 496
Constantine IV, invention of Greek fire, 52
conventional bombs, 280-281
Cooperative Threat Reduction accord (1997), 434
CORONA satellite reconnaissance program, 328-329
Cortés, Hernán, siege of Tenochtitlán and, 66
cranes, 48
Crimean War, 456
Battle of Balaclava, 104-105, 118
Croesus (Lydian king), Battle of Thymbra and, 38
crossbows, 40-41
cruisers, 284-286, 366

Crusade (Atkinson), 412
CSS *Hunley*, 262
CSS *Virginia*, 116-117
Cultural Revolution (1966–1976), 410
Cummings, Samuel, 12, 130-131, 166-167, 442
Custer, George, 104
Cyborg (Caidan), 214
Cyrus the Great, Battle of Thymbra and, 38

D
daggers, 84
Dahlgren gun, 102-103, 116
Dahlgren, John Adolph Bernard, 102-103, 116
d'Annunzio, Gabriele, Italian poet, 80
Darius III, Battle of Gaugamela, 44
Dassault, arms manufacturing, 400, 440, 474
David, slings and, 20-21
Davis, Jefferson, formation of camel cavalry corps and, 38
Davis, Jr., George A., 304
Davis-Monthan Air Force Base, 312
D-Day, 168, 222, 234, 242-243
de Bouillon, Godfrey, halberds and, 72-73
de Córdoba, Gonzalo Fernández, 78
Defeating Braddock (Deming), 88-89
De Gaulle, Charles, 388
De Havilland, Geoffrey, 224-225
de Havilland Mosquito, 224-225
de Milamete, Walter, pots de fer, 76-77
des Portes, Anglophobe Countess, 146
destroyers, 208, 246, 284, 286-287, 366, 408
de Vauban, Sébastien le Prestre, 86
de Vivar, Rodrigo Díaz, sword of, 56
Discover III reconnaissance satellite, 328
Distributed Aperture System (DAS), 498
Doges of Venice, Beretta contract and, 80
dogs, 496-497
dolphins, 480-481
Doolittle, James H. "Jimmy", 228, 230, 272
Dornberger, Walter, 276
Dosé, Curtis, 308

Douglas Aircraft Company, 302
Dow Chemical Company, 306
Dreadnought, battleships and, 282
Dresden, bombing of, 280
Duke of Wellington, 96, 192
Durant, Michael, 404
dynamite, 122-124
E
E-3 Sentry (AWACS), 396-397
Eagles of Mitsubishi: The Story of The Zero Fighter (Horikoshi), 214
Easter Offensive (1972), 362
Edward III
gunpowder and, 64-65
pots de fer, 76-77
Egusa, Takashige, 216
Egyptian Mamelukes, blowguns, 22
Egyptian walls, earliest depictions of spears, 20
EI-du Pont de Nemours & Co., gunpowder mills and, 64
Eilat
Israeli ship, 332
sinking of, 366, 392
Einstein, Albert, 290, 292-293
Eisenhower, Dwight, 230, 242, 314
El Cid, sword of, 56
elephants, 44-45
Elizabeth I, Brown Bess musket, 88
Ely, Eugene B., 284-285, 284
End User Certificate, 442
English longbow, 32
Enola Gay, first atomic bomb, 230, 278
Ericsson, John, 116
Eurofighter Typhoon, 482-483
Excalibur, King Arthur and, 56
Excalibur weapon system, artillery ammunition and, 494-495
Exocet, missiles and, 406-407
Expeditionary Fighting Vehicle (EFV), 500-501
F
FIM-92A Stinger, 417-418
F4F Wildcat, 206-207
F-4 Phantom, combat aircraft, 322, 330-331
F-15 Eagle, combat aircraft, 320, 322, 388, 390-391

F-16 Fighting Falcon, 322, 360, 398-399, 408, 410, 430, 440
F-16 Hornet, 498
F-22 Raptor, 316, 482, 488, 490-491, 498
F-35 Lightning II, 472, 498-499
F-86 Sabre, 300, 304-305
F-117A Nighthawk, 316, 432-433
F/A-18 Hornet, 410, 430-431
Fabbricia D'Armi Pietro Beretta, 80
Fairbairn-Sykes Fighting Knife, 198-199
Fairbairn, William Ewart, 198
Fairey Swordfish, 170-171
faith, 54-55
Falklands War, 364, 400, 406, 418
Farragut, David, 118
Fegelein, Hermann, 146
Ferdinand, Franz, 164
Fermi, Enrico, 292
Fieser, Louis, 306
Firefox, Clint Eastwood film, 424
First Gulf War, 282
First Jewish-Roman War, 50
First Matabele War, 128
Fisher, Bernard F., 302
flails, 60-61
Flak Alleys, 218
flame throwers, 248-249, 306
Flying Tigers, 194, 260
FN Minimi, machine guns, 386-387
Foch, French aircraft carriers, 400
Focke-Wulf 190, 232-233
Fokker, Anthony, 142, 156-157
Fokker Dr. I Dreidecker, 154-155
Fokker E-III, 142-143
Fokker Eindecker, 142-143
Ford, Gerald, 288, 372
Fort McHenry, siege of, 96-97
Foss, Joe, 206
Franco, Francisco, 218
Franco-Prussian War, 138
Fulton, Robert, 116
    naval mines and, 118
    submarines and, 262
Furlong, Rob, 478

G
Gable, Clark, 190
Gabreski, Francis S. "Gabby", 304
Gates, Robert, 488, 490
Gatling guns, 112-113

Gatling, Richard, 114-115
Gavin, James M., 264
General Bonaparte on the Bridge of Arcole (Gros), 94-95
General Dynamics, arms manufacturing, 408, 440
Geneva Protocol of 1925, 446, 448
George I, Brown Bess musket and, 88
Gibson, Guy, 254
Girandoni, Bartholomäus, 92
Glamorgan, British destroyer, 406
Global Positioning System (GPS), 392, 432, 436-438, 454, 492, 494
Goff, Randy, 394
Golan Heights, 294
Goliath, 20
Google maps, 328
Gorbachev, Mikhail, 200
Gordon, Gary, 404
Göring, Hermann, 224, 272
Grant, Ulysses S.
    Cincinnati and, 104
    on John Singleton Moseby, 106
Greek fire, 52-53, 248
Greek hoplites, ancient armor, 28-29
grenades, 250-251, 280, 338, 356
Ground Mobility Vehicle (GMV), 444-445
Groves, Leslie, 290, 292
Grumman F4F Wildcat, 266-267
Grumman, Leroy, 206
Guderian, Heinz, 220, 252-253, 268
Gunn, Paul I. "Pappy", 228
gunpowder, 58, 64-66, 84, 92, 106
    arquebus and, 78
    dynamite, 122
    mortars and, 86-87
    pots de fer, 76-77
Gurevich, Mikhail, 300
H
Haber, Fritz, 446
halberds, 72-73
Hannibal
    biological weapons and, 74
    crossing the Alps and, 44
Hari, Mata, 146-147
Harrier, combat aircraft, 364-365, 450
Harris, Arthur T. "Bomber", 254
Harrison, Benjamin, 114

Hartmann, Erich, 182
hatchets, 30
Hathcock, Carlos, 478
Hawker Hurricane, 186-189
Hawker Typhoon, 222-223
Heckler, Edmund, 126
Heinemann, Edward, 210-211, 302
helicopters
    Aerospatiale SA 341 Gazelle, 384-385
    AGM-114 Hellfire missile system, 426-427
    AH-64 Apache, 438-439
    Bell AH-1 Cobra, 376
    Bell UH-1H Huey, 326-327
    Close Air Support (CAS), 376
    Mi-8 Hip, 336
    Mi-24 Hind, 336
    MiL Mi-24 Hind, 378-379
    SH-60 Seahawk helicopter, 426-427
    Super Cobra, 376, 450
    UH-60 Black Hawk helicopters, 404-405
herbicides, 334-335
Hess, Rudolf, 184
Hezbollah, Iran-Contra affair, 442
Hibbard, Hal, 316
Higgins, Andrew C., 242
High Flight (Magee poem), 202
High Speed Vessel (HSV), 484-485
Hill Air Force Base, 398
Hillenmeyer, Herbert F., 246
Himmler, Heinrich, 276
Hindu mythology, sword Chandrahas (Moon-blade), 56
Hitler, Adolf, 138, 146, 176, 178, 184, 190, 244, 272, 274, 276
Hitler Youth, 264
Hittite Empire, biological weapons and, 74
HMS *Ark Royal*, Fairey Swordfish and, 170
HMS *Sheffield*, sinking of, 400
Hobart, Percy, 240
Holland, John, 262, 408
Holy Roman Empire, ancient armor, 28-29
Homer, slings and, 20
Hopkins, John J., 408

Horikoshi, Jiro, 212, 214

Horne, Barry, 432

horse archery, 32

horses, 32, 104-105

hot oil, 50-51

hot sand, 50

hot water, 50

Hundred Years War, pots de fer, 76-77

Hussein, Saddam, 420, 446, 448, 458

I

Ilyushin Il-2 Shturmovik, 236-237

Immelman, Max, 142

Improvised Explosive Devices (IEDs), 342

incendiaries, 34-35

Indo-Pakistani War (1971), 332

infantry

   ancient armor, 28-29

      halberds and, 72-73

      mail armor and, 62

      morning stars and, 70

      muskets and, 88-89

Innocent II, use of crossbows, 40-41

Intercontinental Ballistic Missile (ICBM), 324-325

International Radio Convention of 1927, 456

Inuit, atlatls and, 24

Invincible, class carriers, 472

Iran Air Flight 655, shooting down of, 366

Iran Contra arms scandal, 172, 442

Iran-Iraq War (1980–1988), 332, 446

Israel Aircraft Industries, 388

Israeli Defense Forces (IDF), 294

J

Jackson, Stonewall, Little Sorrel, 104

Javelin, 464-465

Jernigan, E.J., 286

jihads, 54

Jing-Bow Joy-Ride, P-61 aircraft, 270

Joan of Arc, faith and, 54

Johnson, Clarence "Kelly", 234, 314, 316-317

Johnson, Paul, 394

Johnson, Robert S., 256

Joint Robotics Program (JRP), 452

Joint Variable Message Formatting (JVMF), 492

Joint Venture, High Speed Vessel (HSV), 484

Josephus, Siege of Jotapata and, 50

JU-87 Stuka, 178-179

Jumper, John P., 482

K

Ka-Bar, combat knives and, 198

Kaffa, biological weapons and, 74

Kalashnikov, Mikhail, 296, 298-299

Kargil War, 440

Katyusha rocket launcher, 196-197

Kennedy, John F., 460

Kennedy, Jr., Joseph, 460

Ketley, Donald, 274

Key, Francis Scott, siege of Fort McHenry and, 96-97

Kfir, 388-389

Khaibar, Pakistani destroyer, 332

Khan, Jannibeg, biological weapons, 74

Khashoggi, Adnan, 172-173

Kimpo Airfield, 300

Kindelberger, James H. "Dutch", 228

King Arthur, Excalibur and, 56

King John, Magna Carta and, 62

King Naresuan, killing of Minchit Sra, 44

King Sennacherib, siege of Lachish, 34

Kirishima, battleships and, 282

kirpan, Sikh religion and, 16

knives

   combat knives, 14-17, 198-199

   Fairbairn-Sykes Fighting Knife, 198-199

   Ka-Bar and, 198

Koch, Theodor, 126

Korean Air Lines Flight 007, downing of, 436

Korean War

   flame throwers, 248-249, 248

   Lewis gun and, 132

   M1 Garand and, 174

   M1 Bayonet and, 84

   napalm and, 306

   Thompson submachine gun, 160

Kosovo War, 466

Krupp, Alfried, 138-139

Krupp, Bertha, 136

Kusanagi-no-Tsurugi, Three Sacred Treasures of Japan, 56

Kützer, Klaus, 264

Kuznetsova, Mariya, 200-201

L

Lachish, siege of, 34

Lady in the Dark, P-61 aircraft, 270

Landing Craft Mechanized (LCM), 242

Landing Craft Tank (LCT), 242

Landing Craft Vehicle Personnel (LCVP), 242

Landing Ship Dock (LSD), 242

Landing Ship Tank (LST), 242

Landing Vehicle Tracked (LVT), 242

LandShark, robots and, 488

Last Days of Jerusalem (Church), 50

Lawson, Ted, 228

leadership, 94

Lear, Norman, 190

Lebanese Civil War, 196-197

Ledo Road, use of elephants and, 44

Lee, Robert E., Traveler and, 104

Leopard I Main Battle Tank (MBT), 352-353

Letterkenny Army Depot, 444

Lewis and Clark Expedition, 92-93

Lewis gun, 132-133

Lewis, Isaac Newton, 132

Lewis, Meriwether, 92

Libya, cave art in, 14-15

Lickley, Robert, 188

Lincoln, Abraham, Sharps rifle, 110

The Little Picture: Tales of World War II for My Children (Hillenmeyer), 246

Litvak, Lilya, 200-201

Lockhead Martin, 270, 314, 316, 344, 408, 414, 432, 472, 482, 488, 490, 498

Lockheed P-38 Lightning, 234-235, 270

Lockheed SR-71 Blackbird, 344-345

Lockheed U-2, 314-316

Long Land Pattern, 88

Long Range Sniper Weapon (LRSW), 478

lorica segmentata, ancient armor, 28-29

Lost Battalion, 158

Louis XV, sex and, 146

LTV A-7 Corsair II, 358-359

Luftwaffe, 182, 184, 186, 190, 224, 256, 272, 402, 434-435

Luppis, Giovanni, 120

M

MI Garand, 84, 174-175

MIM-104 Patriot, 420-421

M2 .50-caliber Browning Machine Gun, 162-163

M2 Bradley Armored Personnel Carrier, 412, 416-417

M4 Sherman tank, 246-247

M-16 assault rifle, 348-349

M82 Barrett sniper rifle, 478-479

M-388 Davy Crocket, tactical nuclear weapons, 318

M777A2 howitzer, 494-495

M777 howitzer, 492-493

M1114 Up-Armored Humvee, 468-469

MacArthur, Douglas, 174

mace, 58-59

Magee, Jr., John Gillespie, 202

Magna Carta, signing of, 62

mail armor, 62

Malayan Emergency (1948–1960), 350

Manhattan Project, 290, 292

Maratha Empire, cumberjung and, 60

Marcellus, Marcus Claudius, Second Punic War and, 48

Marine Mammal Program, 480

Marshall, George C., 228, 458

Martin B-26 Marauder, 230-231

Masozane, Tonbogiri (Dragonfly Cutter) spear, 18

Mauser bolt-action rifle, 126

Mauser, Wilhelm, 126

Maxim, Hiram, 128-129

Maxim machine gun, 128-129

MC-130 Combat Talon, 414-415

McCampbell, David, 266

McCartney, Paul, 172

McClean, Samuel, 132

McCloy, John, 138

McConnell, Joseph, 304

McDonnell Douglas, 430, 472

McGuire, Thomas, 234

McMaster, H. R., 412

McMillan Brothers Rifle Company, 478

McMillan Tac-50, sniper rifle, 478

medieval armor, 62-63

Megara, siege of, 46

Meiji Restoration, samurai and, 68

Merchants of Death, 130

Mesopotamia, arrival of Bronze Age, 14

Messerschmitt Bf-109, 182-183

Messerschmitt Me 109, 232

Messerschmitt Me-262, 272-273

Messerschmitt, Wilhelm, 184-185

Mexican War

    Colt pistols and, 108

    Dahlgren gun and, 102

Mi-8 Hip helicopter, 336

Mi-24 Hind helicopter, 336

Middle Ages

    ancient armor, 28-29

    axes and, 30

    ballista and, 42

    halberds and, 72-73

    morning stars and, 70-71

    pots de fer, 76-77

    siege engines, 66-67

MiG-15, 300-301, 304

MiG-17, 308

MiG-21, 308, 410

MiG-21 Fishbed, 322-323

MiG-23 Flogger, 370-371

MiG-25 Foxbat, 372-373

MiG-29 Fulcrum, 430, 434-435

MiG-31 Foxhound, 424-425

Mikoyan, Artem, 300

Milch, Erhard, 184

Military Operations Other Than War (MOOTW), 488

military robots, 452-453

Mills, Heather, 172

MiL Mi-24 Hind, 378-379

Mil, Mikhail Leont'yevich, 378

mines, 118

Minoan civilization, labrys and, 30

Minot Air Force Base, 312

Minuteman III, intercontinental ballistic missiles, 324

Minuteman Missile National Historic Site, 324

Mirage 2000, 410, 440-441

Mirage III, 322, 388

missiles

    AGM-84 Harpoon, 392-393

    AIM-9 Sidewinder missiles, 308-309, 358

    AS-6 Kingfish, 368-369

Exocet, 406-407

FIM-92A Stinger, 418

Intercontinental Ballistic Missile (ICBM), 324-325

Javelin, 464-465

MIM-104 Patriot, 420-421

P-15 Termit, 332

SA-7 Grail, 362-363

Scud tactical ballistic missiles, 420

SS-N-2 Styx, 332

Tomahawk Land Attack Missiles (TLAMs), 454

TOW anti-tank missile launcher, 416

Trident II missile, 422

V-I flying bomb, 244-245

Mitchell, Reginald, 202, 204-205

Mitchell, William "Billy", 190, 228

Mitsubishi G4M Betty, 238-239

Mitsubishi Zero, 180, 194, 200, 206, 208, 212-215, 266

Mk 19 grenade machine guns, 356-357

Modular Lightweight Load Carrying Equipment (MOLLE), 472

Momyer, William W., 304, 340

Moniteur Universe!, propaganda and, 98

MOPP (Mission Oriented Protective Posture) gear, 468

morning stars, 70-71

mortars, 86-87

Moseby, John Singleton, 106

Mount Fujiyama, 82-83

Muhafiz, mine sweeper, 332

Muhammad

    death of, 54

    gift of Zulfiqar (Spinecleaver), 56

Mujahideen, on Soviet helicopters, 378

Musashi, battleships and, 282

muskets, 88-89

Mutually Assured Destruction (MAD), 324

Myers, Wayne "Jump", 302

N

Nagasaki, atomic bomb mushroom cloud over, 290-291

Nagoya Aircraft Works of Mitsubishi Heavy Industries, Ltd., 214

napalm, 306-307

Napoleon I, 496

Napoleonic War, 192

Napoleon III, 456

Napoleon on the field of Eylau (Gros), 98-99

National Air Intelligence Center, 434

National Firearms Act of 1934, 160

Native Americans
    horses and, 104
    muskets and, 88-89
    tomahawks and, 30

Natural History (Pliny the Elder), 46

Naval Construction Battalion Center, 446-447

NAVSTAR Global Positioning System, 436-437

Nazi Germany
    atomic bombs and, 290
    conquest of France and, 176
    Hermann Göring address and, 224
    ICBMs and, 324
    propaganda and, 98-99
    use of poison gas in concentration camps, 446
    V-1 flying bombs and, 244

Nelson, Horatio, 100

Neolithic Age, "ax factories" and, 30

nEUROn, Unmanned Combat Air Vehicle, 474

Night Vision Devices (NVDs), 470-471

Nihongo, Three Great Spears of Japan and, 18

Nimitz, Chester, 210

Nivelle, Robert, 94

Nobel, Alfred, 122-125

non-lethal bullets, 462-463

non-lethal weapon systems, 488-489

Norden bombsight, Precision Guided Munitions (PGMs), 454

North American T-28 Trojan, 340-341

North Atlantic Treaty Organization (NATO), 134, 318, 320, 330, 346, 348, 352, 362, 372, 392, 396, 398, 402, 410, 424, 434, 440, 472, 482

Northrop Grumman, 466, 472

Northrop P-61 Black Widow, 270-271

O

Office of Strategic Services (OSS), 226

O'Grady, Scott, 360, 398-399, 436, 450

O'Hare, Butch, 206

Ohio Class SSBN, 422-423

Okumiya, Masatake, 214

Operation Anaconda, 460, 478

Operation Aphrodite, 460

Operation Arrowhead Ripper, 494

Operation Barbarossa, 196

Operation Citadel, 220, 268

Operation Cyclone, 418

Operation Deny Flight, 360, 398

Operation Desert Shield, 358, 394, 396, 402, 428, 496

Operation Desert Storm (1991), 330, 354, 356, 358, 382, 390, 394, 396, 398, 402, 412, 416, 420, 428, 430, 432, 438, 440, 448, 454, 456, 458, 496

Operation Eager Anvil, 438

Operation El Dorado Canyon, 430

Operation Enduring Freedom, 352, 396, 460

Operation Gothic Serpent, 386

Operation Granby, 428

Operation Husky, 194

Operation Iraqi Freedom (2003), 356, 396, 398, 414, 416, 444, 460, 464, 480, 484, 486

Operation Linebacker, 308

Operation Moolah, 300

Operation Opera, 398

Operation Ranch Hand, 334

Operation Sho-Go, 208

Operation Thunderclap, 280

Operation Torch, 458

Operation Trident, 332

Operation Upshot-Knothole, 318

Operation Urgent Fury (1983), 358, 404

Oppenheimer, J. Robert, 290, 292-293

Otegine, Three Great Spears of Japan, 18

P

P-15 Termit, 332

P-38 Lightning, 238, 256

P-40 Warhawk, 194-195

P-51 Mustang, 188, 190, 256, 258-259, 272

Panavia Tornado, 402-403

Panther tanks, 252, 268-269

panzerfaust, 264-265, 338

Panzerschreck, 232

Paris-Geschütz (Paris Gun), 136

Patterson, Robert, 272

Patton, George S., 12, 412
    Colt pistols and, 108
    leadership and, 94

Peanuts, Sopwith Camel and, 150

Pearl Harbor, raid on, 212-213, 216-217, 234, 238, 288

Peloponnesian Wars, 496

People's Liberation Army Air Force (PLAAF), 410

percussion cap revolver, 106

Pershing II, 318-319

Phantom F-4, 308

Phantom Over Vietnam (Trotti), 330

Philip II, Battle of Bovine (1214), 62

Philip IV, pots de fer, 76

Philip of Macedon, ballista and, 42

Piaroa hunters, blowguns and poison darts, 22

pigs, 46-47

pistols
    Colt M1900, 164
    Colt Model 1911, 134-135

plate armor, 62

Plato, on necessity and, 134

Poisson, Jeanne-Antoinette, 146

Poliorcetus (Appollodorus of Damascus), 22

Polish Soviet War, 148

Popeye, J. Wellington Wimpy and, 192

Porter, David Dixon, 112

Post, Henry A., 110

pots de fer, 76-77

Powell, Colin, 342

Powers, Francis Gary, 314, 316-317

Precision Guided Munitions (PGMs), 454

Predator, 460-461

Predator UAV, military robots and, 452

prehistoric weapons
    knives and, 14-17
    spears and, 14-15, 18-19
    stone knives, 14

Prince of Wales, class carriers, 238, 472

Princip, Gavrilo, 164

propaganda, 98-99

Protestant Reformation, religious wars, 54
public opinion, 458-459
Puntigam, Anton, 164
Pyrrhus of Epirus, 46

Q

quadriremes, warships and, 36
Queen Elisabeth, class carriers, 472
quinquiremes, warships and, 36

R

RADAR, 176-177
Rafale, 474-475
Reagan, Ronald, 436
Reard, Louis, 290
reconnaissance satellites, 328-329
Republic P-47 Thunderbolt, 256-257
Repulse, 238
Rhodes, Cecil, 128
Richard the Lionhearted
    death of, 40
    Siege of Acre (1191) and, 66
Rich, Ben, 314, 344
Rickenbacker, Eddie, 152
Rickover, Hyman George, 310
rifles
    air rifles, 92
    AK-47 assault rifle, 296-299
    Browning Automatic Rifle (BAR), 164-165, 248
    combat shotguns, 350-351
    M1 Garand, 174-175
    M-16 assault rifle, 348-349
    Mauser bolt-action rifle, 126
    Sharps rifle, 110-111
    sniper rifles, 478-479
    Thompson submachine gun, 160-161
robots
    LandShark, 488
    military robots, 452-453
rockets, V-2 rocket, 274-276
Rodenberry, Gene, 190
Roebling, Donald, 242
Roman Empire
    ballista and, 42
    siege engines and, 66-67
    tolerating local religions and, 54
    warships and, 36
Roman legionnaires, ancient armor, 28-29

Rommel, Erwin, 218
Romm, Oskar, 232
Roosevelt, Franklin, 458
Roosevelt, Theodore, 408
Rotmistrov, Pavel, 220
RPG-7 (RPGs), rocket-propelled grenade launchers, 338, 346, 386, 404, 416, 486, 500
Rudel, Hans-Ulrich, 178
Running Gear Entanglement System (RGES), 488
Russian Civil War, 128

S

SSA-6 Gainful, 360-361
SA-7 Grail, 362-363
Saab 37 Viggen, 374-375
Sakai, Saburo, 212
SALT-2, arms control treaties, 380
Samson, suicide attack and, 476
samurai armor, 68-69
Sanitor, Robert, 394
SATCOMs, 456-457
satellites
    communications devices, 456-457
    Global Positioning System (GPS), 392, 432, 436-438, 454, 492, 494
    NAVSTAR Global Positioning System, 436-437
    reconnaissance satellites, 328-329
Satsuma Clan, Japanese samurai of, 82
Saufley, Richard C., 286
SBD Dauntless, 208-210
Scharstein, Victor, 494
Scramble for Africa, 128
Scud tactical ballistic missiles, 420
sea lions, 480
Seamans, Robert C., 372
sea mines, 118
Seattle Times, B-17 Flying Fortress, 190
Second Battle of Ypres, poison gas and, 446
Second Boer War, 126
Second Gulf War (2003), 382
Second Latean Council of 1139, 40-41
Second Punic War
    Archimedes and, 48
    Hannibal crossing the Alps, 44
Seidel, Alex, 126

Seven Years War, 146
sex, 146
SH-60 Seahawk helicopter, 426-427
Shah of Iran, 428
Shakespeare, William, *Julius Caesar* and, 496
Sharps, Christian, 110
Sharps rifles, 110-111
Sheffield, British destroyer, 406
Shenyang J-8 Finback, 410-411
Sherman, Frederick, 266
Sherman, William Tecumseh, 246
ships-of-the-line, 100
Shot Grable, 318
shotguns, combat shotguns, 350-351
Shughart, Randy, 404
siege engines, 66-67
Siege of Antioch (William of Tyre), 66-67
Siege of Carthage, 334
Siege of Jotapata, 50
Sikh religion, kirpan and, 16
Sino-Japanese War (1894), 286
The Six Million Dollar Man, 214
Six Day War (1967), 294, 322, 332, 388, 474
Skunk Works, 314, 316, 344, 432, 488, 490
SLAM-ER (Standoff Land Attack Missile-Expanded Response), 392
Slaughterhouse Five (Vonnegut), 280
slings, 20-21
Smith, James R., 270
sniper rifles, 478-479
Société Pour L'Aviation et ses Dérivés (SPAD), 152
SONAR, 144
Sopwith Camel, 150-151, 154
South Vietnamese Army (ARVN), 348
Soviet-Afghan War (1979–1989), 338, 380
SPAD S.XIII, 152-153
Spanish-American War, 130
    bayonets and, 84-85
    dynamite gun and, 122
    Mauser bolt-action rifle and, 126
Spanish Civil War
    Condor Legion and, 184
    FlaK 36 "88" and, 218
Spanish Conquistadors

atlatls and, 24
  horses and, 104
  plate armor, 62
  warrior groups and, 32
Spanish Tercios, halberds and, 72
spears, 18-19
Speer, Albert, 264, 272, 276
spiculum, spear designs and, 18
Spirit of America (I)
  stealth heavy bomber, 466
Spitfire, 202-203
Sputnik I, 328
SR-71 Blackbird, 316, 372
Sra, Minchit, 44
SS-N-2 Styx, 332
Stalin, Josef, 200, 236
START-I, arms control treaties, 380
Star Trek, Gene Rodenberry and, 190
Stewart, Jimmy, 190, 226
stick weapons, bo and, 82-83
Strike Eagle, 390
submarines (conventional power),
  262-263
submarines (nuclear power), 310
suicide bombers, 476-477
Super Cobra, 376, 450
Super Étendard, 400-401, 406-407
Super Hornet, 430
swords, 56-57, 68-69
Sykes, Eric Anthony, 198

T

T-6 Texan, 180-181
T-34 tank, 196, 218, 220-221, 268,
  298, 338
T-72 Main Battle tank, 382-383
tactical nuclear weapons, 318-319
Tadakatsu, Honda, 18
Taliban
  AGM-114 Hellfire missiles, 426
  F-16s and, 398
  M777 howitzers attack on, 492
  Operation Enduring Freedom, 352
  rocket-propelled grenade launch-
    ers, 338
tanks
  Abrams Main Battle Tank, 412-413
  Centurion tanks, 294-295
  Challenger I Main Battle Tank,
    428-429

Churchill, 240-241
  Leopard I Main Battle Tank
    (MBT), 352-353
  M4 Sherman tank, 246-247
  Panther tanks, 252, 268-269
  T-34, 196, 218, 220-221, 268,
    298, 338
  T-72 Main Battle tank, 382-383, 382
  Tiger tanks, 218, 252-253
Tarawa, amphibious assault ships, 450
Task Force Tarawa, 486
Taylor, Maxwell D., 94
Tennyson, Alfred Lord, Charge of the
  Light Brigade and, 104
Thach, Jimmy, 206
Thanh Hoa "Dragon's Jaw", 358
Thompson, John Taliaferro, 160
Thompson submachine gun, 160-161
Tibbets, Paul, 230, 278, 292
Ticonderoga-class cruisers, 366
Tienamen Square, 410
Tiger in the Mud (Carius), 218, 252
Tiger tanks, 218, 252-253
Tin Can Man (Saufley), 286
Tizona, sword of Rodrigo Díaz de
  Vivar, 56
Tomahawk Land Attack Missiles
  (TLAMs), 454
tomahawks, 30
  Vietnam Tactical Tomahawk, 30
Tonbogiri (Dragonfly Cutter), Three
  Great Spears of Japan and, 18
torpedoes, 118, 120-121, 170
TOW anti-tank missile launcher, 416
trebuchet, siege engines, 66-67
Trident II missile, 422
triremes, 36-37
Trotti, John, 330
Tu-22 Backfire, 380-381
Tupolev Tu-95 Bear, 320-321
Turtle, submarines and, 262
Tutankhamen
  boomerangs and, 26-27
  slings and, 20
Two Knights Fighting in a Landscape (Delac-
  roix), 58-59
Typhoon F2 Eurofighter, 472

U

U-boats, 144, 262

UH-60 Black Hawk helicopters, 404-
  405
Unmanned Aerial Vehicles (UAVs), 460
Unmanned Combat Aerial Vehicles
  (UCAVs), 460
Unmanned Ground Vehicles (UGVs),
  452
Unmanned Surface Vehicles (USVs),
  452
Unmanned Undersea Vehicles
  (UUVs), 452
Upper Paleolithic period, atlatls and,
  24
Urban II, use of crossbows and, 40-41
U.S. Department of Commerce's
  Bureau of Industry and Security,
  End User Certificate, 442

USS Dwight D. Eisenhower, 350, 358-359
USS Enterprise, radar control station
  and, 176-177
USS Hornet, Doolittle raid, 228, 230
USS Houstatonic, 262
USS Iowa, 282
USS John C. Stennis, 400-401
USS John F. Kennedy, 358
USS Kearsarge, 450
USS Missouri, 282
USS Monitor, 116-117
USS Monterey, 288
USS Nautilus, 310
USS New Jersey, 282
USS Ohio, 408-409, 422-423
USS Pennsylvania, 284-285
USS Saufley, 286
USS South Dakota, 282
USS Theodore Roosevelt, 288-289
USS Vincennes, 366
USS Washington, 282
USS Wisconsin, 282-283

V

V-1 flying bomb, 244-245
V-2 rockets, 274-276
van Coehoorn, Menno, 86
Vatican, halberds and, 72
Vauban, military engineer, 250
Verne, Jules, 262
Vickers Wellington, 192-193
Vietnam Tactical Tomahawk, 30

Vietnam War
  Amphibious Assault Vehicles (AAV), 486
  Bell UH-IH Huey, 326-327
  booby traps, 342-343
  Buffalo Hunter remote control airplanes, 460
  conventional bombs, 280
  dolphins and, 480
  Expeditionary Fighting Vehicle (EFV), 500
  flame throwers, 248-249
  herbicides, 334-335
  Lewis gun and, 132
  napalm and, 306
  Precision Guided Munitions (PGMs), 454
  rocket-propelled grenade launchers, 338
  war dogs and, 496
Villa, Pancho, 108
von Braun, Wernher, 274, 276-277
von Lüttwitz, Heinrich, 222
Vonnegut, Jr., Kurt, 280
von Richthofen, Manfred, 148-150, 154, 156
von Zeppelin, Ferdinand, 140

W

Wallace, Bruce, 326
Wallis, Barnes, 204
War of 1812
  Congreve rocket and, 96
  naval mines and, 118
Warsaw Pact, 370
warships
  aircraft carriers and, 208, 284, 288-289, 312, 400
  amphibious assault ships, 450-451
  battleships, 100, 170, 208, 282-284, 286, 288
  cruisers, 284-286, 366
  CSS Virginia, 116-117
  destroyers and, 208, 246, 284, 286-287, 366, 408
  High Speed Vessels (HSVs), 484-485
  ships-of-the-line, 100
  triremes and, 36-37
Wars of the Diadochi, 46

Washington Naval Treaty of 1922, 284
Wasp class Landing Helicopter Dock, 450
Watson-Watt, Robert Alexander, 176
weapons of mass destruction
  atomic bombs, 278, 288, 290-291, 310, 318, 322, 324, 328, 330, 352, 368, 372, 380, 400, 422, 434, 440, 466, 468, 474
  biological weapons, 448-449, 500
  chemical weapons, 446-447, 500
  incendiaries and, 34-35
  tactical nuclear weapons, 318-319
Westmoreland, William, 348, 412
Whitehead, Robert, 120
Whitehouse, Joseph, 92
Whiteman Air Force Base, 466
Whitney, Eli, 90-91
Whittlesey, Charles, 158
"Windbüchse" (wind rifle), 92
Wintgens, Kurt, 142
Wittmann, Michael, 252
Wood, Albert Beaumont, 144
World Peace Foundation, 138
World Trade Center, suicide attacks and, 476-477
World War I
  aircraft carriers and, 288
  biological weapons and, 448
  body armor and, 468
  carrier pigeons and, 158
  Colt Model 1911 pistol and, 134
  destroyers and, 286
  flame throwers, 248-249
  Gatling guns and, 112
  horses and, 104
  leadership and, 94
  Lewis gun and, 132
  Mata Hari and, 146
  mines and, 118
  mortars and, 86-87
  poison gas and, 446
  shotguns and, 350
  torpedoes and, 120
  war dogs of, 496
  Zeppelins and, 140, 176
World War II
  amphibious landing craft, 242-243
  ASDIC and, 144-145

  Bofors 40-mm anti-aircraft gun, 168
  conventional bombs, 280
  D-Day, 168, 222, 234, 242-243
  female spies and, 146
  flame throwers, 248-249
  kamikaze attacks and, 476
  Lewis gun and, 132
  MI Bayonet and, 84
  military robots and, 452
  Mitsubishi Zero, 180, 194, 200, 206, 208, 212-215, 266
  paratroopers in, 62
  RADAR and, 176
  Thompson submachine gun, 160
  torpedoes and, 120
  war dogs and, 496
Wright, Eric, 444
Wright-Patterson Air Force Base, 372, 434
Wright, Wilbur, 156

X

Xenophon, slings and, 20
Xerxes I, Battle of Salamis and, 36

Y

Yak-1, 200-201
Yakovlev, Alexander Sergeevich, 200
Yamamoto, Isoroku, 234, 238
Yamato, battleships and, 282
Yeager, Chuck, 258, 272, 304
Yegorova, Anna, 236
Yemeni jambiya, knives and, 16
Yom Kippur War (1973), 294, 322, 336, 346, 360
Young Man Among Roses, 234–235

Z

Zelle, Margarethe Geertruida, 146-147
Zeppelins, 140-141, 176
Zero! (Horikoshi), 214
ZSU-23-4 Shilka, 346-347
Zulfiqar (Spinecleaver), 56